Factions in House Committees

Factions

in House Committees

Glenn R. Parker
and Suzanne L. Parker

THE UNIVERSITY OF TENNESSEE PRESS / KNOXVILLE

The paper in this book meets the guidelines for permanence and
durability of the Committee on Production Guidelines for Book
Longevity of the Council on Library Resources. Binding materials
have been chosen for durability.

Library of Congress Cataloging in Publication Data

Parker, Glenn R.
  Factions in house committees.

  Includes index.
  1. United States. Congress. House—Committees.
2. United States. Congress. House—Voting. I. Parker,
Suzanne L., 1946–   . II. Title.
JK1429.P37 1985   328.73'0765   85–3150
ISBN 0–87049–467–8 (alk. paper)

In memory of
Grace Raps Parker,
who will never be forgotten.

CONTENTS

TABLES

FIGURES

ACKNOWLEDGMENTS

We would like to acknowledge the assistance and support we have received as we pursued our study of factions in committees in the U.S. House of Representatives. Financial support for this project has been provided by the National Science Foundation in the form of a research grant (SOC-79-10076); Florida State University supplied clerical and computer support. Without such assistance, our efforts would have fallen far short of our goals. We would also like to thank three scholars who provided critical advice in the early stages of our analysis: Joel Aberbach, Leroy Rieselbach, and Herbert Weisberg. Special acknowledgment should be given to Richard Fenno, Larry Dodd, and Walter Stone for their comments on earlier versions of the work, which have had a profound impact on our study of committee factions. While we have benefited from their advice, these scholars bear no responsibility for any inadequacies that appear in the book. Finally, our efforts to study committee decision making have been aided by the encouragement and advice of many friends and colleagues: David W. Brady, Charles S. Bullock III, Joseph Cooper, Roger H. Davidson, Barbara Hinckley, Charles O. Jones, and Samuel Patterson. We hope that our effort to explain committee decision making does justice to the advice and assistance that we have received during the course of this project.

INTRODUCTION

Since the publication of Richard Fenno's (1973) study of congressional committees, *Congressmen in Committees*, scholars have gained a greater appreciation of the ways in which committees differ systematically from one another. One of Fenno's major contributions to the study of committees is the introduction of a framework within which we can compare the similarities and differences among House and Senate committees. This framework has enabled scholars to differentiate among the committees on the basis of the goals of their members and the decision-making environments and processes that characterize them. In writing this book we have had a similar aim: to present a conceptual schema for making cross-sectional and longitudinal comparisons among congressional committees.

The conceptual framework of the book is not designed as a substitute or alternative for Fenno's comparative schema; rather, our conceptual approach is intended to complement Fenno's comparative study of committees. The concepts used by Fenno to describe the operations of committees are compatible with our analysis of the divisions within those committees. In fact, we make considerable use of some of the major concepts Fenno employs to compare individual committees with one another. Our study is designed to suggest another way in which congressional committees can be differentiated from one another—by differences in the types of factions and cleavages within them.

Our framework for comparing committees deviates from Fenno's in several respects. One basic difference is the level of aggregation, or unit of analysis. For Fenno, the individual committee member and his or her goals, assumptions, and expectations are the objects of study. In our study the units for analysis are the blocs of members that appear to form rather consistently within House committees. Hence, we compare committees in terms of the types of voting blocs, or factions, that characterize their decision-making environments.

A second major difference is that our approach uses a new data source for the study of congressional committees: committee roll-call votes. The roll-call votes used here to analyze committee factions cover the years 1973 to 1980 and most House committees. (Three committees were excluded because of the lack of sufficient roll-call votes: District of Columbia, Small Business, and Veterans Affairs.) Until the early 1970s, committee votes were unavailable for public scrutiny. As a consequence, most early studies of congressional committees relied upon interviews with committee members as the basis for generalizations about committee decision making. This constraint limited the scope of most committee research because of the difficulty in obtaining interviews with members of Congress. The present availability of committee votes for public examination has provided congressional scholars with an opportunity to obtain information directly about committee decisions and the voting behavior of committee members.

Our analysis of committees is based upon patterns of agreement in the voting behavior of committee members; these voting patterns are referred to as *factions*. We are not interested in how members vote on specific issues before their committees but in the alignments of committee members that appear to form with some regularity over the entire range of issues that are debated. We assume that the influences critical to decision making will arise during the roll-call stage of committee deliberations, because such decisions are decisive and final. The interplay of the various influences on congressional committees creates divisions, or cleavages, among committee members. Those divisions produce factions, or voting blocs. Thus, in identifying the blocs of members that form into factions, we also identify the major influences on committee decision making: party, ideology, administrations (presidents and executive agencies), and constituencies. The types of factions created by these influences can be used to characterize committees.

Our goals are, first, to describe the influences that create cleavages within each of the committees; second, to compare the committees in terms of these cleavages; third, to describe the sources of change and stability in committee cleavages and factions; and, finally, to demonstrate the impact of cleavages and factions on the types and sizes of coalitions that form in the committees. To meet these goals, we have divided our analysis into three distinct parts.

In the first section of the analysis (Chapters 1–5), we use the committee roll-call votes from the first of two time periods (1973–76 and 1977–80) to describe the influences on decision making and the types of factions that exist in the committees. In Chapters 3, 4, and 5, the committees are organized according to the major influences on decision making. For instance, party and ideology are the primary influences on decision making in the committees included in Chapter 3. Included in Chapter 4 are all the committees in which the executive branch, as well as party and ideology, exerts a significant influence on decision making. Committees that have discernible constituency influences are described in Chapter 5. At the beginning of each of these chapters we briefly explain how the various influences operate within the environment of the committee. The descriptions of the committee factions provide a baseline against which we can compare the same committees in a second time period (1977–80).

In the second part of the analysis (Chapter 6), we present the comparisons of the committees in both time periods. This stage of the study is devoted to evaluating the stability in committee factions and the changes that occurred during the eight-year span of the study. In addition, data from this second time period allow us to assess any shifts in the impact of the executive branch. In the first time period the Republicans controlled the White House and the Democrats the Congress; in the second, the Democrats controlled both branches of government. We can determine, therefore, whether the influence of the executive branch changes under united control of the government. Taken together, the first two stages of the analysis of committee factions provide the necessary conditions for comparing House committees with one another and for examining the degree of change in the decision-making milieus of the committees.

In the final section of the analysis (Chapter 7), we use the information provided in the first two sections to examine a specific aspect of committee decision making—coalition formation. Using the findings about factions, we develop a typology of committees based on the nature of the divisions among members (cleavage patterns). We then apply the typology to explain the size of coalitions that form in the committees. One major purpose of this section is to demonstrate how an understanding of the factional structures can help to explain other aspects of committee decision making.

The four types of factions that we identify serve as the building blocks of coalitions. Factions composed of members with similar or compatible loyalties, attachments, and/or interests form coalitions. The size of such coalitions is influenced by the extent to which partisanship is reinforced or fragmented by the presence of other types of factions. That is, the size of committee coalitions expands in response to the extent to which committee members are cross-pressured by their varying loyalties. When pressures from ideological sentiments, administration loyalties, or constituent interests crosscut party loyalties, a winning coalition must present a broad appeal to secure enough members to win. When partisanship is reinforced by the other influences in the committee, the interests of other committee factions are coincident with partisan sentiments. Hence, such coalitions are smaller because fewer divergent interests need to be accommodated within a winning coalition. Thus, the expansion and contraction of committee coalitions depend on the degree of compatibility among committee factions, especially partisan ones.

Throughout the analysis, a major goal has been to provide a framework for the longitudinal study of committee decision making. The delineation of the factional structures of most House committees establishes a baseline that can be used in future studies to detect changes in committee decision making. Further, the analysis is based on a readily available data source, which increases the opportunity for long-term studies of committee decision making. Finally, a large number of graphs and tables have been supplied to make comparisons easier for later researchers. In sum, our analysis is meant to provide an additional view of committees, based on the divisions between members that appear in committee roll-call voting. The study should shed light on the influences that impinge upon committee decision making, the ways in which these influences divide the committee membership, the impact of such divisions on coalition formation, and the sources of change and continuity in committee decision making.

Factions in House Committees

CHAPTER ONE

The Study of Factions

> The House sits, not for serious discussion,
> but to sanction the conclusions of its
> Committees as rapidly as possible. It
> legislates in its committee rooms; not by the
> determinations of majorities, but by the
> resolutions of specially-commissioned
> minorities; so that it is not far from the
> truth to say that Congress in session is
> Congress on public exhibition, whilst Congress
> in its committee-rooms is Congress at work.
> Woodrow Wilson, *Congressional Government*

Woodrow Wilson's observations on Congress appear to be as accurate today as when he wrote them in 1885. The major work of the House of Representatives in formulating legislation is still done in the committee rooms of the chamber. The major debates on most legislation still take place in the committees; the legislative alternatives considered by the full House membership continue to be defined primarily in the committees. Groups and individuals interested in legislation press their claims in committees by testifying at hearings and by influencing individual committee members just as they did when Wilson wrote about the operation of the House. Thus, one of the most important areas on which to concentrate a study of congression-al policy making has been traditionally and continues to be commit-tee decision making. By concentrating on this topic, we can delineate the major influences on the policies that are eventually considered by the full chamber, since these alternatives are formulated in the com-mittees. It is the objective of this study to focus on decision making in House committees in order to define and to explore the influences that have a major impact on congressional policy making. In the process we will examine such questions as which influences have a particularly important impact on committee decision making. Do these influences vary according to the subject matter of the policies being considered? What types of cleavages exist in committee decision making and how stable are they? What impact do these cleavages have on the coalitions that form in decision making?

In focusing on committee decision making, we benefit from and build upon previous research in this area. Case studies of individual committees provided insights into committee decision making that shaped our thinking in this study. Two excellent examples of this research are Richard Fenno's (1966) *The Power of the Purse* and John Manley's (1970) *The Politics of Finance*. From these studies we gain an understanding of the operation of committees, the behavior of their members, and the influence of forces outside the committee on decision making. The drawback of individual case studies of commit-tees is that unless subsequent studies of committee decision making adopt the same concepts, they provide little opportunity for intercom-mittee comparisons.

There is, therefore, a great advantage to presenting individual case studies of committees within a framework that provides the oppor-tunity to make intercommittee comparisons. A prime example of this approach is Fenno's (1973) *Congressmen in Committees*. Fenno uses two independent and one intervening variable to compare the deci-sion-making processes and resultant decisions in six House commit-tees: member goals and environmental constraints are the independent variables, and strategic premises or decision rules make up the intervening variable. By describing the ways in which these variables affect the legislative behaviors of committee members, Fen-no is able to detect systematic differences in the operation of the committees he examines.

Like Fenno, we attempt in this book to present a framework for the examination of individual committee decision making that provides the opportunity for several types of comparisons. By delineating the voting blocs that result from the examination of committee voting patterns and by defining the environmental influences that affect the formation of these voting blocs, we can detect systematic differences in the impact of environmental influences on committee decision making across the nineteen committees we examine. In addition, since we conceptualize the environmental influences described in this study in a manner similar to that of Fenno (and subsequent works that adopt Fenno's framework), we are able to use earlier studies of committees to compare committee decision making during different time periods. These studies also provide us with information that is useful in describing the major influences on committees (where comparisons can be made) and in identifying the sources of change in committee decision making across time periods. Finally, we hope that our study will provide future researchers with a baseline that could promote systematic, long-term, comparisons of committee decision making.

In delineating voting blocs, which we call factions, we also build and expand upon previous research on floor voting that uses roll-call analysis for describing and explaining voting behavior on the floor of the House. One of the earliest of these works is David Truman's (1959) *The Congressional Party* which sought to define the role of parties in legislative behavior by determining blocs (or clusters) of party members that voted together on issues decided on the floor of the House and Senate. Similar to Truman's, our study examines blocs of members that tend to vote together on roll-call votes, but the focus in our study is committee voting rather than floor voting. Further, we do not confine ourselves to the delineation of blocs within the parties. Instead, using committee members of both parties, we seek to define the blocs that form, and then to determine the underlying factors that influenced members to align in the manner detected. In determining voting blocs, we also rely on a methodology different from that employed in Truman's analysis. In contrast to earlier studies, which relied upon cluster-bloc analysis to define clusters of members, this study employs a factor-analytic technique to define the factional alignments that result from an examination of committee roll-call votes. (A detailed explanation of this technique is provided in Appendix A.)

Unlike studies that focus on the individual vote decision (Clausen, 1973; Kingdon, 1973; Matthews and Stimson, 1975), this study is concerned with patterns in collective decision making. By delineating factions of members that vote together and uncovering the determinates of the factional alignments, we attempt to define the major influences on committee decisions and the major sources of conflict within House committes. This study is not incompatible with theories of member vote decisions; we have, however, shifted the emphasis from the individual to the factions that form among members of a committee.

Our emphasis on committee decision making can be expected to produce findings somewhat different from studies concentrating on floor voting because the nature of decision making in committees differs in several important respects from floor voting. The most obvious difference is in the volume and scope of committee decisions. It has been argued that the great number and range of issues handled on the floor of the House make it impossible for members to make informed, rational decisions on all or even most of them. By contrast, decision making in the committee involves far fewer bills and a much more limited range of topics. Committee jurisdictions thus encourage members to specialize. Further, the stability of committee membership assures that most members are well acquainted with the subject matter under consideration. Increased specialization, as Robert Dahl and Charles Lindblom (1953) note, brings increased opportunity for rational calculation: "When one specializes he focuses his attention on certain categories of repetitive events; by decreasing the number of variables at the focus of attention, specialization enables one to increase his capacity for rational calculations about these particular categories" (p. 63).

Familiarity with the subject area also increases a committee member's ability to understand and deal with the technical complexities of legislation, which can be overwhelming to others on the floor. In the committee, the limited range of issues provides more time for their consideration, as does assistance of committee staff. Because of these differences, it is easier for representatives to make rational decisions in committee than on the floor of the House. Therefore, factors which have only limited impact on the floor, such as ideological considerations (Clausen, 1973), might have a greater impact on committee decisions.

DEFINING COMMITTEE FACTIONS

Committee factions are defined in this study as groups or blocs of members who act in a coordinated fashion to influence committee decisions. The ways in which members align into voting blocs, or factions, reflect the pressures that are produced by influences within the committee's decision-making environment. These influences push and pull committee members in different policy directions, thereby creating factions within the committee and cross-pressures on its members. As a consequence, the committee factions that we uncover are not cohesive groups; members have varying commitments to other factions within the committee while maintaining a primary allegiance to a single committee faction.

These factions are not necessarily organized, either formally or informally, nor do they mobilize only under the influence of formal or informal leaders, though such leadership may add direction. Simply put, while some leadership and organization may underlie the emergence of factions in some congressional committees, members can act in a coordinated fashion to form voting blocs without such explicit direction. For instance, Donald Matthews and James Stimson (1975) observe, "Cue taking is the operational mechanism that translates similar attitudes into similar votes" (p. 87). In such a case, the cue taker and cue giver need not explicitly communicate their preferences to one another or operate under any specific design to register similar votes. They may act in a coordinated manner without deciding explicitly to do so. Similarly, each member of a faction may arrive at the same decision independently, after weighing the forces in his or her field which are in conflict, as John Kingdon (1973) suggests happens when an issue is controversial. In short, we consider the size of the faction and the extent to which members vote with the faction as more relevant information in defining committee blocs than the existence of leaders and organization.

Four types of factions can be identified from the analysis of the roll-call votes within the individual House committees: partisan, ideological, administration, and constituency-interest. Partisan factions are ubiquitous features of committee alignments both in terms of the frequency with which they appear, and the extent to which committee members vote with these factions. We find partisan factions in all but three committees; the three exceptions—Armed Services, Foreign

7

Affairs, and Standards of Official Conduct—deal with policies that are packaged to invoke bipartisan sentiments on the part of committee members. The centrality of the political parties to the legislative process and member behavior helps to explain why they would be important sources of committee factionalism.

Partisan Factions

Political parties can influence a committee's factional structure both directly and indirectly. Since the two major parties are divided in their views of the operation of government—decentralization versus centralization, change versus no change—as well as specific policies, they have the potential of creating major divisions within the House committees. The parties have a direct impact on committe divisions, for instance, when party leaders pressure committee members to follow the party's position on legislation before the committee. In fact, certain committees are expected to function as an arm of the party's congressional leadership (Peabody, 1963, p. 197).

Party leaders may influence the level of partisanship within a committee indirectly through the criteria used in assigning members to a committee. Fenno (1963) provides several examples of this type of influence. Assignment to the Ways and Means Committee, for example, requires that a member display a degree of party orthodoxy. Both parties tend to appoint members who are highly antagonistic to one another to the Education and Labor Committee. As Fenno (1973) observed, "members of the House Committee come from among those in their respective parties who already are in the widest disagreement" (p. 201).

Partisanship may also be reinforced in a less explicit fashion. Since members tend to consult exclusively with those of the same party, the communication network that disseminates information among House members contains a partisan bias. "If congressmen turn to informants with whom they agree," Kingdon (1973, p. 78) observes, "it is only natural that they turn to those within their own party." Party may also supply voting cues by serving as a reference group within Congress (Matthews and Stimson, 1975, p. 97), especially since feelings of compatriotism are a natural by-product of common electoral opposition.

Committee jurisdictions also contribute to the degree of partisanship displayed by the committees, particularly when the work of the committee yields distinct partisan political advantage. For example, congressional committees involved in investigations, such as the House Government Operations Committee, concentrate on errors in the administration of laws, regulations, and programs. The findings of these investigations can provide the party in opposition to the president with ammunition sufficient to embarrass the administration:

> When the congressional majority and the President hold different party allegiances, the opportunity for partisan advantage is vastly increased. In such a situation the minority party in Congress is much more likely to be highly sensitive to criticisms of their President. The majority party, on the other hand, is in such circumstances given an ideal opportunity to carry out investigations under the guise of oversight which embarrass the current Administration. (Henderson, 1970, p. 42)

In this way, partisan interests may serve as an impetus to committee activities. The possibility of partisan investigations means that committee members will pay sharp attention to the political complexion of the committee's work. Under these conditions, committee decision making is likely to proceed along partisan lines.

Finally, there are some political issues on which party positions are matters of historical record; such issues increase the saliency of partisan considerations in committee decision making. The topics of labor, education, and poverty have traditionally divided the parties and appear to exacerbate the level of partisanship exhibited within the House Education and Labor Committee (Fenno, 1973, p. 31). In a similar manner, party stands on trade, social security, taxation, and medicare produce cleavages among Democrats and Republicans on the Ways and Means Committee (Fenno, 1973, p. 24). Partisan disagreement among House Public Works Committee members also occurs on issues which have historically divided the parties, such as

> whether private or public power should be supported; whether the federal government or the state governments should assume responsibility for treating water pollution; how the financial burden of the Interstate and Defense Highway system should be distributed; and finally, whether or not new construction in the District of Columbia should be undertaken. (Murphy, 1974, p. 169)

9

In some cases, issues handled by a committee may change from obscure, nonpartisan matters to salient partisan concerns, thereby introducing greater partisanship into the committee's deliberations. An example is the rise in prominence of environmental issues in the early 1970s. Prior to this period, these issues failed to create major divisions between the parties, because they were not salient to the public. As a result of the increase in the salience of these issues, the parties began to expose different approaches, which in turn, led to partisan conflict in the committee charged with handling these environmental issues—Interior.

Recent congressional research has found a decline in the influence of party: the linear decline in party voting in the House (Brady et al., 1979); the increased dependence upon bargaining and persuasion, rather than command, on the part of House leaders (Cooper and Brady, 1981); and the "routinization" of committee assignments (Gertzog, 1976), formerly a major area of leadership discretion. These trends suggest that political parties are no longer as influential as they once were and might lead one to be skeptical of the importance of party in committee decision making. David Broder's (1971) lament, "the party's over," aptly characterizes this perspective on the declining influence of political parties within the American political system. This study, however, suggests a different perspective on the significance of party in Congress. While we agree with scholars about the declining importance of party, we feel that party is, and will continue to be, a central factor in committee decision making because it serves as a basic reference point for committee members in making policy decisions. Further, although party leaders are not as influential as they once were, they still pressure members to support various party positions. Since the opportunities for partisan pressures both directly and indirectly to influence committee decision making continue to exist, the potential for the formation of partisan factions persists. Therefore, we view party as being a major force in committee decisions because it serves as a prominent and convenient vehicle for coordinating the behavior of committee members.

Ideological Factions

It should not be too surprising that the nature of the House membership leaves its imprint on the committee system. Manley

(1970, p. 20), made a similar observation in his study of the House Ways and Means Committee: "Ways and Means is by no means a perfect microcosm of the House but it is subject to and reflective of the same forces that affect policy-making in the House generally." One characteristic of the House of Representatives that seems likely to be reproduced in committee decisions is the ideological factionalism within and between the political parties. These ideological divisions reflect the difference arising from the historic North-South split within the Democratic party and the differences in ideological outlook between the Democratic and Republican parties. Ideological divisions within the Democratic party are most evident in the behavior of conservative Democrats, particularly those from southern states, who tend to vote less frequently with the Democratic majority than their liberal colleagues. This ideological cleavage among Democrats has led to the formation of a conservative coalition on House floor votes (Brady and Bullock, 1980). If Republicans and southern Democrats vote together on the floor, there is reason to suspect that they will follow the same practice within committees.

Ideological cleavages also divide the two major parties. While committee assignment practices, committee vacancies, and member preferences and characteristics may mediate ideological conflict, whenever the same conditions that exist on the floor of the House also arise within a committee (a substantial number of southern Democrats or sharp ideological differences among committee members, and issues that incite ideological feelings), we can expect ideological factions to surface. Further, there is some evidence that membership turnover during the period under study increased the potential for such conflict. Norman Ornstein and David Rohde (1977) suggest the membership turnover between 1970 and 1975 increased the ideological divisions between the Democrats and Republicans within the House: "At the same time that the Democrats have shifted somewhat to the left, the average conservative coalition score of Republicans has increased, so that the ideological gap between the parties has also increased, from 36 points in the Ninety-first Congress to 43 points in the Ninety-fourth" (p. 191). This type of change increases the potential for partisan-ideological polarization in committee decision making.

Although scholars continue to disagree about the effects of ideology on floor voting (Clausen, 1973; Matthews and Stimson, 1975;

11

Schneider, 1979), a strong argument can be made for ideological voting within congressional committees. One major explanation for the lack of ideological voting on the House floor is that members are unable to identify the ideological context of most legislation (Matthews and Stimson, 1975, pp. 32–37); this inability is a result of the volume of issues that members must vote upon and the lack of a manifest ideological content in most legislative votes. As described previously, the characteristics of the congressional committee system alleviate these impediments to ideological voting. While members may lack a detailed understanding of most of the issues they are called upon to consider, the norm of specialization ensures that members will be better informed about the issues that arise within the committees on which they serve. As a result, members should be better able to detect the ideological positions on issues within their committees' jurisdiction. Frequent participation in committee decisions—a primary criterion for the selection of members in our study—also ensures that committee members will have far greater knowledge of the attitudes and policy interests of other committee members. Hence, cue voting of an ideological nature may be even easier to accomplish within committee than on the House floor. Further, committee members have access to committee staff who can alert them to the underlying issues and nuances and apprise them of the ideological impact of individual amendments. For these reasons, we can expect ideological voting to be salient within committees.

Table 1 illustrates the ideological nature of the core membership of the House committees in our analysis. Core members are defined in this study as committee members who frequently participate in committee decisions; operationally, they are committee members who have participated in at least 70 percent of the recorded votes. Since core members have a greater impact on committee decisions, they help to determine the level of ideological conflict within a committee. On this basis, the most liberal core membership is in the Education Committee; in contrast, Agriculture, Armed Services, Public Works, and Standards of Official Conduct have the most conservative core members. Clearly, the ideological nature of factions is relative to the level of liberalism or conservatism within the committee. For instance, the conservative Republicans on the Judiciary Committee are considerably less conservative than those on Standards or Public Works. The same ideological cleavage is present in both cases, but the

TABLE 1. The Ideological Nature of Core and Committee Membership of House Committees: Mean Conservative Coalition Support Scores for the 93d–96th Congresses (in percentages)

Committee	Mean Committee Vote		Mean Core Vote	Mean Committee Vote		Mean Core Vote
	93d Cong.	94th Cong.	93d–94th Congs.	95th Cong.	96th Cong.	95th–96th Congs.
Agriculture	60	53	61	56	58	56
Appropriations	54	53	55	51	46	53
Armed Services	62	61	62	65	63	68
Banking, Finance, and Urban Affairs	38	42	38	41	45	40
Budget	—	49	50	43	43	40
Education and Labor	36	36	27	37	42	33
Foreign Affairs	41	37	40	38	40	—
Government Operations	42	39	44	40	44	41
House Administration	46	49	46	44	43	44
Interior and Insular Affairs	50	50	43	45	47	45
Interstate and Foreign Commerce	52	46	51	43	50	45
Judiciary	42	41	38	46	47	46
Merchant Marine and Fisheries	48	35	—	48	42	44
Post Office and Civil Service	44	40	45	41	47	36
Public Works and Transportation	55	51	62	57	60	57
Rules	48	44	46	39	39	38
Science and Technology	51	46	43	48	53	52
Standards of Official Conduct	58	65	69	55	65	—
Ways and Means	52	48	49	50	46	50

Note: Dashes indicate that there were insufficient votes to include in the analysis.

divisions occur at different places on the liberal-conservative continuum in the three committees. Thus, the most "liberal" block of committee members may still be "conservative," but *less so* than other factions in the committee.

For the most part, there is very little ideological shift in the composition of the core membership of the House committees that we examine: the core membership in most committees rarely changes in ideological direction by more than a few percentage points (table 1). The largest ideological shifts occur on two of the more liberal committees (the Judiciary Committee and the Science and Technology Committee) and on two relatively conservative committees (the Post Office and Civil Service Committee and the Rules Committee). These committees move in opposite ideological directions during the span of this analysis: the core membership of the liberal committees becomes more conservative, and the core membership of the conservative committees moves to the left. Although these ideological shifts represent changes in the strength and power of individual committee factions, they have little impact on the creation of *new* cleavages within these committees.

Basically, the core membership of a committee is fairly representative of the ideological composition of the committee. That is, the core membership is as conservative (or liberal) as the full membership of that committee (table 1). There are two exceptions to this general rule: the core membership of the Education and Labor Committee is more liberal than the full membership in all four Congresses, and the core membership of the Public Works Committee is somewhat more conservative than the full membership during the Ninety-third and Ninety-fourth Congresses. These differences may reflect the greater involvement in committee deliberations on the part of the dominant committee majority. For example, liberals dominate the Education Committee in the same way that conservatives dominate the Public Works Committee. Committee members who are at ideological odds with the vast majority of the members of a committee may have little incentive to participate actively in the committee deliberations, since they consistently find themselves outnumbered and outvoted. Thus, the ideological domination of liberals and conservatives on the Education and Labor Committee and the Public Works Committee, respectively, may deter ideological opposition from actively participating in committee deliberations. For a detailed description of the ideological divisions between Democratic and Republican committee members, see Appendix B.

Administration Factions

The jurisdiction of committees appears to be one variable that explains the differing levels of interest shown by the executive branch in committee decision making. When the administration has a strong interest in issues falling within a committee's jurisdiction, factions of executive-branch supporters and adversaries are apt to arise. Those committees that have jurisdictional responsibilities that impinge upon important executive functions, such as the maintenance of the national defense (Armed Services), the development of foreign policy (Foreign Affairs), and the level of governmental spending and revenue (Appropriations and Ways and Means), are the most likely targets of executive influence. The area of foreign policy is a good example of such a jurisdiction, because it has constitutionally and historically been an area of executive responsibility, and the cleavages within the House Foreign Affairs Committee reflect this historic tug-of-war between the president and Congress.

In those cases where there is disagreement *within* the administration, committee factions may reflect the contending positions. Although the president may have many powerful allies both inside and outside of the committee, an obstinate agency may wield equal or greater influence within that committee. The mutually supportive relationships between agencies, groups, and congressional committees ensure that some members will be more swayed by agency arguments than by the logic of the president's position. Moreover, when an agency's expenditures favor particular congressional districts, many congressmen rally to the support of the agency's position: "Bureaucrats allocate expenditures both in gratitude for past support and in hopes of future congressional support; and congressmen support agencies both because they owe them for past allocations and because they desire future allocations" (Arnold, 1979, p. 36).

The influence of the administration on committee decision making can appear as a mixture of presidential persuasion and partisanship. In fact, partisanship can obscure the impact of presidential power on committee decisions. Party loyalty is, after all, an appeal that presidents invoke in trying to influence members within their own party, but party and administration loyalties differ even among congressmen from the president's own party. Not all members of the president's party are successfully courted, nor are all party members susceptible to pleas for loyalty. Further, the president is not averse to crossing the aisle to form a successful coalition of administration supporters, as in the House Foreign Affairs Committee (Fenno, 1973, p. 90). Finally,

15

the influence of the executive branch may depend on whether the party in control of the White House also commands a majority in Congress. Hence, executive influence may vary from committee to committee and from member to member, as well as from one time period to the next.

Constituency-Interest Factions

Interest groups create factions within committees in the natural pursuit of their legislative objectives. Normally, groups restrict their lobbying efforts to those who are sympathetic to their causes, avoiding those in opposition to their positions. As a result, committee members supportive of the group's interest coalesce around the group's position, and those opposed to that same interest, either because of attitude, ideology, or loyalty to other groups, also close ranks.

In addition, the common practice among interest groups of rewarding friends and punishing enemies (Fenno, 1973; Magida, 1975; Salaman, 1975) is likely to create differing group attachments. The AFL-CIO, for example, "devotes enormous resources of manpower, money, and organization to help elect liberal Democratic Presidents and Congressmen—including members of the Education and Labor Committee" (Fenno, 1973, p. 34). Such differential treatment serves to solidify group attachments. Factions within committees can result, therefore, from groups entering the political fray and mobilizing supporters and/or opponents.

Constituency interests are especially important to the calculus of committee decision making when the policies being debated concern the distribution of benefits relevant to individual constituencies. In many cases, committee assignments are determined on the basis of constituent needs (Masters, 1961, p. 354; Price, 1975, p. 6), and members who serve similar constituent interests can find it strategically beneficial to organize as a bloc in order to ensure that these interests are accommodated within the framework of any policy decision. Thus, factions can reflect the alignments of committee members with similar constituent interests. According to previous research, this seems the case among House Agriculture Committee members who represent the specific commodity interests of their constituencies (Jones, 1961).

While it is possible to find two independent cleavages representing constituency interests *and* the influence of organized groups, it is also possible for a hybrid of the two to appear. Interest groups are most effective and influential where they have linkages to the congressmen's constituencies. As Kingdon (1973, pp. 143–46) notes, interest groups have little effect on the votes of congressmen when they lack this constituency connection. Further, members seek to accommodate their "strongest supporters" in their "reelection constituency" (Fenno, 1978, p. 19) because these supporters provide the financial aid and campaign assistance that help the incumbent to stave off electoral defeat. When such support comes from interest groups within the member's constituency, the effects of interest groups and constituency influences are collinear and impossible theoretically or empirically to separate. Therefore, in interpreting committee factions we consider interest group influence as also reflecting constituency effects. When such a combination of forces appears within committees, we refer to the influences as reflecting *constituency interests,* or for simplicity, constituency pressures.

Constituency-interest factions are found in few congressional committees. Aside from the obvious conclusion that such influences have little impact on congressional committees, there are at least two explanations for the lack of constituency factions. First, factions created as a result of constituency concerns and interest groups demands may be obscured by the influence of party and ideology. For example, the absence of cleavages created by the conflicts between environmentalists and commercial users on the Interior Committee (Fenno, 1973) may be the result of the collinearity between positions on land use and ideological and partisan sympathies: liberal Democrats support the demands of environmentalists and conservative Republicans promote the interests of commercial users.

Second, the influence of such interests may be absent because a consensus has developed over the distribution of particularistic benefits for constituencies or groups. We suggest that a consensus of this nature may have developed among Armed Services Committee members. In a similar vein, the House Public Works Committee appears to have developed a consensus over the requirements for the funding of constituency projects (Murphy, 1974). Constituency concerns and interest group demands may be important influences that already have been accommodated, and therefore they no longer promote

TABLE 2. Characteristics of the Voting Participation of Committee Members Included in the Analysis, 1973–1976 and 1977–1980

| | 1973–1976 | | |
Committee	Mean Voting Participation (%)	SD in Voting Participation (%)	Range in Voting Participation (%)
Agriculture	82.7	7.4	72.7–98.0
Appropriations	85.3	8.3	70.0–100.0
Armed Services	88.3	8.1	69.7–100.0
Banking, Finance, and Urban Affairs	81.6	5.2	76.0–91.2
Budget	92.7	8.0	70.6–100.0
Education and Labor	88.2	7.4	74.4–98.8
Foreign Affairs	85.5	9.9	71.4–100.0
Government Operations	89.2	7.2	75.9–100.0
House Administration	82.7	9.1	70.0–98.3
Interior and Insular Affairs	86.8	6.2	69.8–97.7
Interstate and Foreign Commerce	83.7	7.7	70.1–96.3
Judiciary	89.7	7.7	71.8–98.8
Merchant Marine and Fisheries	—	—	—
Post Office and Civil Service	89.5	8.1	76.0–100.0
Public Works and Transportation	91.7	7.6	77.8–100.0
Rules	88.2	7.3	73.2–99.3
Science and Technology	87.6	10.0	72.2–100.0
Standards of Official Conduct	84.4	10.0	73.3–100.0
Ways and Means	89.5	9.4	71.7–99.2

Note: Dashes indicate that there were insufficient votes to include in the analysis.

TABLE 2. Continued

| Number of Members | 1977–1980 | | | Number of Members |
	Mean Voting Participation (%)	Standard Deviation In Voting Participation (%)	Range in Voting Participation (%)	
18	86.6	6.5	75.6–94.9	33
35	86.5	9.8	71.4–100.0	42
22	87.5	7.8	70.0–100.0	29
15	83.9	6.9	71.0–97.8	30
25	97.5	2.5	93.8–100.0	14
22	84.2	8.7	70.1–97.9	22
20	—	—	—	—
20	88.7	8.0	70.3–100.0	29
16	84.8	9.4	70.2–98.2	23
21	88.9	7.3	70.5–97.7	30
23	83.1	6.0	71.9–92.6	28
28	89.8	6.6	71.2–96.5	24
—	82.9	8.6	69.7–100.0	23
11	83.5	7.7	70.2–94.7	19
24	89.6	8.1	70.6–100.0	33
13	85.8	7.0	75.0–95.2	10
26	88.7	7.9	70.0–100.0	23
9	—	—	—	—
19	93.4	5.1	77.5–100.0	29

conflict over the distribution of benefits. The consensus may take the form of agreement on formulas for the distribution of constituency benefits, as in the Public Works Commitee (Murphy, 1974), or the resolution of conflict through partisan mutual adjustment processes (Lindblom, 1965).

THE SIGNIFICANCE OF FACTIONS

There are three reasons why we can expect the factions we uncover to be influential in committee decisions. First, since frequent participation in committee decisions serves as a basic criterion for the selection of members for analysis, the factions we describe represent the alignments of those members who are influential in committee decisions. As is shown in table 2, the members in our analysis participate frequently in committee deliberations: the mean level of voting participation is above 80 percent in every committee and close to 90 percent in about one-half of the committees. These members represent the *core* of a committee, those who consistently influence commitee decisions. Multiple committee assignments have become common, and few members can give equal attention to each of them. This practical consideration combines with the norm of specialization (that members should specialize in narrow policy matters) to force members to concentrate their energies. As a consequence, each committee develops a core of members who are most likely to guide committee actions and structure its agenda than less-active participants. Committee members who participate infrequently in committee deliberations are less influential because they are perceived as lacking sufficient expertise and/or information to contribute to the deliberations. Further, a committee member's lack of participation could easily be construed by committee colleagues as evidence of a loss of interest in a policy area; such perceptions can drastically diminish a member's influence in committee decisions.

Second, factions reflect the distribution of power within congressional committees. Individually and collectively, committee members with the greatest amount of influence in a policy area are able to derive a disproportionate share of the benefits generated by it (Ferejohn, 1974). In most committees, power is more apt to reside in groups or factions than in the hands of individual members. This is not to refute the notion that some members wield considerable influence over certain policies and policy areas within a committee. Clearly, subcommittee leaders exercise greater influence in guiding subcommittee deliberations than other subcommittee members, and the same can be said about committee leaders. Rarely, however, can a single member *consistently* influence committee decisions over a *whole range* of issues; it is more likely that groups of members, or factions, act to influence policy decisions within a committee. As we noted earlier, such alignments can materialize without an explicit or organized effort to form voting blocs. In short, without support from committee colleagues, a member's influence is apt to be limited, no matter how powerful he or she is otherwise. Finally, factions that exist in committee provide the basic ingredients of coalitions. Those factions with similar attitudes, policy orientations, or loyalties (Hinckley, 1972)—that is, factions that represent mutually accommodative interests—tend to coalesce. In sum, members who find themselves pushed in the same policy directions by the interplay of environmental pressure form factions. Committee decisions can be viewed, therefore, as resulting from the emergence of a majority faction, or the merging of several smaller factions representing mutually accommodative interests.

HOW FACTIONS ARISE

The environment of a congressional committee is a milieu composed of the major forces that shape legislative behavior: parties, ideologies, constituencies, presidents, agencies, policies, and interest groups. Pressures from these forces constitute the political context in which members make their individual decisions regarding the policy matters before the committee. These environmental influences operate in at least three ways to influence the decisions of committee members: (1) through subjective identification, (2) through interpersonal communication and influence, and (3) through shared interests.

These mechanisms of influence correspond to three major sources of social influence: identification, compliance, and internalization (Kelman, 1958). The desire on the part of individuals to gain the

21

acceptance of and to maintain a satisfying relationship with other individuals or groups is the motivating factor behind the conformity that is induced by *identification*. For instance, labels (e.g., "conservationists," "hawks") and symbols of identification can induce "partisans" to close ranks behind a party, constituency, administration, or other group-identified position on an issue.

Compliance occurs when an individual adopts certain behaviors because there are specific rewards or punishments associated wih conformity. This mechanism of influence is evident when political actors representing salient influences (parties, groups, constituents, or executive agencies) lobby, promise, pressure, cajole, and generally attempt to persuade committee members to follow certain positions on matters before the committee.

Finally, some behavior occurs because it is congruent with an individual's *internalized predispositions* (attitudes, values, beliefs). Where these predispositions are shared by a number of committee members, some form of unconscious "cue voting" may materialize as committee members with similar interests coalesce. Therefore, members may vote together because they identify with other members who vote similarly, because they comply with the pressures operating on them in order to secure specific benefits or avoid punishments, or because they share certain predispositions with other members.

As the environmental influences compete for the support of committee members, they create divisions or cleavages within the committees; these cleavages appear as voting blocs, or factions. Pressures from environmental forces create the four types of factions that we observe within House committees: partisan, ideological, constituency-interest, and administration factions. This is not to suggest that committee members never vote "their conscience" on policy matters before the committee. We contend only that there are distinct patterns in the voting behavior of committee members and that the existence of committee factions can account for some of the variation in that behavior.

The relationships between the political environment, policy cleavages, committee cleavages, and committee factions—the basic relationships that underlie this analysis—are shown in figure 1. It should be clear from our schema that we expect environmental pressures to create policy cleavages as well as committee cleavages. Policy cleavages arise from the effects of environmental influences when pressures

Figure 1

HOW COMMITTEE FACTIONS EMERGE

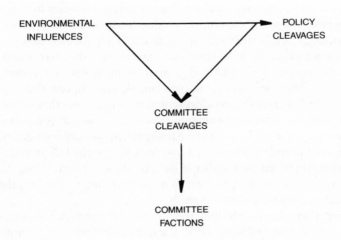

from these influences become solidified into consistent policy differences. For instance, policies relating to urban housing or mass transportation reflect the pressures from constituency influences; similarly, labor legislation reflects the interests of labor groups. These policy cleavages are then translated into committee cleavages, which appear as factions within committees. In sum, environmental influences have a direct and indirect impact on the formation of committee factions. This is not to ignore the specificity of policy cleavages; however, we do not feel that the uniqueness of such policy cleavages is sufficient to produce the factions that we observe. Some factions may be policy-oriented, but party, ideology, constituency, and administration influences seem to go further in explaining the attachments of members to specific committee factions (Parker and Parker, 1979).

The terms committee "cleavages" and committee "factions" are often used interchangeably to describe the factional alignments with-

23

in House committees. The difference between the two concepts is that committee cleavages are inferred, while committee factions are defined empirically. We infer the types of cleavages that exist from the factions that appear; hence, there is a natural correspondence between the types of factions that we observe and the cleavages that characterize the committee.

This distinction is necessary in some cases because a single faction may be the result of pressures from several different environmental influences. For example, ideological and partisan pressures from the environment of many committees produce polarized factions where Democratic liberals align with one faction and Republican conservatives form another. Such polarization occurs because the two environmental pressures push and pull committee members in the same directions. Thus, we can refer to partisan, ideological, constituency-interest, and administration *cleavages* in the same sense that we use these terms to describe committee factions. Our use of committee "cleavages" to describe the factional alignments is only intended to avoid any misunderstanding that may arise due to the lack of correspondence between the number of factions in the committee and the types of environmental pressures that are operating to produce the particular factional configuration.

There is another benefit from the inclusion of committee cleavages within our conceptual framework. The relationship between committee factions and cleavages provides a means for analyzing the stability and change in committee factions over time. It is difficult to identify the stability of committee factions from the factional alignments of committee members, since the composition of the factions will normally change even over a relatively brief period of time. For example, members may shift their allegiance to other committee factions, or new members may form a different faction. Such conditions complicate attempts to determine the stability in the factional composition of the committee.

No matter how members rearrange themselves within the committee over time, if the factional structure is stable the same *types* of cleavages should appear unless there has been an alteration in the types of environmental pressures operating on the committee. Thus, we can compare the factional structures of individual committees in terms of the types of cleavages that can be inferred from the factions that we uncover. This avoids the problems inherent in interpreting factional stability and change where membership turnover, or shifts in member support, produce different factional alignments at different points in time. In sum, we can monitor the changes in the factional structure within committees by determining the stability or change in the types of cleavages that underlie the factions within a committee at different points in time.

DATA AND METHODS IN THE STUDY OF COMMITTEE FACTIONS

This study of committee factions depends on the analysis of committee roll-call votes, a new data base in the study of committee decision making (Appendix A). Previous studies of committee decision making have relied upon observations and interviews because committee roll-call votes were unavailable for public scrutiny. Analysis of committee votes can add to our understanding of decision making in committees and can complement previous committee studies by providing additional specification of the decision-making forces within committees. In addition, roll-call votes are likely to become a major data source for the study of committee decision making because the rapidly expanding demands on the time of House members may limit the opportunities for extensive elite interviewing. The methods outlined in this analysis can serve as an example for the design of these future studies.

The data for this study are based on a subset of roll-call votes in congressional committees between 1973 and 1980—the Ninety-third through the Ninety-sixth Congresses. Since procedural issues frequently elicit partisan responses (Froman and Ripley, 1965), they will be analyzed separately. We have adopted this method to prevent biasing our analysis toward uncovering partisan conflict and factions in committees. Near-unanimous committee votes, defined as those where at least 90 percent of the committee members vote on the same side, are also analyzed separately, because our measure of vote agreement among committee members (the product-moment correlation coefficient) can be severely distorted by skewed distributions (Chapter 2). Since the uneven workload across committees resulted in little roll-call voting in some committees during the span of this analysis,

TABLE 3. The Study of Committee Factions: Characteristics of the Data, 1973–1976 and 1977–1980

| | 1973–1976 | | | | |
| | No. of Committee Votes | | No. of Non-procedural, Non-unanimous Votes | | No. of Committee Members in the |
Committee	93rd Cong.	94th Cong.	93rd Cong.	94th Cong.	Analysis
Agriculture	59	103	31	65	18
Appropriations	49	16	9	11	35
Armed Services	48	82	18	15	22
Banking, Finance, and Urban Affairs	146	105	100	68	15
Budget	—	23	—	17	25
Education and Labor	89	66	56	28	22
Foreign Affairs	36	40	23	19	20
Government Operations	42	34	16	13	25
House Administration	44	77	24	36	16
Interior and Insular Affairs	57	69	41	45	21
Interstate and Foreign Commerce	71	130	43	91	23
Judiciary	109	96	19	66	28
Merchant Marine and Fisheries	—	—	—	—	—
Post Office and Civil Service	29	23	11	14	11
Public Works and Transportation	13	29	12	24	24
Rules	133	109	79	73	13
Science and Technology	2	33	0	18	26
Standards of Official Conduct	10	102	0	13	9
Ways and Means	100	283	67	175	19

Note: Dashes indicate that there were insufficient votes to include in analysis

TABLE 3. Continued

Percentage of Continuing Committee Members	Number of Committee Votes		No. of Non procedural, Non unanimous Votes		No. of Committee Members in the Analysis	Percentage of Continuing Committee Members
	1977–1980					
	95th Cong.	96th Cong.	95th Cong.	96th Cong.		
90	88	61	52	26	33	92
81	25	11	21	7	42	84
69	96	46	28	23	29	83
63	136	67	90	48	30	86
—	72	79	62	63	14	100
88	107	51	64	33	22	96
67	—	—	—	—	—	—
86	55	43	36	28	29	97
89	65	23	44	13	23	100
74	62	68	38	50	30	91
79	81	122	55	80	28	85
96	100	127	71	99	24	100
—	23	16	19	14	23	74
65	75	17	47	10	19	100
92	23	23	18	16	33	94
100	71	77	61	63	10	83
57	27	37	10	20	23	88
75	—	—	—	—	—	—
89	198	151	139	97	29	97

committees' votes are pooled for the Ninety-third and Ninety-fourth Congresses and for Ninety-fifth and Ninety-sixth Congresses. This type of aggregation also allows a comparison of committee factional structures under both a Democratic and a Republican administration and under unified and divided control of the government.

In addition, aggregating the votes over the four-year periods (1973–76, 1977–80) ensures that the derived factions demonstrate some degree of stability. Therefore, intersession and inter-Congress analyses are ignored. The unreliability of intersession analysis stems from the differences in number and representativeness of the roll-call voting that occur during a single legislative session. In some cases, legislative cycles (e.g., election years, budgetary deadlines) dictate the nature of committee decisions and votes; hence, the substance of such votes may differ between legislative sessions, introducing an uncontrolled source of error into the analysis. Aggregating committee votes over four legislative sessions should offset the effects that any one session could have on the structure of committee voting. Reliability is another consideration in aggregating the roll-call votes: the smaller the size of the data base, the less confidence we can have in the conclusions. The limited number of issues that are voted upon in a single legislative session in most committees would further weaken any inferences that one may wish to draw from these data.

Inter-Congress analyses may also be suspect because they are apt to capture the specificity of individual Congresses on committee voting. The factions within the House Judiciary Committee, for example, could conceivably change between the Ninety-third and Ninety-fourth Congresses as the impeachment question vanishes from the committee's agenda. In short, inter-Congress analyses may confound the stability of committee factions and the comparisons of factions over time. Aggregating committee votes over two Congresses should reduce the impact of the specificity of any one Congress on the formation of factions within committees.

Aggregating committee votes requires that members in the study must have served continuously on the committee during a four-year period.[1] As table 3 illustrates, the study includes at least 70 percent of the continuing members in two-thirds of the committees in the initial

1. This requirement is relaxed only where a committee's roll-call votes are distributed in such a way that a member could in a single Congress vote on over 70 percent of the nonunanimous roll-call votes in two Congresses.

analysis (Ninety-third and Ninety-fourth Congresses); the percentages of continuing members increase further during the replication period (Ninety-fifth and Ninety-sixth Congresses). Extending the time-period requirement to continuous service in three or four Congresses would only serve to limit the number of members who could qualify for inclusion in the analysis. The requirement adopted in this analysis of committee factions (four years of committee membership) maximizes the number of committee members included in the study, while ensuring that the included factions exhibit stability. In addition to the above requirement, the pool of committee members is restricted to those who have voted on at least 70 percent of the substantive committee roll calls (core membership). This additional requirement limits the effects of factoring a product-moment correlation matrix where the correlations themselves are based on varying numbers of votes. At the same time, the requirement is not overly restrictive in determining the number of members included in the analysis (see table 2).

A member's attachment to a committee faction is reflected in his or her correlation (factor loading) with that specific faction. The stronger the correlation of a member with a faction, the more frequently the member votes with that faction. The square of this correlation provides a measure of the strength of attachment of a member to a faction. In the tables describing the factional alignments (tables 6, 8–41), we have included factor loadings less than .50 *only* where we feel they will clarify the interpretation of the factions. Displaying the factor loadings in this manner will illuminate the salient features of the factional alignments within a committee. Committee members with the highest correlations with a faction are characterized as the *nominal leaders* of the faction for the purposes of identifying the voting bloc; this should *not* be construed as imputing any leadership to such members or any organization of committee factions.

INTERPRETING FACTIONS

A variety of sources of information have been used in interpreting the factional alignments within congressional committees. Group ratings are extremely useful in determining the *partisan* (Democratic party unity,[2] presidential support) and *ideological* (Americans for Democratic Action [ADA], Americans for Constitutional Action [ACA], Committee on Political Education [COPE], Chambers of Commerce of the United States [CCUS], the National Farmers' Union [NFU], and Conservative Coalition scores) loyalties of committee members. These ratings reflect an interest group's evaluation of a member's legislative support of a salient group interest. Some of our interpretations are based upon the consistency in the patterns of correlations between factional alignments and diverse group ratings. Conceptually similar and strongly intercorrelated variables are treated as measurements of the same underlying dimension. We feel that this strategy is preferable to interpreting individual ratings, which tend to be less reliable than multiple-item measures. We are also reluctant to reduce the variables to a few scales, because some of the specificity of a group's interests or concerns may be obscured. Our analysis attempts to strike a balance between these two approaches in order to maximize the benefits of each. The interpretation of factions relies upon the patterns that appear in the correlations; at the same time, we display the correlation for each group to allow the reader to examine the different impact of individual group ratings.

Unfortunately, the absence of direct measures of the effects of administration or constituency influences creates obstacles to the identification of these types of factions. The problem is further exacerbated by the possibility that the effects of constituency and administration pressures will be obscured by the impact of party and ideology. For instance, party support and presidential support are inextricably linked when the same party controls both Congress and the White House. This should not be construed to mean that constituency and administration factions can be identified only when the effects of party and ideology are weak or nonexistent. We have tried to probe beneath the partisan and ideological nature of committee factions to see if other forces might also be at work by examining additional statistical and nonstatistical properties of individual factions. Our approach has been to suspect partisan and ideological factionalism within committees but to distrust our suspicions. As a result, we have been able to identify administration and constituency-

2. The variable party unity is coded in terms of *Democratic* party support; hence, Democratic factions should have a positive correlation with party unity; Republican blocs, a negative correlation.

interest factions even in House committees where ideology and party appear to dominate the organization of committee factions.

In identifying administration and constituency-interest factions we have placed special reliance upon three sources of information about committee factions: the political and biographical information about committee members; the subcommittee assignments and positions (leadership) of committee members; and the policy cleavages associated with individual factions. Biographical and political profiles of individual committee members who form the same faction provide information regarding the constituency interests of members and their political sympathies. Subcommittee assignments are useful pieces of information because they often delineate the policy interests of committee members and the types of environmental influences that might have a stake in subcommittee decisions. The significance of subcommittee decisions on the outcome of committee legislation and the decentralization of Congress have enhanced the relevance of subcommittee rule, making subcommittee leaders and members appropriate targets for constituent, group, and administration pressures.

Salient policy cleavages within committees (policy dimensions) are another source of information for identifying administration and constituency-interest factions. The policy cleavages are determined through an R-component analysis of the votes taken within individual committees and provide insights into the types of policies that divide committee members. The relationship between policy cleavages and committee factions provides a basis for inferences regarding the nature of the committee's factional structure and the types of environmental pressures that are relevant to committee decision making. Policy cleavages, like committee factions, also result from environmental pressures, especially constituent, group, and administration pressures. The reason may be that the effects of policies are immediate and direct for constituents, presidents, agencies, and interest groups; hence, certain policies may be closley identified with such influences. In any event, the association between policy cleavages and specific committee factions provide a clue to the nature of the environmental pressures underlying committee factions and the associated policy cleavages. (These policy cleavages are described in fuller detail in Chapter 2.) We have relied upon *all* of these sources in interpreting the factional alignments in committees, although some pieces of

31

information have been more useful than others. In interpreting our data, however, we direct the reader's attention *only* to that information directly relevant to interpreting the factional structure of a congressional committee.

In order to simplify comparisons of committee cleavages, we present two-dimensional representations of the major vote divisions within each committee (figures 4–28, 30–38). Committee members' coordinates on the graphs are their correlations with each of the two dimensions (factor loadings). Since every committee's factional structure is reduced to the same number of dimensions, these graphic illustrations provide a common basis for identifying similarities and differences in the major cleavages across House committees. In addition, the two-dimensional representations provide some indication of the coalitions that form from the factions: the closer a member is to a cluster of committee colleagues, the greater the likelihood that the committee member will vote with that cluster to form a coalition.

The two dimensions reflected in the graphs generally represent the major cleavages within Congress and its committee system—party and ideology. The most important features of the graphs are the distance between clusters of committee members and the degree to which members cluster into small groups or are dispersed across the defined space. Tight clusters of committee members reflect the polarization of partisan and ideological loyalties within the committee; the greater the diffusion of committee members and clusters, the greater the likelihood that forces other than party and ideology are at work in creating cleavages within the committee. The distance between clusters provides a rough indication of the size of the gulf that separates factions and coalitions.

The graphs also provide another means for determining the long-term stability and change in a committee's factional structure. Comparisons of the two-dimensional graphs at different time points provide information for determining continuity in a committee's factional structure: similarities in the spatial configurations of committee members across the two dimensions at different points in time serve as an indication of factional stability. In most instances, the stability or instability in committee factions that results from comparisons of committee cleavages across time is also evident.

In Chapter 2 we explore the nature of policy conflict within the House committees. Chapters 3–5 present detailed descriptions of the factional structure of individual committees. The committees have been classified according to the salient sources of conflict within the committee: in Chapter 3 we examine committees in which conflict is entirely partisan and ideological in nature; committees which reflect pressures from the executive branch are discussed in Chapter 4; and Chapter 5 deals with committees displaying signs of the influence of constituencies and groups. We begin each of these chapters with a brief description of the operation of the environmental influence (parties, ideologies, presidents, agencies, groups, and constituencies) within congressional committees. These discussions are intended to suggest the types of actors and processes that might account for the composition of the factional structure within a committee. In Chapter 6 we compare the committee factions in both time periods (Ninety-third and Ninety-fourth Congresses and Ninety-fifth and Ninety-sixth Congresses) in order to delineate stability and change in the factions. In the final chapters (7 and 8) we examine the relationship between committee cleavages and coalition size and explore sources of stability and change in committee decision making.

CHAPTER TWO

Issue Conflict
and Consensus

Committee roll-call votes can be divided into three general categories: substantive, procedural, and final-passage votes. Substantive votes amend legislation; they determine what will or will not be included in the legislation that may someday become government policy. Procedural votes include reconsideration votes, points of order, referrals to subcommittees, recommit votes, instructions on handling legislation on the floor, postponement of committee action, votes on limiting debate, and motions to table legislation. Final-passage votes are taken after the amending process has been completed, the compromises have been wrought, and the legislation is ready to proceed to floor consideration. In many committees, these votes are *pro forma*, or procedural, issues, and are dealt with routinely by the committee. Since the major concern of this study is with policy making within committees, our analysis uses only substantive roll-call votes.

Two aspects of the three categories of votes merit further consideration before we move on to our analysis of decision making in committees. The first question to consider is the degree of unanimity among members in decision making. Because cleavages and factions do not appear when members are in agreement on the matter to be decided, it is necessary to focus on conflict within the committees, which may minimize or obscure the degree of consensus displayed by the committee. Therefore we will first examine the degree of conflict or consensus a committee displays on each type of vote (procedural, substantive, and final-passage). In the last section of our analysis we will once again return to the question of conflict and consensus within committees when we examine the relationship between cleavages and the size of winning coalitions on substantive issues before the committee.

The second question to be investigated is the degree to which procedural and final-passage votes reflect partisan influences. Previous studies of legislative behavior give us reason to suspect that on these votes the party will be better able to hold their partisans in line than on substantive matters.

> [Party] Leaders are also more likely to prevail with specific requests at relatively invisible points in the legislative process. That is, if a member perceives that his position might cause some negative reaction in his constituency, he would feel insecure in honoring a leadership request on a final roll call on the floor. His action in a committee, however, is likely to go unnoticed at home by either the press or public whereas his action on the floor is likely to be reported. Leaders are also more likely to gain converts on issues that are defined in substantive terms. For example, a motion to adjourn may really be a motion that will kill a bill. A person who may mildly favor the bill can still claim that position and yet vote with his party leaders in favor of adjournment and rationalize his action—if he is ever questioned—as "only procedural." (Ripley, 1978, pp. 220-21)

Hence, on procedural votes within the committee, which tend to be relatively invisible, the predominant influence on the vote is likely to be party. The same can be said of final-passage votes, because they are both invisible and likely to be defined as "procedural" in nature. Final-passage votes have thus been excluded from our anlysis of factions because of the possibility that their inclusion would bias our analysis toward finding a higher degree of party influence than actually present.

UNANIMOUS AND NEAR-UNANIMOUS ROLL-CALL VOTES

Although roll-call votes can be thought of as a means of resolving conflict, some unanimous votes do occur.[1] In some instances, roll-call votes on final-passage decisions are mandated by committee rules. The decision to close a committee meeting to the public is also normally determined by a roll-call vote. In this last case, a committee that must hold many meetings in closed session because of national security considerations would be expected to have a large number of unanimous votes in this category. In fact, the largest percentage of unanimous roll-call votes could be expected in the final-passage category because by the time this stage is reached most conflicts have already been resolved. The mere act of calling for a roll-call vote on a substantive issue, however, generally denotes that there is some conflict over the matter. Consensual issues can be disposed of quickly and easily by a show of hands or a voice vote. A roll-call vote on a substantive issue forces committee members publicly to declare a position on a particular issue. Since such votes cannot be hidden or obscured as easily as a voice vote or a show of hands, roll-call votes should occur primarily on salient conflicts within the committee. For this reason, we expect that the smallest percentage of unanimous votes will occur on substantive amendments.

The delineation of unanimous votes is important to the study of conflict because it provides a context in which to view the conflicts that are uncovered. For instance, conflict may arise in a committee on several substantive issues, but those issues may make up only a small percentage of all the substantive roll-call votes taken in the committee, the majority being unanimous. Concentrating merely on the conflict and failing to note the large degree of consensus would present a distorted picture of the nature of decision making in the committee. It is impossible, of course, to delineate all the areas of consensus within a committee with roll-call votes, because many consensual issues are decided by means other than roll-call votes. Examination of the number of unanimous votes provides a method of comparing not only the degree of consensus in each of the vote

1. Henceforth, such votes will be referred to as "unanimous," or "consensual," votes. In this study unanimous votes are defined as those on which 90 percent of the members voting support one side (yes or no).

categories but also the amount of consensus on various types of votes in each of the committees.

The largest number of unanimous *procedural* votes during the Ninety-third and Ninety-fourth Congresses (table 4) occur in the Standards of Official Conduct (80 percent unanimous) and Armed Services committees (70 percent unanimous). All of the unanimous roll-call votes in the Standards Committee, and all but two of the unanimous votes in the Armed Services Committee, deal with decisions to go into executive session. In Standards, closed meetings are used to take testimony on pending investigations, and in Armed Services they are used to discuss national defense matters. A substantial number of unanimous votes also occur in the Foreign Affairs Committee (28 percent of the *procedural* votes); once again, all of the consensual votes are decisions to go into executive session. In six committees (Budget, Interior and Insular Affairs, Judiciary, Post Office and Civil Service, Public Works and Transportation, and Science and Technology) there are no unanimous roll-call votes on procedural issues. In the remaining nine committees, between 5 percent and 21 percent of the procedural votes are unanimous.

The pattern of consensus on procedural issues established in the Ninety-third and Ninety-fourth Congresses appears to hold in the Ninety-fifth and Ninety-sixth Congresses (table 4). When the Public Works Committee is excluded (only one procedural vote), the three committees which show the greatest degree of consensus on procedural issues are Standards (90 percent), Armed Services (78 percent), and Foreign Affairs (73 percent). Consistent with the earlier findings for the 1973–76 period, the bulk of these votes concern decisions to go to executive session.

The number of consensual votes on substantive issues is small (table 4) in both time periods.[2] In the Ninety-third and Ninety-fourth Congresses, four committees (Appropriations, Budget, Interstate and Foreign Commerce, and Rules) have no unanimous votes on substantive roll calls, and twelve committees range between 1 percent and 11 percent consensual votes. In the Standards Committee, 63 percent of all substantive roll-call votes are unanimous; the majority of these

2. Two committees, Public Works and Merchant Marine, could not be compared because they had no recorded roll-call votes on procedural issues. Both the Rules and Standards committees have no final-passage votes; patterns in both procedural and final-passage votes for these two committees are not presented.

TABLE 4. Issue Consensus in House Committee Voting, 1973–1980

Committee	Procedural Votes			Substantive Votes			Final-Passage Votes		
	No. Unani- mous	Total	% Unani- mous	No. Unani- mous	Total	% Unani- mous	No. Unani- mous	Total	% Unani- mous
Agriculture									
1973–76	4	30	13	6	105	6	8	22	36
1977–80	0	13	0	5	83	6	29	46	63
Appropriations									
1973–76	4	42	10	0	20	0			
1977–80	2	7	29	0	28	0	0	1	0
Armed Services									
1973–76	44	63	70	4	35	11	14	26	54
1977–80	39	50	78	5	56	9	27	33	82
Banking, Finance, and Urban Affairs									
1973–76	1	21	5	13	184	7	15	46	33
1977–80	3	9	33	13	151	9	24	43	56
Budget									
1973–76	0	3	0	0	17	0	0	2	0
1977–80	0	8	0	3	132	2	0	10	0
Education and Labor									
1973–76	3	16	19	10	96	10	18	38	47
1977–80	4	14	29	5	103	5	12	25	48
Foreign Affairs									
1973–76	5	18	28	5	47	11	2	11	18
1977–80	11	15	73	1	14	7	5	7	71
Government Operations									
1973–76	2	11	18	3	32	9	18	22	82
1977–80	0	8	0	3	67	4	11	18	61
House Administration									
1973–76	4	19	21	18	78	23	5	19	26
1977–80	3	12	25	5	62	8	1	11	9
Interior and Insular Affairs									
1973–76	0	17	0	1	88	1	5	18	28
1977–80	0	16	0	3	91	3	4	16	25
Interstate and Foreign Commerce									
1973–76	3	46	7	0	144	0	2	12	17
1977–80	0	30	0	1	136	1	3	31	10

TABLE 4. Continued

Committee	Procedural Votes			Substantive Votes			Final-Passage Votes		
	No. Unanimous	Total	% Unanimous	No. Unanimous	Total	% Unanimous	No. Unanimous	Total	% Unanimous
Judiciary									
1973–76	0	11	0	2	84	2	11	23	48
1977–80	0	16	0	4	173	2	12	34	35
Merchant Marine and Fisheries									
1973–76[a]									
1977–80	0	1	0	1	34	3	1	3	33
Post Office and Civil Service									
1973–76	0	4	0	1	27	4	8	16	50
1977–80	1	11	9	2	59	3	7	17	41
Public Works and Transportation									
1973–76	0	1	0	2	38	5	1	1	100
1977–80	1	1	100	1	35	3	2	8	25
Rules									
1973–76	7	81	9	0	160	0			
1977–80	0	19	0	4	128	3			
Science and Technology									
1973–76	0	2	0	1	16	6	12	14	86
1977–80	2	6	33	6	36	17	14	18	78
Standards of Official Conduct									
1973–76	52	65	80	25	40	63	2	2	100
1977–80	94	105	90	12	22	55	1	1	100
Ways and Means									
1973–76	7	108	6	3	245	1	1	24	4
1977–80	0	49	0	2	238	1	7	36	19

[a]The Merchant Marine and Fisheries Committee had only one recorded roll-call-vote in 1973–76; the vote was not unanimous.

votes concern establishing procedures for the investigation of specific complaints. While the House Administration Committee displays a modest degree of unanimity (23 percent unanimous) on substantive issues in the Ninety-third and Ninety-fourth Congresses, the number of consensual votes in the Ninety-fifth and Ninety-sixth Congresses drops (8 percent). In contrast, the number of consensual substantive roll calls in the Standards Committee remains relatively high (55 percent) during the Ninety-fifth and Ninety-sixth Congresses. In the latter two Congresses, the percentage of unanimous roll-call votes ranges between 0 and 9 percent in the vast majority (seventeen) of the committees.

The figures for the final-passage votes indicate that the greatest percentage of unanimous votes occur in this category. During the Ninety-third and Ninety-fourth Congresses (table 4) only the Ways and Means Committee shows a percentage of unanimous votes less than 17 percent. The relatively high degree of unanimity on final-passage votes is also evident in the Ninety-fifth and Ninety-sixth Congresses. The large number of consensual votes on final-passage decisions can be explained in two ways: by the time final-passage votes are taken, the compromises on the legislation have already been hammered out; further, in many committees final-passage votes are pro forma actions dictated by committee rules.

These findings confirm earlier speculations about unanimous votes: they are least likely to occur on substantive issues; the largest percentage of unanimous votes are found in those committees in which release of information to the public must be safeguarded; and finally, by the time the legislation reaches the final vote, the battle over substantive matters has already been won or lost during the amending phase of deliberations. The next place that battles will be fought is not on the final-passage vote in committees, but on the floor of the House. As a result, the greatest degree of consensus occurs on final-passage votes.

PARTISANSHIP IN PROCEDURAL AND FINAL-PASSAGE VOTES

In the previous chapter we suggested that nonunanimous procedural and final-passage votes tend to be partisan in nature. The fear of introducing a partisan bias into the analysis is the justification for the exclusion of these two types of votes. To include these votes in the analysis might strengthen the effect of partisan forces to the point that they obscure other salient influences in a committee's environment. In this section, patterns in the correlations between party and procedural and final-passage votes are examined; the phi-coefficient is calculated for each nonunanimous procedural and final-passage vote in each committee. The party correlations for each type of vote in each committee are then averaged to determine the average party correlation (figures 2 and 3). Caution should be exercised in interpreting patterns in average correlations that are based on a small number of votes, and interpretations of such correlations should be considered tentative.

If the party correlations with *both* procedural *and* final-passage votes are examined in each committee, five possible patterns can emerge. A committee could be consistently partisan: that is, both procedural and final-passage votes display a substantial degree (ϕ $\rangle$ .50) of partisanship in both time periods. The obverse would also be a notable pattern: a committee could be consistently nonpartisan (ϕ $\langle$ .50) during both time periods. More mixed patterns could also emerge from the examination of party correlations in both vote categories. A committee may exhibit higher party correlations in both categories in one time period than in the other time period. In contrast, a committee might increase (or decline) in partisanship in only one category of vote (procedural or final-passage) from one time period to the next. Finally, one vote category may display partisan correlations and the other nonpartisan correlations.

Three committees display correlations that are consistently above .50 on both procedural and final-passage votes: Budget, Education and Labor, and Government Operations committees (figures 2 and 3). Two other committees with fairly consistent partisan patterns that fall just shy of the stated criterion of .50 are the House Administration (ϕ = .49) and Post Office committees (ϕ = .49). Consistent nonpartisan patterns are maintained in three committees. Both the correlations for procedural issues and for final-passage votes are below .50 for the entire span of the analysis in the Appropriations, Armed Services, and Foreign Affairs committees (figures 2 and 3).

The remaining committees display mixed patterns for procedural and final-passage votes. For example, the Banking, Finance, and Urban Affairs Committee is more partisan in the 1977–80 period for

41

Figure 2

AVERAGE CORRELATION BETWEEN PROCEDURAL VOTES AND PARTY
(1973—1980)

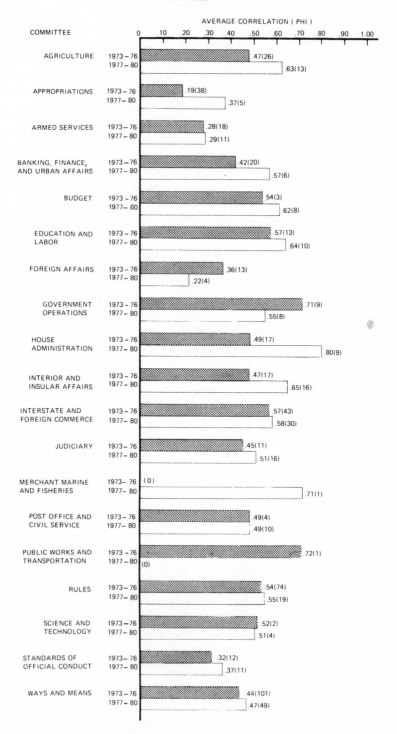

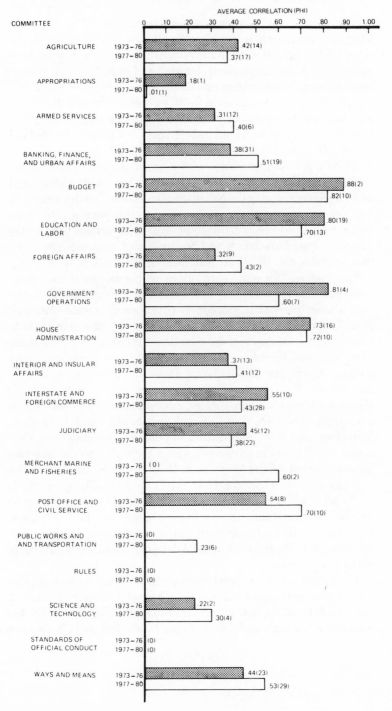

Figure 3

AVERAGE CORRELATION BETWEEN FINAL-PASSAGE VOTES AND PARTY

(1973–1980)

both procedural and final-passage votes than in the 1973–76 period. Three committees show a noticeable increase only in party correlations for *procedural votes* in the Ninety-fifth and Ninety-sixth Congresses (1977–80): Agriculture, Interior, and Judiciary. Final-passage votes are more partisan than procedural votes during the Ninety-fifth and Ninety-sixth Congresses in the Ways and Means and the Science and Technology committees, where party correlates are above .50 for procedural votes (ϕ = .55 in 1973–76; ϕ = .51 in 1977–80) and well below .50 for final-passage votes (ϕ = .22 in 1973–76; ϕ = .30 in 1977–80). All the committees with a mixed pattern examined thus far show increased partisanship in one or both areas (procedural and/or final passage) during the Ninety-fifth and Ninety-sixth Congresses. The one committee that is an exception to this pattern is Interstate and Foreign Commerce; in this committee, final-passage votes are less partisan in the Ninety-fifth and Ninety-sixth Congresses (ϕ = .43) than in the Ninety-third and Ninety-fourth Congresses (ϕ = .55).

The tendency for party correlations with procedural votes to be more partisan in the Ninety-fifth and Ninety-sixth Congresses becomes more marked if procedural issues are examined separately from final-passage votes. Of the seventeen committees that could be compared, five committees show moderate increases in party correlations with procedural issus during the later two congresses: Agriculture, Appropriations, Banking, House Administration, and Interior (figure 2). In ten committees, the correlations remain essentially the same (Armed Services, Budget, Education, Interstate and Foreign Commerce, Judiciary, Post Office, Rules, Science and Technology, Standards, and Ways and Means). In only two committees are there noticeable declines in partisanship from the earlier to the later congresses: Foreign Affairs (ϕ = .36 in 1973–76; ϕ = .22 in 1977–80) and Government Operations (ϕ = .71 in 1973–76; ϕ = .55 in 1977–80). While these declines may be influenced by the small number of procedural votes in these committees, the Government Operations Committee remains partisan according to the earlier criterion (ϕ .50), and the Foreign Affairs Committee remains consistently nonpartisan.

The patterns in party correlations are not as clear on final-passage votes as they are on procedural votes. Three of the fifteen committees compared (Banking, Foreign Affairs, and Post Office) display modest increases in the party correlations in the Ninety-fifth and Ninety-sixth

Congresses (figure 3).[3] Eight committees (Agriculture, Armed Services, Budget, House Administration, Interior, Judiciary, Science and Technology, and Ways and Means) have correlations that remain essentially the same in both time periods. The major difference between procedural and final-passage votes is that four committees register declines in the correlations between party and final-passage votes. The Education and Government Operations committees show declines in the partisanship of final-passage votes (figure 3), but still remain above our standard (.50) for classification as partisan. In the Appropriations Committee the number of votes (one) is too small to create much confidence in the correlation. The remaining committee to register declines is Interstate and Foreign Commerce. As mentioned earlier, Interstate and Foreign Commerce is the only committee in which the decline in partisanship in 1977–80 moves the final-passage votes from a partisan categorization to a nonpartisan one.

These findings suggest that caution is warranted in determining which votes to include in the analysis of committee factions. Although in the correlations for procedural *and* final-passage votes some committees (Budget, Education, and Government Operations) display unambiguously partisan patterns while others (Appropriations, Armed Services, and Foreign Affairs) show nonpartisan ones, the majority of the committees exhibit a more mixed pattern, where correlations fluctuate from one time period to the next. Inclusion of final-passage and procedural votes as data in the analysis of some committees would definitely introduce a partisan bias into the interpretation of committee factions. In the case of a mixed pattern, one could not be sure to what extent a bias was present. Hence, the most prudent course for handling procedural and final-passage votes appears to be to separate them from substantive votes and to analyze them separately.

The examination of each type of vote (procedural and final-passage) indicates that the majority of the committees examined (fifteen) either show noticeable increases in partisanship on procedural issues or remain the same in the later time period (1977–80). There are two possible sources of the increases; committee turnover may have resulted in the addition of partisan members. Alternatively, the shift in

3. In four committees comparisons are not possible because of the lack of votes during one time period: Merchant Marine, Public Works, Rules, and Standards.

party control of the presidency between the Ninety-third and Ninety-fourth Congresses and the Ninety-fifth and Ninety-sixth Congresses may have stimulated increased partisanship on the part of Democrats in some committees and resulted in increased partisanship on procedural votes. The ambiguous pattern in final-passage votes—with about as many committees revealing increases in party correlations as show declines—may be explained by two additional factors. The subject matter of the legislation being considered and the amount of discussion, compromise, and amending that preceded the final-passage vote could conceivably influence the degree of partisanship displayed on such votes. Some of these sources of change are explored in later chapters (Chapters 6 and 8).

POLICY CONFLICT IN HOUSE COMMITTEES

Policy areas and particular legislation are more likely to create conflict when they touch upon cleavages that are salient within the committee. Partisan loyalties may be aroused, for instance, by legislation that falls into certain policy areas. This is especially true when the parties hold opposing views on the scope, goals, and restraints that should guide policy in particular areas. Other legislation can incite ideological conflict. Often on ideological issues we find Democrats divided between conservative and liberal positions. Finally, conflict in certain policy areas can result from the pressures of particular interests on committee members; for instance, these pressures may reflect constituency or group interests. Although it is not possible to pinpoint particular pressures in examining the partisan and ideological conflict, the absence of partisan and ideological conflict suggests that perhaps other influences are at work. The occurrence and impact of organized groups or interests is examined in later chapters (Chapters 5 and 6).

Policy dimensions can help in the interpretation of factions when other variables such as party, ACA and ADA, or presidential support scores cannot explain the formation of voting blocs. The identification of areas of policy conflict also aids in uncovering new issues that emerge in committees. By delineating the areas of policy conflict and describing the pieces of legislation over which the conflict arises, we can pinpoint changes in the nature of conflict. In the same way, areas of stability in policy conflict can be located and can serve as indicators of the type of legislation that is likely to continue to generate either partisan or ideological conflict.

The connection between the jurisdictions of the committees and the policy issues they handle suggests that stability can be expected to exist in most committees. In fact, the immutability of jurisdictional lines is attested to by the failure of attempts to reform the committee system. However, jurisdictional boundaries are broad, and some issues generate salient conflict while others do not. Changing events and societal conditions catapult certain issues into prominence at the expense of other issues that were formerly important. Change is possible, therefore, despite the stability of committee jurisdictions. Although not the only factor of importance, the emergence of new issue conflicts is instrumental in changing the factional alignment in a committee. New issues may crosscut older lines of conflict; when these new issues become salient in the committee, they break older factions and lead to the formation of new alignments that reflect the pressures from these issues and the political actors with an interest in the issues. Changes in the salience of particular policy areas can be helpful, therefore, in describing the increased salience of new cleavages in committees.

References to the policy dimensions in later chapters refer to the policy conflicts described in this chapter. These policy dimensions are derived from an R-component analysis of all substantive, non-unanimous amendments voted upon by at least 70 percent of the members included in the analysis (see Appendix A for a fuller explanation). Since party and ideology are generally recognized as salient sources of legislative conflict, two indicators of ideology (ADA and ACA ratings of individual members) and one indicator of party (support for the Democratic party) are correlated with each policy dimension in order to determine the degree to which the conflicts underlying the policy dimensions are ideological and/or partisan in nature.[4] This procedure enables us to determine to what extent ideology and party are components of the issue conflicts within the committee.

---

4. Since a yes vote is coded 1 and a no vote is coded 2; a negative correlation indicates support for the ideological and/or partisan indicators and support for (a yes vote) the amendment(s).

TABLE 5. The Ideological and Partisan Nature of Policy
Cleavages within House Committees, 1973–1980

Committee	Policy Dimension	Party	Ideology ADA	Ideology ACA
Agriculture				
1973–76	I. Food Stamps	.89*	87*	−.89*
1977–80	II. Assistance to Farmers	.22	−.09	−.06
	I. Food Stamps and Wheat and Feed Grains Legislation	.88*	.67*	−.89*
Appropriations				
1973–76	I. Restricting Military Expenditures	−.50*	−.66*	.64*
	II. Budget Reductions	.52*	.43	−.35
1977–80	I. Reducing Military Procurements	.31	.45*	−.35*
	II. Reducing Agency Appropriations	.82*	.63*	−.76*
Armed Services				
1973–76	I. Military Strength Reductions	−.61*	−.73*	.65*
	II. Military Procurement Reductions	.07	.02	−.18
1977–80	I. Administration Recommendations	.31	.65*	−.34
	II. Increases in Defense Spending	.60*	.50*	−.61*
	III. Increases in Aircraft Procurements	.10	.08	−.17
Banking, Finance, and Urban Affairs				
1973–76	I. Banking and Economic Policy	.84*	.72*	−.84*
	II. Limitations on Housing and Urban Programs	.42	.31	−.44
1977–80	I. Monetary Policy	.67*	.24	−.57*
	II. Banking Regulation	.44*	.55*	−.51*
	III. Housing and Urban Programs	.37	.52*	−.44*
Budget				
1973–76	I. Reductions in "Education, Manpower, and Social Services" Expenditures	.89*	.77*	−.87*
	II. Increases for Income Security Programs	−.34	−.41	.34
1977–80	I. Reductions in Nondefense Expenditures	.81*	.66*	−.84*
	II. Reductions in Defense Expenditures	−.46	−.59*	.45
Education and Labor				
1973–76	I. Labor and Education	.93*	.81*	−.89*
1977–80	I. Labor and Education	.86*	.64*	−.77*
Foreign Affairs				
1973–76	I. Limits on Presidential Discretion	−.34	−.40	.26
	II. Sanctions	−.53*	−.55*	.63*
	III. Military Assistance	−.10	−.29	.11
1977–80	(Not enough votes)			

TABLE 5. Continued

Committee	Policy Dimension	Party	Ideology ADA	Ideology ACA
Government Operations				
1973–76	I. Revenue Sharing and Agency Regulation	−.85*	−.86*	.78*
1977–80	I. Agency Regulation and Fiscal Assistance	.83*	.66*	−.83*
	II. Revenue Sharing	−.25	−.59*	.30
House Administration				
1973–76	I. Administration of the House	.73*	.54	−.61*
	II. Federal Elections Campaign Regulation	.46	.37	−.50
1977–80	I. Regulation of Campaigns	.89*	.67*	−.83*
	II. Congressional Reforms	.23	.32	−.22
Interior and Insular Affairs				
1973–76	I. Land-Use and Surface-Mining Regulation	.78*	.81*	−.87*
1977–80	I. Land-Use and Water-Use Regulation (Wilderness Areas)	−.87*	−.92*	.84*
Interstate and Foreign Commerce				
1973–76	I. Energy	.95*	.91*	−.87*
1977–80	I. Energy and Health Care Costs	.94*	.87*	−.93*
Judiciary				
1973–76	I. Illegal Practices and Crime Control	.76*	.69*	−.66*
	II. Gun Control	−.23	−.44*	.40
1977–80	I. Ethics in Government	.84*	.69*	−.83*
	II. Additional Judges	−.06	−.14	.06
	III. Individual's Rights	.29	.31	−.27
Merchant Marine and Fisheries				
1973–76	(Not enough votes)			
1977–80	I. Panama Canal Treaty Implementation	.81*	.61*	−.80*
	II. Environmental Protection	−.05	−.36	−.02
	III. Shipping U.S. Oil Imports on U.S. Flagships	.27	−.11	−.20
Post Office and Civil Service				
1973–76	I. Limiting Presidential Discretion	−.86*	−.77*	.84*
	II. Federal Salaries	.42	.38	−.41

49

TABLE 5. Continued

| Committee | Policy Dimension | Party | Ideology | |
			ADA	ACA
	III. Postal Regulations	.04	−.09	.08
1977–80	I. Political Activities of Federal Employees	.81*	.51*	−.89*
	II. Civil Service Reform—Executive-Level Employees	−.18	−.13	.01
	III. Civil Service Reform—Rights and Protections of Federal Employees	.28	.41	−.18
Public Works and Transportation				
1973–76	I. Mass Transportation	.79*	.55*	−.68*
	II. Airport Regulation	−.39	−.63*	.47*
1977–80	I. Transportation Policy	.83*	.65*	−.80*
	II. Regulation	.24	.32	−.19
Rules				
1973–76	I. Amending Rules to Modify Substantive Legislation	.58	.45	−.64*
	II. Modifying Normal House Procedures	.38	.75*	−.69*
1977–80	I. Modification of Rules	.89*	.87*	−.88*
	II. Internal House Procedures	.35	.03	−.35
Science and Technology				
1973–76	I. Fossil Fuel Research and Development	.33	.56*	−.43*
	II. Synthetic Fuels Loan Guarantees	.39	−.54*	.47
	III. ERDA Funding	.63*	.37	−.47*
1977–80	I. Nuclear Research	−.39	−.66*	.45*
	II. Alternative Technologies Research	−.77*	−.30	.71*
Standards of Official Conduct				
1973–76	I. Daniel Schorr Case	.86*	.85*	−.85*
	II. Michael Harrington Case	−.26	−.32	.11
	III. Disciplinary Action	.06	.11	−.13
	IV. Decisions on Complaints	.33	.23	−.33
1977–80	(Not enough votes)			
Ways and Means				
1973–76	I. Individual and Corporate Taxes	.81*	.69*	−.27*
	II. Oil and Gas Depletion	.41	.47	−.53*
1977–80	I. Taxing Oil Profits	.76*	.57*	−.74*
	II. Individual Income Tax Deductions	−.38	−.64*	.35

Note: Pearson correlations marked with asterisks are significant at the .01 level.

Agriculture

Two policy dimensions are salient in the Agriculture Committee during the Ninety-third and Ninety-fourth Congresses (table 5). Conflict between conservatives and liberals is evident in Policy Dimension I, which concerns establishing eligibility standards for the Food Stamp Program. The high correlation (*r*) of this dimension with liberal and conservative measures (ADA = .87; ACA = −.89) indicates that liberals are opposed to the proposed amendments that would tighten eligibility criteria. In contrast, conservatives favor restraints. The high correlation with party (.89) indicates that the conflict is not entirely ideological; Democrats oppose the amendments and Republicans tend to support them. The second salient policy conflict (Policy Dimension II) deals with assistance to farmers. The legislation represented by this dimension includes the Rural Environment Assistance Program; target prices for wheat, feed grains, cotton, and milk; and research on wheat and feed grains. Since the correlations with partisan and ideological measures are not significant, it appears that the conflict on this dimension centers on something other than ideology and party.

Although only one policy dimension emerges during the Ninety-fifth and Ninety-sixth Congresses, the same policy areas mark the conflict. Eleven of the nineteen amendments associated with Policy Dimension I concern food stamp legislation. The remaining amendments relate to wheat and feed grain legislation (i.e., wheat reserves, loan levels for 1980 and 1981 crops of feed grains and wheat, and the purchase of embargoed wheat). The correlations reveal that liberal Democrats continue to oppose restrictions on the Food Stamp Program and increased subsidies for wheat and feed grains, whereas conservatives tend to support both of these positions. It appears that the change in the number of policy dimensions has not altered the nature of the conflict in the Agriculture Committee.

Appropriations

In the Ninety-third and Ninety-Fourth Congresses, military appropriations and other budget cuts inspire ideological conflict in the Appropriations Committee. Conservatives (ACA = .64) oppose and liberals (ADA = −.66) support cuts in such areas as the anti-ballistic missile (ABM) program and the military construction program and in funding for fighting in Southeast Asia (Policy Dimension I, table 5). On Policy Dimension II, Democrats (party = .52) oppose proposed spending levels in various areas, including military assistance to Laos and South Vietnam.

As might be expected of a committee that decides how money is to be spent, budget reductions continue to be a salient source of conflict in the Ninety-fifth and Ninety-sixth Congresses. Military procurement reductions such as rescinding money for nuclear carriers and the conversion of the USS *Long Beach* are associated with Policy Dimension I. The second area of conflict (Policy Dimension II) concerns reductions in agency programs (Health, Education, and Welfare [HEW] and foreign assistance programs). The conflict on this dimension pits liberal Democrats (ADA = .63; party = .82), who oppose the cuts, against conservatives (ACA = −.76), who support them. Disagreements over military spending and budget reductions in nonmilitary areas seem to be continuing sources of conflict in the Appropriations Committee.

Armed Services

Two policy dimensions are defined in the Armed Services Committee during the Ninety-third and Ninety-fourth Congresses. Policy Dimension I represents liberal Democratic (ADA = −.73; party = −.61) support for cuts in military strength and conservative (ACA = .65) opposition to these cuts. The amendments connected to this dimension propose cuts in overseas troop strength and in U.S. support for Vietnamese and local Laotian forces. The second policy dimension (Policy Dimension II) contains amendments that would result in reductions in military procurements (i.e., the A-10 aircraft).

In the Ninety-fifth and Ninety-sixth Congresses, the number of salient policy dimensions changes from two to three. Policy Dimension I represents conflict over whether to increase defense spending beyond the requests of the Carter administration. Liberals (ADA = .65) support the president's requests, are opposed to the increases in navy planes and the MX basing mode, and support amendments to reduce funding for Air Force projects. Policy Dimension II also represents conflict over increases in defense spending. In this latter case, conservatives support (ACA = −.61) increases in army helicopters and A-10 aircraft; these increases are opposed by liberal Democrats (ADA = .50; party = .60). The final policy dimension (Policy

Dimension III) concerns increases in aircraft procurement. The lack of significant correlations prevents further interpretation of this dimension. In sum, increases in procurement and other defense areas are a continuing source of conflict within this committee.

Banking, Finance, and Urban Affairs

Two salient policy dimensions emerge in this committee during the Ninety-third and Ninety- fourth Congresses (table 5). The first of these policy dimensions (Policy Dimension I) is characterized by partisan (party = .84) and ideological (ADA = .72; ACA = −.84) acrimony over banking regulations and economic policy. Conservative Republicans and liberal Democrats clash over the extension of the Economic Stabilization Act of 1970 (providing wage and price guidelines) and over such banking regulations as the extension of section 14(b) of the Federal Reserve Act and audits by the General Accounting Office (GAO) of the Federal Reserve Board banks and branches. There are no significant correlations associated with Policy Dimension II; the policy area in dispute here is housing and urban programs. Included in the amendments associated with Policy Dimension II are legislation to provide for greater home ownership opportunities for the middle class and for substantial increases for urban mass transportation.

The number of salient policy dimensions in the Banking Committee increases to three in the Ninety-fifth and Ninety-sixth Congresses, but the nature of the policy areas in dispute remains constant. Conservative support (ACA = −.57) and Democratic opposition (party = .67) characterize Policy Dimension I disputes over monetary policy. Issues include the Chrysler loan package, legislation concerning monetary policy, and competitive equality between financial institutions. Banking regulations are the subject matter of Policy Dimension II; conservatives (ACA = −.51) and liberal Democrats (ADA = .55; party = .44) argue over regulation of reserve limits for federally insured financial institutions, consumer credit and electronic funds transfers, and regulation of depository institutions. The conflict over housing and urban programs in the Ninety-third and Ninety-fourth Congresses is repeated in the later time period on Policy Dimension III. In the Ninety-fifth and Ninety-sixth Congresses, liberals (ADA = .52) oppose amendments supported by conservatives (ACA = −.44) about housing, community, and neighborhood development programs. Although there is an increase in the number of policy dimensions, the policies that cause conflict remain fairly stable from one time period to the next.

Budget

Conservative support (ACA = −.87) for reducing funding levels for social programs and liberal Democratic opposition (party = .89) to these reductions result in the policy conflict we see in Policy Dimension I (table 5). The programs earmarked by the conservatives for reductions include health, full employment, food stamps, and income security. Disagreement over spending for social programs also marks Policy Dimension II; however, disagreements center on *increases* to such programs as public service jobs and income security. In contrast to Policy Dimension I, the conflict on this dimension cannot be characterized as ideological or partisan, since none of the correlations is statistically significant (.01 level).

In the Ninety-fifth and Ninety-sixth Congresses, policy disputes broaden to include defense spending as well as nondefense spending. The same liberal Democratic (ADA = .66; party = .81) and conservative (ACA = −.84) disagreements over funding levels in nondefense areas noted in the Ninety-third and Ninety-fourth Congresses can be distinguished in Policy Dimension I. The conflict in Policy Dimension II revolves around liberal support (ADA = −.59) for cuts in defense spending (reductions in the national defense budget category). While reductions and increases in different budget categories are a stable feature of the conflict in the Budget Committee, the emergence of a new area of conflict—defense spending—is noted in the Ninety-fifth and Ninety-sixth Congresses. Nevertheless, it seems unlikely that this policy area will create a new factional alignment, because the issue appears to cut the committee along the same partisan and ideological lines as earlier policy conflicts.

Education and Labor

The same types of legislation cause policy conflicts within the Education and Labor Committee over the eight-year span of this analysis (table 5). Conservative Republicans support amendments that would place limitations on eligibility and cut funding for labor and education programs. Liberal Democrats oppose these efforts on the part of the Republican conservatives. In the Ninety-third and Ninety-fourth Congresses, the legislation in the area of education, associated with Policy Dimension I, includes the Elementary and Secondary School Amendments, Vocational Education Act Amendments, Education for All Handicapped Children Act of 1975, and the National School Lunch Program. Labor legislation such as funding for the Comprehensive Employment and Training Act (CETA), providing employment opportunities and training for the unemployed and underemployed, establishing a youth conservation corps, and increasing and expanding the minimum wage are also associated with Policy Dimension I. During the Ninety-fifth and Ninety-sixth Congresses the labor legislation that causes conflict are proposed amendments to the Fair Labor Standards Act, the National Labor Relations Act, and common situs picketing legislation. Legislation in the area of education that causes conflict is that dealing with the inspection of schools • for asbestos; the extension of certain elementary, secondary, and other educational programs; and the Education Amendments of 1981.

Foreign Affairs

During the Ninety-third and Ninety-fourth Congresses, there are three salient policy dimensions in the Foreign Affairs Committee. Attempts to limit the president's discretion define Policy Dimension I. This dimension reflects legislation that cuts aid to various Southeast Asian countries (Cambodia and South Vietnam) and dictates how the pull-out from South Vietnam should be handled (table 4). Liberal Democratic (ADA = −.55; party = −.53) support for sanctions against South Vietnam, South Africa, and South Korea, and conservative opposition (ACA = .63) to these proposals mark Policy Dimension II. Legislation concerning restrictions on military assistance, particularly aid to Greece, is associated with Policy Dimension III. Unfortunately, there are not enough roll-call votes in the Ninety-fifth and Ninety-sixth Congresses to analyze this committee; as a result, no comparisons of policy dimensions are possible.

Government Operations

During the Ninety-third and Ninety-fourth Congresses, liberal Democrats (ADA = −.86; party = −.85) clash with conservatives

(ACA = .78) over the administration of the Federal Energy Agency (FEA) and revenue sharing (Policy Dimension I, table 5). Liberal Democrats support amendments to regulate the actions of FEA employees in order to prevent conflicts of interest, to give the GAO easy access to the books and records of companies whose services are regulated, and to establish citizen advisory committees on revenue sharing. These amendments are opposed by conservatives.

Revenue sharing and the regulation of a federal agency are also salient policy concerns during the Ninety-fifth and Ninety-sixth Congresses; however, they make up two separate policy dimensions in the later Congresses. The salient amendments associated with Policy Dimension I (table 5) pertain to the establishment of the Department of Education. Liberal Democrats (ADA = .66; party = .83) oppose attempts by conservatives (ACA = −.83) to transfer certain training programs to the Department of Labor and to provide a congressional veto on decisions by the Department of Education to withhold funds from local and state governments. In addition, fiscal assistance (countercyclical aid), also associated with Policy Dimension I, generates conflict between liberal Democrats and conservatives. Conservatives are opposed by liberal Democrats in their attempts to reduce the amount of, and establish limitations on, these funds. In Policy Dimension II, there is evidence of liberal (ADA = −.59) support for increases in funding for the revenue- sharing program. Clearly, there is a high degree of stability in the types of policies that generate conflict within this committee.

House Administration

Disagreement over the administration of House business and attempts to change the laws governing campaigns and voter registration set the tone of the conflict in the House Administration Committee during the Ninety-third and Ninety-fourth Congresses (table 5). Policy Dimension I represents Democratic opposition (party = .73) to amendments by conservatives (ACA = −.61). Further, there is conservative opposition to Democratic amendments to increase allowances for members and to increase the pay of certain House employees. Policy Dimension II is marked by conflict over financing voter registration programs and amending rules governing campaign contributions. None of the correlations with Policy Dimension II is statistically significant.

The controversy over the regulation of campaigns and elections continues in the Ninety-fifth and Ninety-sixth Congresses. Liberal Democrats (ADA = .67; party = .89) oppose amendments by conservatives (ACA = −.83) to legislation that encourages greater voter registration and that amends the Federal Elections Campaign Act (Policy Dimension I). Conflict that arises over the recommendations of the Committee on Administrative Review for House reforms is also represented in Policy Dimension II. Neither the ideological nor the party support measures correlate highly with this policy dimension (II).

Interior and Insular Affairs

Land-use and surface-mining regulations emerge as the most salient policy conflicts (Policy Dimension I) in this committee during the 1973–76 period (table 5). Amendments that create exceptions to legislated environmental requirements are opposed by liberal Democrats (ADA = .81; party = .78) and supported by conservative (ACA = −.87) Republicans. While land use remains a salient area of conflict, the legislation in question in the Ninety-fifth and Ninety-sixth Congresses concerns water use (Reclamation Reform Act) instead of surface-mining regulations (Policy Dimension I). In addition, the designation of wilderness areas also creates conflict (Alaska lands, Idaho wilderness, and wild and scenic rivers). Conservatives (ACA = .84) support amendments that would reduce the size of wilderness areas and leave the development of water conservation in the hands of state and local governments, while opposing attempts by liberal Democrats (ADA = −.92; party = −.87) to increase federal regulation of land and water use. Land-use regulation seems to be a stable component of policy conflicts within his committee; however, the focus of that regulation shifts from surface mining in the 1973–76 period to water use and wilderness areas in the 1977–80 period.

Interstate and Foreign Commerce

Only one salient policy dimension is present in the Commerce Committee during the eight-year span of this analysis. In all four

Congresses energy legislation generates liberal Democratic support and conservative Republican opposition (table 5) to such issues as energy conservation and synthetic fuels production. One additional policy area which did not appear in the Ninety-third and Ninety-fourth Congresses, health care costs, is salient during the Ninety-fifth and Ninety-sixth Congresses. Thus, conflict over energy legislation appears to be a stable element in the policy conflicts in the Interstate and Foreign Commerce Committee.

Judiciary

Liberal Democratic (ADA = .69; party = .76) opposition to conservative (ACA = −.66) attempts to dilute legislation to curb illegal and deceptive practices by industry (competition in the food industry) and government (Government in Sunshine Act) is one of the conflicts associated with Policy Dimension I in the Ninety-third and Ninety-fourth Congresses (table 5).[5] In addition, liberal Democrats oppose amendments by conservatives that would weaken legislation providing compensation to victims of crime. The second area of policy conflict within the committee during the Ninety-third and Ninety-fourth Congresses concerns gun control legislation (Policy Dimension II). The only significant correlation associated with this policy dimension is liberal support for such legislation (ADA = −.44).

The nature of the policy conflicts within the Judiciary Committee changes during the Ninety-fifth and Ninety-sixth Congresses: three policy dimensions instead of two are salient. Policy Dimension I deals with legislation setting ethical standards of behavior for public officials. The amendments to the legislation associated with this policy dimension are opposed by liberal Democrats (ADA = .69; party = .84) and supported by conservatives (ACA = −.83). The correlations are too small to allow for interpretation of the types of members who tend to support, or oppose, legislation associated with Policy Dimensions II and III. It is possible, however, to describe the policies that cause the conflict. Policy Dimension II concerns attempts to increase the number of circuit and district judges in particular regions. The final dimension, Policy Dimension III, contains legislation that ex-

5. Impeachment votes are excluded from the analysis of policy dimensions and committee factions because of their unusual nature.

tends and protects individual rights—rights of institutionalized individuals, establishment of a Commission on Wartime Relocation and Internment of Civilians, and amendments of federal rules of criminal procedures and evidence. It is evident that the number and nature of the policy conflicts in this committee changes between the earlier and later Congresses under study. Whether the new issues crosscut older lines of cleavage within the committee can be determined only by an examination of the factional alignments over the eight-year span (Chapters 3 and 6).

Merchant Marine and Fisheries

There were not enough votes during the Ninety-third and Ninety-fourth Congresses to permit analysis of the policy conflicts within the Merchant Marine and Fisheries Committee; however, we can describe the policy dimensions that emerge during the Ninety-fifth and Ninety-sixth Congresses (table 5). The Panama Canal Treaty incites the partisan (party = .81) and ideological (ACA = − .80; ADA = .61) conflict captured by Policy Dimension I. Conservative attempts to maintain greater control over the Panama Canal through amendments to legislation to implement the Canal Treaty are met by liberal Democratic opposition. Interest in environmental legislation is reflected in Policy Dimension II. The amendments associated with this dimension pertain to Alaska lands, environmentally sound development of the seabeds, and ocean dumping. The final policy dimension (Policy Dimension III) concerns legislation to require that U.S. oil imports be carried on U.S. flagships.

Post Office and Civil Service

Three areas of conflict are present in the Post Office Committee in the Ninety-third and Ninety-fourth Congresses (table 5). Attempts to limit the discretion of the president (determining the size of the White House staff) in areas which fall into the committee's jurisdiction are supported by liberal Democrats (ADA = − .77; party = − .86) and opposed by conservative (ACA = .84) Republicans (Policy Dimension I). Liberal Democrats and conservative Republicans also clash over setting postal rates for first- and fourth-class mail (Policy Dimension I). PolicyDimension II represents disagreement over the president's proposals for increasing executive, legislative, and judicial salaries. The final policy dimension (Policy Dimension III) concerns conflict over postal regulations. The correlates are not helpful in interpreting the last two policy dimensions.

We also find three policy dimensions during the Ninety-fifth and Ninety-sixth Congresses; all three concern a particular aspect of civil service reform. Legislation to loosen some of the Hatch Act restrictions on the political activities of public employees is associated with Policy Dimension I. Liberal (ADA = .51) Democrats (party = .81) oppose conservative (ACA = −.89) amendments to this portion of the civil service reform on Policy Dimension II, but in this instance the area of controversy centers on high-level executive-branch personnel. The amendments associated with this dimension deal with regulation of the Senior Executive Service; ideology and party are not useful in characterizing this conflict. The same is true of the correlates of Policy Dimension III; the policy conflict here concerns personnel policies for civil servants—protections and rights of federal employees. In this committee there is a noticeable shift in the policies that generate conflict. In the Ninety-third and Ninety-fourth Congresses, conflict arises over postal matters and presidential discretion; civil service matters dominate during the Ninety-fifth and Ninety-sixth Congresses.

Public Works and Transportation

The two policy dimensions during the Ninety-third and Ninety-fourth Congresses reflect conflicts over mass transportation (Policy Dimension I) and airport regulation (Policy Dimension II). Support of Policy Dimension I (table 5) represents opposition to the allocation of money and projects for urban mass transportation. Conservatives (ACA = −.68) support amendments that are designed to limit the allocation of funds to urban areas, and they are opposed by liberal Democrats (ADA = .55; party = .79). Policy dimension II reflects liberal (ADA = −.63) support for amendments that propose airport regulations that would effectively ban the supersonic transport; their efforts are opposed by conservatives (ACA = .47).

Transportation policy and regulation divide the committee in the Ninety-fifth and Ninety-sixth Congresses as well. Once again, liberal

Democrats (ADA = .65; party = .83) oppose conservatives (ACA = −.80) over amendments to transportation policy (Policy Dimension I). Policy Dimension II is made up of a hodgepodge of regulatory policies (i.e., aviation safety and noise reduction, navigation development). The correlations give no clue to the nature of the conflict underlying Policy Dimension II.

Rules

Attempts to amend rules to allow modification of substantive legislation (Policy Dimension I) receives the support of conservatives (ACA = −.64) on the Rules Committee during the Ninety-third and Ninety-fourth Congresses (table 5). Liberals (ADA = .75) and conservatives (ACA = −.69) also oppose one another over modification of normal House procedures (such as waiving rules) on Policy Dimension II. Partisan (party = .89) and ideological (ADA = .87; ACA = −.88) conflicts mark Policy Dimension I during the Ninety-fifth and Ninety-sixth Congresses; once again, the area in contention is the modification of rules. The second policy dimension (Policy Dimension II) in the Ninety-fifth and Ninety-sixth Congresses concerns rules governing such internal House matters as select committees (Select Committee on Ethics, and Select Committee on Intelligence) and television and radio coverage of floor proceedings. The absence of significant correlations with ideological and partisan measures suggests that party and ideology are not significant factors in the latter conflict.

Science and Technology

The topic of energy generates all the conflict within this committee over the entire eight-year span of the analysis. In the earlier two Congresses all three policy dimesions are identified with some type of energy legislation. On Policy Dimension I (table 5), liberals (ADA = .56) and conservatives (ACA = −.43) disagree over the emphasis that should be placed on fossil fuel research and development. Policy Dimension II reflects conflict over synthetic fuels development. The legislation on this latter dimension opposes synthetic fuel development and is supported by liberal (ADA = −.54), who favor fossil fuel development. The final policy dimension (Policy Dimension III) represents disagreement between Democrats (party = .63) and conservatives (ACA = −.47) over funding for the Energy Research and Development Administration (ERDA); the conservatives support cuts in energy research funding while Democrats oppose these decreases.

Energy research continues to be a source of controversy during the Ninety-fifth and Ninety-sixth Congresses. Policy Dimension I concerns nuclear energy research and reflects liberal (ADA = −.66) support for amendments to reduce or eliminate breeder reactor programs. Conservatives (ACA = .45) oppose these liberal attempts. Democrats (party = −.77) oppose conservative Republicans (ACA = .71) over the issue of funding for alternative technologies research (i.e., support for appropriate technology research, vehicle propulsion research, and geothermal research)—Policy Dimension II.

Standards of Official Conduct

Disciplinary action against Daniel Schorr for leaking classified information incites the greatest ideological (ADA = .85) and partisan (party = .86) conflict (Policy Dimension I) of any of the four policy conflicts distinguishable in the Ninety-third and Ninety-fourth Congresses (table 5). There is opposition to pursuing the Daniel Schorr investigation from moderate committee Democrats; conservative Republicans support the investigation. Another investigation, the Michael Harrington (D-Mass.) case, also results in policy conflict (Policy Dimension II). Harrington, like Schorr, was charged with leaking classified information to the press. In the Harrington case, Robin L. Beard Jr. (R-Tenn.) alleged that Harrington had made public classified information about CIA activities in Chile that had been disclosed in an executive session of the Armed Services Investigations subcommittee. The lack of significant correlations suggests that the conflict over the Harrington case is neither ideological nor partisan. The final two policy dimensions (III and IV) are difficult to define because they encompass so few issues. It appears that they deal with disciplinary actions (Policy Dimension III) and decisions on disciplinary complaints (Policy Dimenion IV), but these descriptions should be treated with caution. There are not enough votes in this committee to determine the areas of policy conflict in the Ninety-fifth and Ninety-sixth Congresses.

Ways and Means

The Ways and Means Committee experiences ideological and partisan conflict over the issue of individual and corporate income taxes (Policy Dimension I) in the Ninety-third and Ninety-fourth Congresses (table 5). Liberal Democrats (ADA = .69; party = .81) oppose amendments by conservative (ACA = −.27) Republicans in the area of individual income tax deductions. In addition, conservative Republicans oppose liberal Democratic amendments to increase taxes on oil and gasoline. Policy Dimension II concerns the oil depletion allowance; conservatives (ACA = −.53) support the existing allowance and resist amendments proposing a phaseout of the allowance.

The taxing of oil and individual tax deductions are also the subject matter of Policy Dimensions I and II during the Ninety-fifth and Ninety-sixth Congresses. On Policy Dimension I, conservative Republicans (ACA = −.74; party = .76) and liberal Democrats (ADA = .57) split over the rate at which oil profits should be taxed and the exemptions oil companies should be allowed. Liberals (ADA = −.64) support personal income tax exemptions (Policy Dimension II) such as a one-time exemption from capital gains on the sale of a house and educational tax credits for higher and vocational education; they also support the repeal of certain entertainment deductions. Thus, there is little change in the types of policies that generate conflict within this committee over the eight years.

The most notable feature of conflict in committees is the stability of salient policy conflicts. Very few of the committees examined undergo noticeable shifts in the policies that create dissension among committee members. As suggested earlier, this stability can probably be attributed to the unchanging nature of committee jurisdictions. The legislation considered by a committee varies within certain set boundaries. If the importance of the issues considered within those boundaries does not change significantly, then stability in issue conflicts can be expected to be the norm. Change in factional alignments, however, does not depend solely on changes in salient issue conflicts. Membership turnover, and shifts in party control of the White House can also shape factional alignments. Nevertheless, our analysis suggests that the emergence of new issues is likley to result in new factions in only a few of the committees examined.

Only four committees during the eight-year analysis (of the fifteen committees that could be compared) display changes in the nature of conflict. The conflict over nondefense spending in the Budget Committee during the Ninety-third and Ninety-fourth Congresses broadens to include disputes over defense spending as well as conflict over other nondefense budget categories (1977–80). Yet, this new dispute cuts the committee along the same partisan and ideological lines as in the earlier two Congresses. In the Interior Committee, we note a shift in the focus of the legislation that creates conflict; land-use regulation is a continuing source of conflict, but the emphasis changes from determining strip-mining regulations (Ninety-third and Ninety-fourth Congresses) to designating wilderness areas and regulating water use.

The most significant changes in the content of policy conflict occurs in the Judiciary Committee and in the Post Office and Civil Service Committee. The two policy dimensions uncovered in Judiciary in the 1973–76 period concern legislation on crime control and illegal and deceptive practices and on gun control. In the 1977–80 period, the salient conflicts center on ethics in government, appointment of judges, and rights of individuals. The Post Office and Civil Service Committee is also characterized by a significant change in the topics that cause salient conflict. The earlier time period (1973–76) is marked by disputes over postal regulation, limits on presidential discretion, and salary recommendations; the nature of the conflict in the later time period (1977–80) focuses on civil service reform legislation. It cannot be automatically assumed that the changing nature of the conflict in these four committees will result in new factional alignments of committee members. Only if the new disputes alter earlier lines of conflict can they be expected to affect the alignment of members within the committee. Determination of whether the policy shifts in these four committees have cut across older lines of cleavage and created new alignments is left to the following chapters.

CHAPTER THREE

Partisan and
Ideological Cleavages

In the first chapter we defined four influences that could be expected to have an impact on the formation of factions in committees: party, ideology, the administration, and constituency interests. In this and the two following chapters, we will group the committees according to these major influences. This chapter focuses on the committees in which party and ideology can be used to explain all the factions that form in the committee. In Chapter 4 we examine the committees in which the executive branch, in addition to party and ideology, can be identified as a dominant influence in the decision-making environments: Appropriations, Armed Services, Foreign Affairs, Post Office and Civil Service, and Ways and Means Committees. Interest groups, as well as party and ideology, are found to be particularly salient in the environments of the committees examined in Chapter 5: Agriculture, Banking, and Education and Labor.

Even among committees displaying factions influenced predominantly by party and ideology, the underlying factional structures are not identical. We can determine the differing impact of party and ideology on these structures by making comparisons between them, for instance, according to the degree of polarization caused by the overlap of party and ideology. Some of the committees examined in this chapter are characterized by bipolar factions where party and ideology are impossible to separate. The opposing blocs can be distinguished by the strongly positive or negative attachments (loadings) to the faction. In the two-dimensional graphs, these polarized decision-making environments are characterized by two tightly clustered groups of members which are diametrically opposite to one another. In decision making, the two groups of members that are identified with the bipolar factions can be expected to be strong adversaries who consistently oppose one another on committee decisions. That is, members with positive loadings on the faction are opposed by members with negative loadings on the faction. One example of this type of factional alignment occurs in the Budget Committee, where the intense partisan-ideological split in the committee results in the opposition of conservative Democrats and Republicans to liberal Democrats.

A comparison of the two-dimensional graphs presented with each committee description will reveal the degree to which the factional structures are dispersed in the partisan and ideological committees. A high degree of collinearity between party and ideology results in the bipolarized configuration mentioned earlier. When ideology and partisanship are not so highly collinear and there are several ideological blocs represented in the committee, the two-dimensional graphs show a high degree of dispersion. In contrast to structures like those in the Interior and Commerce Committees that are characterized by a high degree of polarization, both the Judiciary and the Science and Technology committees have factional structures that display a high degree of dispersion. In these latter two committees members are spread across the graphs rather than clustered into two distinct groups. Unlike polarized committees where two antagonistic groups consistently opposed one another, decision making in the committees with more dispersion could be expected to involve coalition formation among several of the factions.

In addition to analyzing committees' factional structures, we examine the findings of relevant previous studies of the committees. These literature reviews can be used to compare the findings of committee studies in earlier periods with the findings presented in our analysis.

The five House committees with jurisdictional responsibilities that yield partisan advantages—Budget, Government Operations, House Administration, Rules, and Standards of Official Conduct—tend to divide into partisan and/or ideological factions. The Budget Committee establishes the expenditure limits on functional categories in the federal budget; these limits reflect the legislative priorities established by Congress and the legislative leadership. The participation of party leaders in setting policy priorities guarantees that party will be a major environmental force. The major task of the Government Operations Committee is to oversee the functioning of the executive branch. Errors in agency administration, once detected, can provide useful ammunition for political attacks on the president's party. Control of the House Administration and Rules committees provides the majority party with influence over the perquisites of party control and internal procedures. Finally, the Standards Committee deals with such sensitive topics that attempts are made to mute partisanship by assigning equal numbers of Democrats and Republicans to the committee.

Budget

The Budget Committees in Congress, established by the Congressional Budget Act of 1974, were the result of an attempt by Congress to reassert control over the budgetary process. Charged with the responsibility of coordinating authorization, revenue, and appropriations decisions made in Congress, the committees are responsible for producing two budget resolutions per year. The first of these establishes budget targets for authorizations in functional categories, revenue raising, deficits, and the public debt based on requests submitted by the relevant committees in the chamber. The second budget resolutions by the two budget committees reflect the spending actions taken by Congress during the authorization and appropriations processes. The jurisdiction of the House Budget Committee overlaps that of the major substantive committees as well as the jurisdictions of the Appropriations and Ways and Means committees.

An examination of several characteristics of the House Budget Committee leads to the speculation that conflict in this committee would be partisan and ideological in nature. The membership on the committee rotates, with a limitation of no more than six years of service in any ten-year period. This stipulation provides little incentive for members to develop strong attachments to the committee; unlike other committees in the House where longer tenure on the committee leads to increased power, a member joining the Budget Committee knows that his or her tenure is of finite duration. Further, the overlapping jurisdiction of the committee leaves little room for the development of an area of expertise from which a member could derive a degree of status and/or deference in the House. Hence, members on the committee are encouraged to maintain a major committee assignment. As Allen Schick (1980) notes, this fact has an impact on decision making in the committee: "The members of the Budget Committees are brought together to deal with matters on which they are divided in their everyday legislative work. All bring their particular specialities into the meeting room, and throughout the process of budgeting most exhibit identities as members of the other committees on which they sit" (p. 110).

Further enhancing the policy differences between the members are the assignment strategies employed by each of the parties in choosing members for the committee. Prior to the Ninety-fifth Congress, the Democrats tried to maintain a membership on the committee which reflected the ideological division of Democrats in the House. In contrast, the Republican committee members represented the most conservative wing of the party. This practice provided the potential for a conservative, Democratic-Republican coalition in the committee that could override the preferences of the moderate and liberal Democrats. In response, the Democrats employed a new strategy for determining membership in the Ninety-fifth Congress; conservative and moderate Democrats were replaced with liberal members, which resulted in a significantly more liberal Democratic membership on the committee. In this study, this ideological split in membership is expected to result in committee cleavages that reflect the ideological differences between the members.

As the discussion of the assignment practices of the two parties illustrates, the parties are not averse to using the committee to promote their political stands.

> House Republicans view the budget resolution as the great divide between the two parties, as one of the few contemporary issues on which there ought to be a clear-cut demarcation between Republican and Democratic positions. They regard the budget as a political statement about the reach and purpose of the federal government, its

economic role, and the national priorities of the United States. For House Republicans, the budget resolutions sum up the essential differences between the two parties; the dollar disputes, accordingly, do not merely reflect conflicts over money but go to the heart of the American political process. (Schick, 1981, pp. 9–10)

In light of this, partisanship is also expected to play an important role in defining the nature of the conflicts in committee decision making.

Finally, the nature of the issues debated by the Budget Committee provides a ready arena for the venting of the ideological and partisan outlooks of the members. Issues such as the size of the federal government, the tradeoffs between inflation and unemployment, and the size of the national debt are not debated directly by the committee, but decisions on the size of social spending and military spending reflect these underlying issues. Thus, such decisions are likely to engender partisan and ideological conflict. As we noted in chapter 2, the most devisive issues in the committee concern the level of spending for social programs, such as health, full employment, and food stamps. John Ellwood and James Thurber (1981) note that in the House, too, these issues create conflict: "Budget votes in the House almost always are close, with liberals disgruntled over military expenditures and conservatives concerned about spending for social programs" (p. 260). Because Budget is a new committee, there are no committee norms which could serve to mute such conflicts. It is expected, therefore, that the House Budget Committee will display the characteristics of a committee polarized by ideological and partisan conflict.

The impact of party and ideology on the Budget Committee is evident in the committee's factional structure (table 6). Faction 1 represents the alignment of committee Republicans (Garner E. Shriver, [Kans.], Delbert L. Latta [Ohio], Elford A. Cederberg [Mich.], Herman T. Schneebeli [Pa.], James T. Broyhill [N.C.], Del Clawson [Calif.], Marjorie S. Holt [Md.], and Barber B. Conable, Jr. [N.Y.]); this faction also attracts some support from southern Democrats Omar Burleson [Tex.] and Phil M. Landrum [Ga.]). The bipolarity of this faction reflects the intense ideological (ACA, $r = .88$) and partisan (party unity, $r = -.94$) cleavages within the committee. Committee Democrats also divide along ideological lines: Faction 2 can be characterized as an alignment of partisan (party unity, $r = .89$) and basically liberal Democrats (ACA, $r = -.90$) that includes the

TABLE 6. Factions in the Budget Committee, 1973–1976

Committee Member	Factions 1	Factions 2	Factions 3	Explained Variation (%)
Garner E. Shriver (R-Kans.)	.96			100
Delbert L. Latta (R-Ohio)	.95			99
Elford A. Cederberg (R-Mich.)	.95			99
Herman T. Schneebeli (R-Pa.)	.95			99
James T. Broyhill (R-N.C.)	.95			99
Del Clawson (R-Calif.)	.95			99
Marjorie S. Holt (R-Md.)	.86	−.59		100
Barber B. Conable, Jr. (R-N.Y.)	.82			88
Omar Burleson (D-Tex.)	.57	(−.46)	.61	91
Phil M. Landrum (D-Ga.)	.52	(−.47)	.64	90
Parren J. Mitchell (D-Md.)	−.63	(.48)	−.53	91
Louis Stokes (D-Ohio)	−.62	(.49)	−.54	91
Sam Gibbons (D-Fla.)	−.46	(−.41)		39
Jim Wright (D-Tex.)	−.50	.83		96
Elizabeth Holtzman (D-N.Y.)	−.56	.72		90
Patsy Mink (D-Hawaii)	−.54	.69		97
Robert L. Leggett (D-Calif.)	−.68	.53		90
James G. O'Hara (D-Mich.)	−.70	.53	(−.46)	98
Robert N. Giaimo (D-Conn.)		.89		85
Thomas P. O'Neill, Jr. (D-Mass.)		.89		99
Brock Adams (D-Wash.)		.87		91
Neal Smith (D-Iowa)		.85		88
Thomas L. Ashley (D-Ohio)		.73		53
Butler Derrick (D-S.C.)			.84	81
Harold Runnels (D-N.Mex.)			.78	68

Correlates of Facitonal Alignments			
Presidential support	.93*	−.79*	.49*
Conservative coalition	.88*	−.84*	.70*
Party unity	−.94*	.89*	−.62*
ADA	−.84*	.78*	−.66*
COPE	−.93*	.93*	−.66*
NFU	−.93*	.88*	−.68*
CCUS	.90*	−.82*	.70*
ACA	.88*	−.90*	.72*
Reductions in Social Services Expenditures (I)	−.82*	.98*	−.43
Increases in Income Security Programs (II)	.49*	.01	.59*

Note: Pearson correlations marked with asterisks are significant at the .01 level.

Speaker of the House (Thomas P. O'Neill [Mass.]), the majority leader (Jim Wright [Tex.]), and the committee chairman (Brock Adams [Wash.]). Faction 3 represents a bloc of southern Democrats and reflects the liberal-conservative (North-South) division in the Democratic party. This conservative alignment of southern Democrats (ACA, $r = .72$) tends to vote with the Republicans (Faction 1) to form a conservative coalition ($r = .55$).[1]

In light of these partisan and ideological differences among committee members, it is not surprising to find that the major policy cleavage within the committee—the reduction of expenditures for programs in the areas of education, manpower, and social services—is also partisan (party unity, $r = .89$) and ideological (ACA, $r = -.87$) in substance. The conservatives on the committee, located primarily in Faction 1, support reductions in programs that have been historically supported by the Democratic party (Reductions in "Education, Manpower, and Social Services" Expenditures, $r = -.82$). These cuts are strongly opposed by the Democratic liberals on the committee (Faction 2). The partisan-ideological conflict that is reflected both in the factional alignments of committee members and in the major policy cleavage within the committee is also evident in the two-dimensional representation of the patterns of vote agreement within the Budget Committee.

Figure 4 reveals two distinct clusters of committee members diagonally opposite one another: the conservative members cluster in the lower-right quadrant of the figure while the liberal Democrats occupy the opposite (left quadrant) of the graph. This configuration reflects the ideological-partisan polarization of these groups. The southern Democrats Butler Derrick (S.C.), Harold Runnels (N.M.), and Sam Gibbons (Fla.) fall between these tight clusters of Democrats and Republicans, perhaps reflecting the cross-pressures created by the divergence between partisan loyalties and ideological sympathies.

In the case of Butler Derrick, there is some evidence to support this speculation. Schick identified Derrick as one of the few members who placed his commitment to the budget process above his concern for the substantive outcomes of the process.

---

1. The correlations between factions used throughout this study are the correlations among vectors of factor loadings, *not* the interfactor correlations that result from oblique factor rotations.

Figure 4. Two-Dimensional Representation of Cleavages in the House Committee on Budget: 1973-1976.

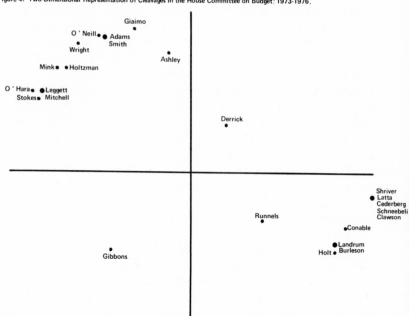

The most "socialized" members of the Budget Committees have been those whose activity has focused primarily on procedural matters. Rather than viewing the process as a means for advancing their program interests, they have perceived it as a mechanism for bringing budgetary discipline to Congress. Representative Butler Derrick's case offers a clear example of this behavior in the House. Derrick was assigned to HBC [House Budget Committee] as a freshman before he had established legislative interests on other committees. . . . As a new member from a conservative state (South Carolina) Derrick voted against the first budget resolution in 1975. But his commitment to the budget process spurred a turnaround in his voting record and he subsequently supported the budget resolution. (Schick, 1980, pp. 111–12)

The cross-pressures between loyalty to the budget process and loyalty to his party and his ideological and constituent interests are illustrated by Derrick's position on the two-dimensional graph.

In Runnel's case, as well, there is some evidence of cross-pressuring; Runnel's request to maintain his committee membership for the second two years of what was originally a four-year term was denied by the Democrats (Schick, 1980, p. 98). The denial occurred at a time when the Democratic leaders were attempting to replace conservative and moderate members on the committee with more liberal members. This suggests that Runnel's position is at least partially attributable to cross-pressuring due to his partisan and ideological loyalties. These interpretations of the partisan and ideological nature of cleavages corresponds to the observations of Schick and of Ellwood and Thurber. In sum, when committee battles come down to roll-call votes, partisan and ideological factions are apt to appear in the Budget Committee.

Government Operations

The jurisdictional responsibilities of the Government Operations Committee include oversight of the operations of executive agencies. The committee functions primarily as a "post-audit agent, examining the efficiency of bureau expenditures" (Henderson, 1970, p. 22). Most of the committee's investigations consist of exposures of administrative misfeasance, inquiries into constituent and congressional complaints, and critiques of the effectiveness of agency procedures.

When the majority party controls both branches of government—Congress and the presidency—the incentives for partisan inquiries into agency performance dwindle. However, when the House and the presidency are controlled by different parties, the opportunities for partisan advantage are significantly increased: "In such situations, the minority party in Congress is much more likely to be highly sensitive to criticisms of their President. The majority party, on the other hand, is in such circumstances given an ideal opportunity to carry out investigations under the guise of oversight which embarrass the current Administration" (Henderson, 1970, p. 42).

Since Congress is controlled by the Democrats and the presidency by the Republicans during the span of this part of the analysis (1973–76), sharp partisan cleavages can be expected in this committee. In fact, as Norman Ornstein and David Rohde (1977) noted in their analysis of the committee in the early 1970s, the increased attractiveness of the committee during this period was due at least in part to the investigation of the Nixon administration.

> One staff member noted, "In 1975 we got ten new members, later eleven when Reuss resigned. The second, third and fourth termers who requested to get on the committee demonstrated their recognition of a new enhanced role of Government Operations—this was partly the role of Brooks in investigating the Nixon administration. That role becomes clear when we see that three of the five new nonfreshmen Democrats came from Judiciary [where Brooks also serves]." (P. 198)

During the period 1970 to 1975, Ornstein and Rohde (1977) reported, the Democratic membership on the committee became more liberal, while the Republican members became more conservative. Further, the liberal members who joined the committee were among the most activist members of the House.

The increased attractiveness of this committee to liberal and southern Democrats (table 7) adds an ideological dimension to the existing partisan conflict. Between the Eightieth and Ninety-first Congresses, Government Operations was ranked fifteenth in attractiveness among southern Democrats and tenth (9.5) among northern Democrats. During the next five Congresses the prestige of the committee jumped to seventh among southern Democrats (6.5) and fourth among northern Democrats. As a consequence, it is not surprising to find that partisanship (party unity) and liberalism (ACA) are strongly correlated

TABLE 7. Index of House Committee Prestige and Corresponding Rank, 80th–96th Congresses

Committee	80th–91st Congresses						92d–96th Congresses					
	Index of Prestige[a]			Committee Rank			Index of Prestige[a]			Committee Rank		
	Rep.	S. Dem.	N. Dem.	Rep.	S. Dem.	N. Dem.	Rep.	S. Dem.	N. Dem.	Rep.	S. Dem.	N. Dem.
Ways and Means	1.00	1.00	1.00	1	2	1.5	1.00	1.00	1.00	1.5	2	2
Appropriations	.98	1.00	.98	2	2	3	.97	1.00	1.00	3	2	2
Rules	.95	1.00	1.00	3	2	1.5	1.00	1.00	1.00	1.5	2	2
Armed Services	.91	.80	.74	4	4	6	.45	.50	.60	7	6.5	6
Foreign Affairs	.84	.67	.94	5	6	4	.88	.40	.44	4	9	11.5
Education and Labor	.70	.43	.14	6	13	17	.21	.00	.11	18	18.5	20
Judiciary	.58	.68	.68	7	5	7	.57	.00	.31	6	18.5	17
Interstate and Foreign Commerce	.57	.64	.84	8	7	5	.73	.00	.50	5	18.5	10
Internal Security[b]	.50	.25	.00	9	16	20						
Banking, Finance, and Urban Affairs	.44	.45	.22	10	11.5	14	.06	.13	.57	21	14	7
Agriculture	.42	.47	.54	11	10	8	.44	.50	.44	8.5	6.5	11.5
Public Works and Transportation	.31	.50	.41	12	8.5	9.5	.29	.33	.43	13	11	13.5
District of Columbia	.25	.42	.17	13.5	14	15.5	.25	.00	.17	15.5	18.5	19
Science and Technology	.25	.45	.36	13.5	11.5	11	.33	.33	.23	11.5	11	18
House Administration	.24	.12	.30	15	17	12	.08	.50	.40	20	6.5	15
Interior and Insular Affairs	.16	.50	.17	16	8.5	15.5	.22	1.00	.53	17	15	9
Veterans Affairs	.14	.08	.10	17	19	18.5	.38	.00	.38	10	18.5	16
Post Office and Civil Service	.11	.05	.10	18	20	18.5	.25	.00	.00	15.5	18.5	21
Merchant Marine and Fisheries	.10	.11	.26	19	18	13	.33	.33	.43	11.5	11	13.5
Government Operations	.08	.33	.40	20	15	9.5	.27	.50	.88	14	6.5	4

Note: Rep. = Republican; S. Dem. = Southern Democrat; N. Dem. = Northern Democrat.
[a]Index is based upon the relative attractiveness of the committee in terms of the net number of members that transfer to it.
[b]Dissolved in the Ninety-fourth Congress.
Source: Data for 80th–91st Congress are from Bullock, 1973, p. 94.

in this committee ($r = -.92$), and the major policy cleavage is both partisan (party unity, $r = -.92$), and ideological (ADA, $r = -.86$) in nature (table 5, Chapter 2).

Faction 1 (table 8) represents the vote agreement among liberal committee Democrats (ACA, $r = -.83$); this strongly partisan block (party unity, $r = .91$) is concerned with exercising control over executive agencies (Federal Energy Administration) and programs (Revenue Sharing and Agency Regulation, $r = -.92$). The disagreements between the liberal Democrats in Faction 1 and committee Republicans in Faction 2 mirror the intense partisan and ideological conflict within the committees. It should also be noted that Faction 1 reflects the vote agreement among several subcommittee leaders: Benjamin S. Rosenthal (D-N.Y.; Commerce, Consumer, and Monetary Affairs), William S. Moorhead (D-Pa.; Conservation, Energy, and Natural Resources), William J. Randall (D-Mo.; Government Activities and Transportation), Bella S. Abzug (D-N.Y.; Government Information and Individual Rights) and Floyd V. Hicks (D-Wash.; Manpower and Housing). The other liberal Democrats that align with this faction are members of the subcommittees that these leaders chair. This pattern could lead to the inference that Faction 1 reflects the organization of an antiadministration bloc of committee members. While this is a tempting interpretation, it requires a far greater inferential leap than the data permit. Party and ideology may confound the identification of factions that organize in response to the influence of the executive branch in the committee's environment. Clearly, the salient ideological and partisan cleavages between liberal Democrats and Presidents Nixon and Ford could easily obscure the unique impact of the executive branch on the formation of committee factions. Still, since Faction 1 can easily be differentiated from the other committee factions on the basis of party and ideology, we prefer to use these characteristics in defining this voting bloc.

Faction 2 is a bloc of strongly partisan (presidential support, $r = .71$) Republicans who are less conservative than the Republicans who consistently vote against Faction 1 (Garry Brown [Mich.], Sam Steiger [Ariz.], Charles Thone [Nebr.], John N. Erlenborn [Ill.], and Clarence J. Brown [Ohio]). In fact, some of the more liberal and moderate Republicans on the committee vote with this faction: Gilbert Gude (Md.), Paul N. McCloskey, Jr. (Calif.), Joel Pritchard (Wash.), and Frank Horton (N.Y.). Despite this ideological difference among Re-

TABLE 8. Factions in the Government Operations Committee, 1973–1976

Committee Member	Factions			Explained Variation (%)
	1	2	3	
Dante B. Fascell (D-Fla.)	.87			76
John E. Moss (D-Calif.)	.86			100
Fernand J. St. Germain (D-R.I.)	.85			94
Benjamin S. Rosenthal (D-N.Y.)	.85			93
Bella S. Abzug (D-N.Y.)	.84			76
John Conyers, Jr. (D-Mich.)	.81		(.44)	91
William S. Moorhead (D-Pa.)	.72		.51	80
Floyd V. Hicks (D-Wash.)	.71			51
William J. Randall (D-Mo.)	.59		.56	68
Gilbert Gude (R-Md.)	.50	.60		61
Clarence J. Brown (R-Ohio)	−.82	(.45)		97
Sam Steiger (R-Ariz.)	−.81		(−.42)	94
Charles Thone (R-Nebr.)	−.81	(.47)		96
John N. Erlenborn (R-Ill.)	−.80			87
Garry Brown (R-Mich.)	−.79			85
John W. Wydler (R-N.Y.)		.81		77
Alan Steelman (R-Tex.)		.79		68
Paul N. McCloskey, Jr. (R-Calif.)		.78		73
Frank Horton (R-N.Y.)		.72		66
Joel Pritchard (R-Wash.)		.69		61
Don Fuqua (D-Fla.)		(.26)		09
Leo J. Ryan (D-Calif.)			.86	75
Jack Brooks (D-Tex.)			.77	78
Jim Wright (D-Tex.)		(−.40)	.70	65
L.H. Fountain (D-N.C.)			(−.37)	15

Correlates of Factional Alignments			
Presidential support	−.88*	.71*	−.51*
Conservative coalition	−.81*	.53*	−.40
Party unity	.91*	−.69*	.53
ADA	.80*	−.55*	.32
COPE	.92*	−.77*	.65*
NFU	.87*	−.57*	.54*
CCUS	−.83*	.49*	−.37
ACA	−.83*	.53*	−.47*
Revenue Sharing and Agency Regulation (I)	−.92*	.69*	−.36

Note: Doublets: Fuqua (D-Fla.) and Steelman (R-Tex.); Gude (R-Md.) and Randall (D-Mo.). Pearson correlations marked with asterisks are significant at the .01 level.

publicans, Faction 2 does not waiver in its opposition to the attempts of committee Democrats to exercise control over executive agencies (Revenue Sharing and Agency Regulation, $r = .69$). There is a similar split among committee Democrats with liberals (Faction 1) and conservatives (Faction 3) organizing into separate blocs. Conservative committee Democrats like Leo J. Ryan (Calif.), Jack Brooks (Tex.), and Jim Wright (Tex.) are the nominal leaders of Faction 3, which is neither as liberal (ACA, $r = -.47$) nor as partisan (party unity, $r = .53$) as the committee Democrats that form Faction 1. Nevertheless, Factions 1 and 3 frequently join forces ($r = .51$) to create a partisan Democratic coalition.

These ideological differences within the parties and between Democrats and Republicans also appear in the two-dimensional representation of the alignments within the committee (figure 5). Committee Democrats and Republicans cluster into quadrants that are directly opposite one another. Within these quadrants, it is possible to detect the ideological splits within the parties. In the upper-left quadrant, the more moderate and liberal Republicans (McCloskey, Horton, Pritchard, and Alan Steelman [Tex.]) divide from the more conservative Republicans like Steiger, Thone, Clarence Brown, and Erlenborn; in the lower-right quadrant, the more liberal Democrats (Abzug; Fernand St. Germain [R.I.]; Rosenthal; John Conyers, Jr. [Mich.]; and John E. Moss [Calif.]), split away from their more conservative colleagues (Ryan, Brooks, and Wright). There also appear to be a few committee members who find themselves cross-pressured by their party attachments and ideological sentiments. For example, conservative Democrats Don Fuqua (Fla.) and L. H. Fountain (N.C.), and liberal Republican Gude (Md.) are positioned between the partisan-ideological clusters of Democrats and Republicans. The two-dimensional graph confirms that party and ideology are salient environmental influences on members of the Government Operations Committee.

House Administration

The House Administration Committee handles issues related to the internal operations of the House of Representatives (e.g., the assignment of office space, travel allowances, office perquisites, elections). While some matters that enter the committee's jurisdiction seem

Figure 5. Two-Dimensional Representation of Cleavages in the House Committee on Government Operations: 1973-1976.

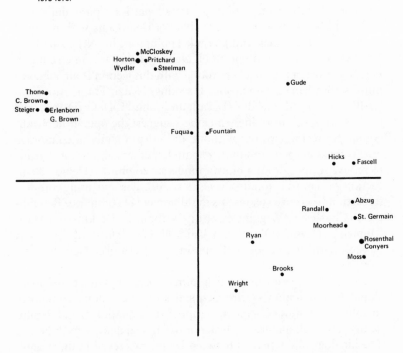

relatively nonpartisan (e.g., management of the Library of Congress and the services of the House), partisan differences over the administration of the House and campaign regulations are sufficiently intense to overcome whatever incentives exist for bipartisan cooperation. Committee partisanship is also apt to have an ideological color because party (party unity) and ideology (ACA) are strongly intertwined ($r = -.96$).

Faction 1 (table 9) represents a strongly partisan (party unity, $r = .96$) and liberal (ACA, $r = -.91$) bloc of Democrats with nominal leaders John Brademas (Ind.), Frank Thompson, Jr. (N.J.), Augustus F. Hawkins (Calif.), and Lucien N. Nedzi (Mich.). It is interesting to note that most of the members voting with this faction chair subcommittees (Brademas, Thompson, Hawkins, Nedzi, Frank Annunzio [D-Ill.], Joseph M. Gaydos [D-Pa.], and John H. Dent [D-Pa.]. The leadership positions of these members suggest the operation of subcommittee reciprocity, but without an in-depth study of committee norms this interpretation must remain hypothetical. Faction 1 tends to receive support from a bloc of moderate committee Democrats in Faction 2 on most committee votes ($r = .50$). The remaining committee faction (Faction 3) represents the alignment of committee Republicans (Charles E. Wiggins [Calif.], William L. Dickinson [Ala.], Samuel L. Devine [Ohio], and James C. Cleveland [N.H.]) that is strongly partisan (presidential support, $r = .92$) and conservative ACA $r = .73$).

The partisan nature of this committee is captured in a two-dimensional representation of the factional structure among committee members: committee Democrats (upper-right quadrant) and Republicans (lower-left quadrant) cluster into diagonal quadrants (figure 6). The ideological differences between Democrats result in the organization of two Democratic factions and the dispersion of committee Democrats within the quadrant (upper-right quadrant). Once again, a southern Democrat (Dawson Mathis [Ga.]) is cross-pressured by the ideological and partisan nature of the cleavages within the committee. As a result, Mathis's voting behavior appears to fall between the clusters of Democratic and Republican committee members.

Rules

The Rules Committee has a central position in the internal functioning of the House of Representatives:

TABLE 9. Factions in the House Administration Committee, 1973–1976

Committee Member	Factions 1	2	3	Explained Variation (%)
John Brademas (D-Ind.)	.93			93
Frank Thompson, Jr. (D-N.J.)	.92			92
Augustas F. Hawkins (D-Calif.)	.84	(.41)		90
Lucien N. Nedzi (D-Mich.)	.77			71
Frank Annunzio (D-Ill.)	.55	.70		84
Joseph M. Gaydos (D-Pa.)	.53	.70		83
James C. Cleveland (R-N.H.)	−.65		(.26)	54
Samuel L. Devine (R-Ohio)	−.74		.56	86
William L Dickinson (R-Ala.)	−.77		.56	91
Robert H. Mollohan (D-W.Va.)		.93		94
Wayne L. Hays (D-Ohio)		.85		85
Ed Jones (D-Tenn.)	(.42)	.82		88
John H. Dent (D-Pa.)	(.49)	.76		84
Dawson Mathis (D-Ga.)		.59		37
Bill Frenzel (R-Minn.)		−.57	.72	88
Charles E. Wiggins (R-Calif.)	(−.44)		.82	91

Correlates of Factional Alignments

Presidential support	−.91*	−.76*	.92*
Conservative coalition	−.94*	−.36	.72*
Party unity	.96*	.48	−.81*
ADA	.85*	.17	−.62*
COPE	.91*	.74*	−.87*
NFU	.95*	.64*	−.83*
CCUS	−.85*	−.35	.67*
ACA	−.91*	−.40	.73*
Administration of the House (I)	.75*	.74*	−.90*
Federal Election Campaign Regulation (II)	.51	.36	−.27

Note: Pearson correlations marked with asterisks are significant at the .01 level.

Rules is to a large degree the governing committee of the House. To it the House has largely delegated the power to regulate procedure vested in the House itself by the Constitution. Furthermore, by virtue of its influence in determining the order and the content of floor business, the committee may also function as a "steering" committee, steering the House in whatever directions the exigencies of the hour appear to demand. (Kravitz, 1969, p. 6)

The power to schedule the release of bills for floor action provides the Rules Committee with a great deal of control over legislation. The

Figure 6. Two-Dimensional Representation of Cleavages in the House Committee on House Administration: 1973-1976.

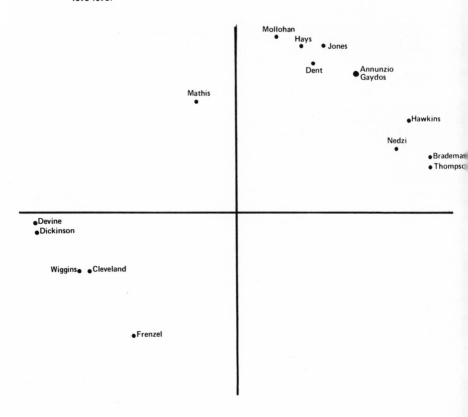

committee also determines the manner in which legislation will be debated and amended. The power to determine the types of amendments and the instances when rules will be waived is crucial to House decision making. For instance, the committee can restrict or prohibit amendments to legislation by attaching a "closed rule" to the legislative measure. The Rules Committee functions as a legislative "traffic cop" by determining whether or not a bill will reach the House floor (refusal to grant a rule to a legislative measure normally "kills" that bill), when and how a bill will be debated, and how long such debate will continue.

Historically, the Rules Committee has operated with a great degree of independence from the parties and their leaders. In fact, it often obstructed the consideration of legislation that the majority of the committee opposed, even when such legislation had the support of the majority party's congressional leaders. Membership turnover within the committee, congressional reforms, and enlargement of the membership of the committee, however, have made the Rules Committee more responsive to the majority faction (liberal) of the Democratic party. The successful attempt of Sam Rayburn to enlarge the committee's membership and to fill these additional committee slots with loyal Democrats, helped to offset the dominant conservative bias of the committee (Peabody, 1963); one consequence of this maneuver was that the committee became more sensitive to leadership directives. Additional leadership control over the Rules Committee resulted from House reforms that curtailed the power of committee leaders and forced them to stand for reelection each Congress, thus removing a major impediment to leadership control of the committee. Finally, as members have left the committee, Democratic leaders have ensured that the replacements are staunchly loyal to the party. Such efforts seem to be having the desired effect. Democratic members of the committee perceive their role as one of agreeing with the party leadership, "if not being subservient to it" (Matsunaga and Chen, 1976, p. 8), but coexisting with the desire to adhere to the wishes of the party leadership is the goal of committee members to establish a degree of independence for the committee.

The degree of party leadership control in the 1970s and its effect on the party loyalty of the committee have been documented by Spark Matsunaga and Ping Chen (1976).

. . . the Democratic leadership, by its initial insistence on party loyalty, has been able to exercise a degree of control over the Rules Committee members. This assumption can be further substantiated by the fact that the Rules Committee evidences a higher minimum party unity score for Democratic appointments than the two other exclusive committees [Ways and Means and Appropriations]. (p. 61)

Although the Republican leadership does not exercise as much control over its members as the Democrats, the net effect is essentially the same:

The minority status of the Republican Party has weakened the Republican leadership's claim for their party's complete identity with the Rules committee. However, the homogeneous character of the House Republican establishment has cancelled out the disadvantages of not being able to exert complete dominance over the membership recruitment process. The end result is that only members philosophically acceptable to the Republican leadership are appointed to the Rules committee from the Republican ranks. (Matsunaga and Chen, 1976, pp. 55–56)

In both cases, it is necessary to distinguish between loyalty to the legislative party and loyalty to the national party with the president as titular head. Rules Committee members, while exhibiting loyalty to the legislative leadership, feel no particular ties to the president. Hence, we would expect party to be a salient influence on decision making in the committee, but we would not expect presidential influence to be important.

Along with the desire to serve the leadership, Rules members would also like to maintain a degree of independence for the committee. "The authors conclude that this study supports the position that the history of the Rules Committee is one of the committee's accommodating the leadership on the one hand and seeking independent status on the other" (Matsunaga and Chen, 1976, p. 143). Increasing this urge for independence were the House reforms in the early 1970s which opened executive meetings of the committee. Members' votes on bills concerning their constituencies were even more visible following the reforms than they were previously.

In the 93rd Congress, the committee made a practice of holding open business meetings. With this turn of events, a member who was concerned with constituency repercussions obviously was not in the position to remain loyal to the leadership. Bereft of that veil of secrecy which formerly shielded Rules Committee members, he was forced to vote in support of constituent interests. (Matsunaga and Chen, 1976, p. 131)

Ideology, therefore, can be expected to have an impact on committee decision making and to play an important role in the formation of factions in this committee. Because the loyalty displayed by members is to the legislative party, we expect that presidential influence will play no role in the formation of factions.

Partisan-ideological conflict within the Rules Committee is captured by the bipolarity of Faction 1 (table 10): the more liberal (ACA, $r = -.92$) and partisan (presidential support, $r = -.94$) Democrats have positive associations (correlations) with this voting bloc, while conservative Republicans (James H. Quillen [Tenn.], Del Clawson [Calif.], and Delbert Latta [Ohio]) have equally large negative correlations to this faction. The remaining committee faction (Faction 2) appears to represent a more conservative bloc of partisan (presidential support, $r = -.60$) Democrats (John Young [Tex.], B. F. Sisk [Calif.], Gillis W. Long [La.], and James J. Delaney [N.Y.]). The partisan nature of Faction 2 might go unnoticed, since only one of the direct measures of party support is statistically significant. Although members of this faction may not be unusually supportive of Democratic party policies on the floor of the House, they are supportive of their party's position on critical partisan measures within the committee: votes on rules that modify normal congressional procedures for the purpose of altering substantive legislation (Amending Rules to Modify Substantive Legislation, $r = .86$). These are, of course, critical decisions for the majority party, since these modifications can yield partisan advantage. Thus, Faction 2 can best be described as a bloc of more conservative Democrats who are supportive of the party's position on critical decisions relating to the modification of House procedures and who frequently vote with their Democratic colleagues in Faction 1 ($r = .53$).

The two-dimensional representation of factional alignments in the Rules Committee illustrates the partisan nature of committee cleavages and the strains on party loyalty that result from the ideological differences within the parties (figure 7). For example, conservative Democrats like Delaney, Sisk, and Young do not cluster with their

TABLE 10. Factions in the Rules Committee, 1973–1976

| Committee Member | Factions | | Explained Variation (%) |
	1	2	
Ray J. Madden (D-Ind.)	.88		81
Spark M. Matsunaga (D-Hawaii)	.82		72
Claude Pepper (D-Fla.)	.78		65
Morgan F. Murphy (D-Ill.)	.70		64
Richard Bolling (D-Mo.)	.69		56
Gillis W. Long (D-La.)	(.46)	.56	52
James H. Quillen (R-Tenn.)	−.87		77
Del Clawson (R-Calif.)	−.87		79
Delbert L. Latta (R-Ohio)	−.83		73
John Young (D-Tex.)		.85	75
B.F. Sisk (D-Calif.)		.63	54
James J. Delaney (D-N.Y.)		.41	22
John B. Anderson (R-Ill.)	(−.32)		14
Correlates of Factional Alignments			
Presidential support	−.94*	−.60*	
Conservation coalition	−.95*	−.34	
Party unity	.72*	.48	
ADA	.87*	.27	
COPE	.95*	.71*	
NFU	.92*	.65*	
CCUS	−.91*	−.56	
ACA	−.92*	−.53	
Amending Rules to Modify Substantive Legislation (I)	.72*	.86*	
Modifying Normal House Procedures (II)	.62*	−.05	

Note: Pearson correlations marked with asterisks are significant at the .01 level.

Democratic colleagues (Morgan F. Murphy [Ill.], Richard Bolling [Mo.], Spark M. Matsunaga [Hawaii], Claude Pepper [Fla.], and Ray J. Madden [Ind.]); the same can be said of maverick Republican John B. Anderson (Ill.).

Anderson's position at a distance from his Republican colleagues can be explained by his own statement to Matsunaga and Chen: (1976) " 'In view of the fact that the minority leadership does not have the function of programming legislation, I don't think that the minority Rules members are bound by the same degree of responsibility to it

Figure 7. Two-Dimensional Representation of Cleavages in the House Committee on Rules: 1973-1976.

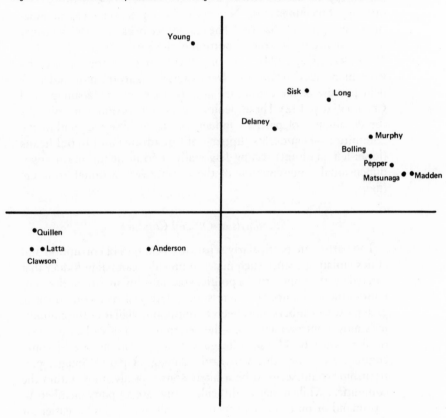

as the majority members are to the majority leadership' " (p. 132). It is obvious from figure 7 that Anderson followed this conviction in his voting on substantive amendments in the Ninety-third and Ninety-fourth Congresses. The deviance of the group of Democrats in this period appears to reflect the pull of their conservative ideology. The opening of meetings in the Ninety-third Congress served as an impetus to this type of behavior. "The committee began to display greater independence in the second portion of the 93rd Congress (October, 1973-December, 1974). The constituent interest factor was used by Chairman Madden and other Democrats to justify the more independent posture of the committee and its decisions" (Matsunaga and Chen, 1976, p. 142). These ideological differences should not obscure the dominance of partisan influences on the cleavages within the committee—Democrats (upper-right quadrant) and Republicans (lower-left quadrant) occupy diagonally opposite quadrants in a two-dimensional representation of the committee's factional structure (figure 7).

Standards of Official Conduct

The parties are particularly sensitive to charges of corruption and ethics violations, since such material provides campaign fodder that can reduce the popularity of political parties—an important determinant of the outcomes of congressional elections. As a consequence, each party's members must keep a continuous vigil over the committee's most controversial task—the determination of violations of official conduct by House colleagues. Since violations of ethics and conduct are issues that can easily damage a party's image, partisanship would seem to be a likely source of divisions within the committee. While it may be difficult in any case for party members to reprimand or punish one of their own colleagues, it is far easier for them to assign blame to members of the opposition party than to members of their own party. The problem of partisan conflict was recognized when the committee was instituted, and to minimize the impact of partisanship, party ratios were made identical. In addition, members were chosen with care:

> Created in 1966 in response to several scandals involving House members, the Committee on Standards of Official Conduct was apparently intended by Speaker John McCormack to be noncontroversial. As one

TABLE 11. Factions in the Standards of Official Conduct
Committee, 1973–1976

Committee Member	Factions		Explained Variation (%)
	1	2	
Melvin Price (D-Ill.)	.98		95
Thomas S. Foley (D-Wash.)	.96		95
Albert H. Quie (R-Minn.)	.51		33
Edward Hutchinson (R-Mich.)	−.51	.50	51
Thad Cochran (R-Miss.)	−.47		25
Charles E. Bennett (D-Fla.)	(.34)	−.59	47
John J. Flynt, Jr. (D-Ga.)		.88	83
Floyd Spence (R-S.C.)		.83	70
James H. Quillen (R-Tenn.)		.51	33

Correlates of Factional Alignment		
Presidential support	−.72*	.18
Conservative coalition	−.90*	.42
Party unity	.88*	−.53
ADA	.83*	−.47
COPE	.70	−.29
NFU	.74*	−.38
CCUS	−.89*	.61
ACA	−.81*	.44
Daniel Schorr Case (I)	.79*	−.74*
Michael Harrington Case (II)	.01	−.29
Disciplinary Action (III)	.39	.58
Decisions on Complaints (IV)	.39	−.02

Note: Doublet: Bennett (D-Fla.) and Cochran (R-Miss.). Pearson correlations marked with asterisks are significant at the .01 level.

Select Committee member said, "My impression is that the committee's function is to sweep things under the rug and not make waves. It's made up of senior men—compatible and isolated." (Davidson and Oleszek, 1977, p. 149)

The partisanship of Standards is reflected in the factional structure of the committee (table 11): Although Faction 1 is largely composed of Democats and Faction 2 has the greater number of Republicans, neither faction is solely partisan in nature. Republican Albert H. Quie (Minn.) aligns with the Democrats in Faction 1, and the southern Democrat John J. Flynt, Jr. (Ga.) votes with the Republicans in Faction

2, suggesting that ideology also influences these alignments. Quie may vote with Faction 1 because this bloc is less conservative (ADA, $r = .83$) than Faction 2; conversely, Flynt may have more in common with conservative Republicans that identify with Faction 2. This contention is supported by the fact that Flynt unfailingly votes with the conservative coalition on the House floor. Some of the ideological nature of Faction 2 is reflected in the relationship between votes on issues related to the investigation of Daniel Schorr and identification with this faction ($r = -.74$): the Schorr case itself creates ideological strains among committee members (ADA, $r = .85$). The association of the Daniel Schorr case with liberal and conservative positions on the responsibilities and obligations of the news media accounts for some of the ideological voting on this issue. In fact, no other case or set of decisions—disciplinary action, decisions on complaints, the Michael Harrington complaint—is as closely associated with the ideological divisions between committee members.

The two-dimensional representation of the factional alignments among the nine members of the Standards Committee illustrates ideological cleavages that divide committee members (figure 8). Members of Faction 1—Melvin Price (D-Ill.), Thomas S. Foley (D-Wash.), Charles E. Bennett (D-Fla.), and Republican Quie (lower quadrants)—are located opposite to Faction 2—Edward Hutchinson (R-Mich.), James H. Quillen (R-Tenn.), Floyd Spence (R-S.C.) and Democrat Flynt (upper quadrants). Republican Thad Cochran's (Miss.) voting behavior may be difficult to interpret because the factional structure explains only about 25 percent of the variation in his voting.

Several committees have jurisdictional responsibilities that encompass some of the most divisive ideological issues of the day: land and surface mining (Interior and Insular Affairs), energy regulation (Interstate and Foreign Commerce), defendants' rights and gun control (Judiciary), federal regulation (Public Works and Transportation), and the development of synthetic and nuclear fuels (Science and Technology). As a consequence, cleavages within these committees appear to mirror the ideological cleavages within society; the close association between party and ideology during the span of this analysis adds a partisan component to these ideological conflicts.

Figure 8. Two-Dimensional Representation of Cleavages in the House Committee on Standards of Official Conduct: 1973-1976.

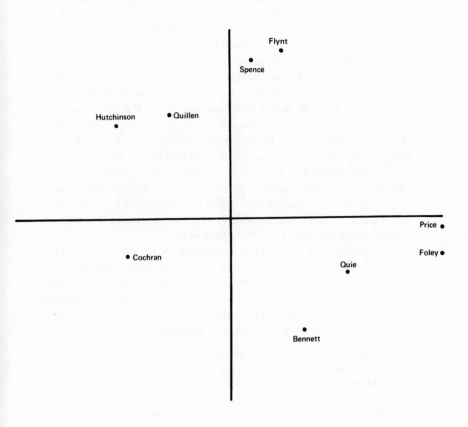

Interior and Insular Affairs

Partisan and ideological elements within the environments of the Interior and Insular Affairs Committee and the Interstate and Foreign Commerce Committee polarize the sympathies of committee members. Two factors account for this ideological- partisan polarization. First, the jurisdictions of these committees stir both types of conflict, and partisan and ideological attitudes move committee members in the same directions. The major policy dimension in Interior, for instance, relates to land and surface mining and is strongly correlated with measures of ideology (ACA, $r = -.87$) and partisanship (party unity, $r = .78$). The major policy dimension in the Interstate and Foreign Commerce Committee deals with energy issues and is also strongly correlated with measures of ideology (ADA, $r = .91$) and party (party unity, $r = .95$). Second, the ideological differences between Democrats and Republicans reinforce their partisan attachments. In fact, in both Interior and Commerce the influences of party and ideology are virtually impossible to disentangle ($r \rangle .90$). As a consequence, both committees have factional structures that are polarized along partisan and ideological lines.

This portrayal of the Interior Committee is at odds with Fenno's (1973) interpretation in *Congressmen in Committees*, which examined the committee in the late sixties. In this earlier period, partisanship played no role in the committee, because partisan conflict would have been detrimental to the achievement of members goals and contradictory to the committee's strategic premises.

> Interior Committee members uniformly describe their committee as low in partisanship. And the reason is clear. Neither of its decision rules could be implemented under conditions of partisanship. Its members could not meet their reelection goals and the clientele groups with which they are in greatest sympathy would not be served. To the contrary, crossparty cooperation is absolutely essential if members are to get projects for their districts and extend sympathetic treatment to Western-oriented interests. (Fenno, 1973, pp. 92–93)

The mode of operation in this earlier period was to resolve potential conflicts that might hinder the passage of constituent-oriented bills by accommodating those interests that might be opposed. Committee members were thus able to ensure passage of legislation that brought benefits to their districts. One indicator of this success at pursuing reelection goals is the amount of benefits committee members were able to bring back to their districts. A 1971 examination of the committee found that while per capita expenditures by the Interior Department averaged $10 nationwide, in committee members' districts the average was $64 per capita (Ralph Nader Congress Project, 1975).

The most salient conflict in the committee in the 1960s concerned user and conservation interests; however, the committee membership at that time heavily overrepresented western interests. Because the environmental movement had not achieved the salience it did in the 1970s, the conflicts that arose were more likely to mirror regional differences rather than ideological cleavages. The issues dealt with were local rather than national in scope and unlikely to excite the interests of a national constituency. Further, the clientele groups with which the committee interacted changed from issue to issue. As a result, these groups were not likely to form a coalition with the goal of national policy. Hence, Fenno (1973) characterized the committee as operating in a clientele-led environment and displaying partisan conflict only over policies that could be construed in terms of public versus private power. In contrast, we find that party and ideology play a major role in the formation of factions in the Ninety-third and Ninety-fourth Congresses.

The bipolar nature of the factional alignments among committee members (table 12) reflects the partisan-ideological polarization of the Interior Committee. Faction 1 represents the vote agreement among conservative (ACA, $r = .87$), partisan (party unity, $r = -.82$) Republicans (with the addition of Harold T. Johnson, an anticonservationist Democrat from California) and the opposition of liberal Democrats like Philip Burton (Calif.), Jonathan B. Bingham (N.Y.), Robert W. Kastenmeier (Wis.), John F. Seiberling (Ohio), Patsy T. Mink (Hawaii), and Morris K. Udall (Ariz.). Conversely, Faction 2 represents a mixture of partisan (party unity, $r = .87$) and ideological (ACA, $r = -.75$) voting among Democratic committee members. The two-dimensional representaton of these alignments (figure 9) illustrates the relatively tight clustering of Democrats (upper-left quadrant) and Republicans (lower-right quadrant) in diagonally opposite quadrants of the graph that is characteristic of the ideological-partisan conflict in the committee.

There are several factors that could lead to the differences between

TABLE 12. Factions in the Interior and Insular Affairs
Committee, 1973–1976

Committee Member	Factions 1	Factions 2	Explained Variation (%)
Don H. Clausen (R-Calif.)	.83		70
Donald E. Young (R-Alaska)	.81		75
Sam Steiger (R-Ariz.)	.79	−.52	89
Harold T. Johnson (D-Calif.)	.75		56
Keith G. Sebelius (R-Kans.)	.72		66
Steven D. Symms (R-Idaho)	.69	−.67	93
Manuel Lujan, Jr. (R-N.Mex.)	.62	−.59	73
Joe Skubitz (R-Kans.)	.57	−.51	58
Phillip Burton (D-Calif.)	−.80	.57	97
Jonathan B. Bingham (D-N.Y.)	−.70	.65	91
Robert W. Kastenmeier (D-Wis.)	−.69	.64	90
John F. Seiberling (D-Ohio)	−.69	.51	74
Patsy T. Mink (D-Hawaii)	−.69	.62	86
Morris K. Udall (D-Ariz.)	−.58	.66	78
Antonio Wo Pat (D-Guam)		.88	91
Lloyd Meeds (D-Wash.)		.82	79
Joseph P. Vigorito (D-Pa.)		.82	78
John Melcher (D-Mont.)		.78	62
Teno Roncalio (D-Wyo.)		.64	41
Phillip E. Ruppe (R-Mich.)	(.33)		11
Roy A. Taylor (D-N.C.)	(.27)	(.26)	14

Correlates of Factional Alignments

	1	2
Presidential support	.81*	−.58*
Conservative coalition	.90*	−.65*
Party unity	−.82*	.87*
ADA	−.87*	.84*
COPE	−.80*	.76*
NFU	−.88*	.73*
CCUS	.88*	−.69*
ACA	.87*	−.75*
Land-Use and Surface-Mining Regulation (I)	−.88*	.75*

Note: Pearson correlations marked with asterisks are significant at the .01 level.

Figure 9. Two-Dimensional Representation of Cleavages in the House Committee on Interior and Insular Affairs: 1973-1976.

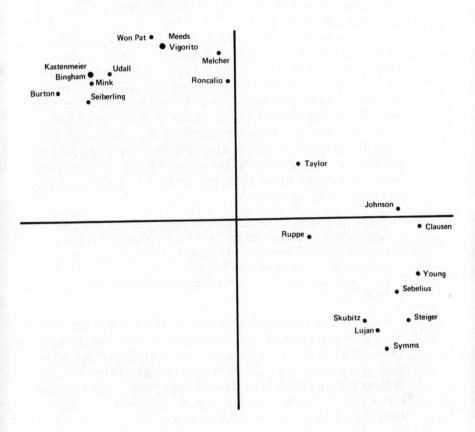

our findings and those of Fenno (1973). The environmental move-ment had not blossomed into the national movement it became in the early 1970s. As this movement became more salient to the public, the conflict over the environment took on more partisan and ideological tones. The nature of the issues handled by the Interior Committee correspondingly began to change. We find that the issues that tended to divide the committee in the time frame investigated here concerned land-use and surface-mining regulations and, in particular, amend-ments that would allow exceptions to legislated environmental stan-dards (Chapter 2). Further, the stands on these issues are attached to distinct ideological positions—conservatives support the exceptions while liberals oppose them. Finally, the parties also began to develop opposing stands on environmental issues: the Republicans with their ties to business and their heavy representation in the West tended to support user interests and the Democrats began to champion en-vironmental causes. Fenno (1973), himself, remarks on the possibility for change in the committee:

> But the winds of change are blowing through the committee to a degree not present in the period from 1955 to 1966. . . . Should more policy-oriented members come to the Committee, we would expect to see Interior—the most fragile of our "corporate" committees—move from the "corporate" toward the permeable end of the committee spec-trum. (p. 287)

Fenno was not amiss in his observations. As a matter of fact, there was a great deal of membership turnover in the committee between 1966 and 1972. In 1967, there was an infusion of liberal Democrats to the committee (Burton, Kastenmeier, John G. O'Hara [Mich.], William F. Ryan [N.Y.], Mink, Lloyd Meeds [Wash.], and Abraham Kazen [Tex.]). This membership turnover and the House reforms strengthened the environmentalist position in the committee (Ralph Nader Congress Project, 1975). The final factor that may have con-tributed to the change in the committee was the defeat of Wayne Aspinall in 1972. As chairman, Aspinall exercised tight control over decision making within the committee. Much like Wilbur Mills in Ways and Means, he was able to work out compromises between opposing interests, which contributed to the muting of conflict in the committee. Fenno (1973) reported that "like Mills, Aspinall agrees with his Committee's decision rules and has used his chairmanship to help implement them. Thus he works to pass a large number of bills through the Committee and the House and to protect Western user interests in more controversial cases. The members, in turn, grant him his pre-eminence" (p. 118).

While Aspinall's successors (James A. Haley [D-Fla.] and Harold T. Johnson [D-Calif.]) were frequently characterized as antienvironmentalists (Ralph Nader Congress Project, 1975), the reforms in the House so strengthened the subcommittees in Interior that committee leaders could not be expected to exert the same influence over the committee that Aspinall did. Consequently, these four conditions—growth of the environmental movement, membership turnover, committee reforms, and the defeat of Aspinall—seem sufficient to explain the growth of partisan and ideological conflict in the committee.

Interstate and Foreign Commerce

Several important characteristics of the Interstate and Foreign Commerce Committee are described by David Price (1975, 1978, 1981). According to Price the jurisdiction of the committee and the issues handled do not generate the interests of strong clientele groups such as organized labor. Business interests do seek legislation, but they generally concentrate on industry-specific exceptions to proposed regulations.

> In the first place, the committees do not deal extensively with the "peak associations" seeking "redistributive" policies. The "distributive" and "regulatory" measures with which the committees generally work involve organized labor only peripherally and seldom raise the spectre of a massive reallocation of national resources. . . . The result is an environment in which group conflict is, while sometimes intense, generally limited in scope. (Price, 1978, p. 550)

Cleavages over the distribution of constituency benefits are unlikely to arise for another reason; all members are able to gain from particularistic decisions.

The issues dealt with by the committee rarely are a high priority for the president (Price, 1978); consequently, the influence of the executive branch in the environment of the committee is slight. Finally, Price (1975, p. 54) finds that the minority party members and majority members maintain a relatively harmonious relationship, although it is more harmonious in the Senate than in the House.

Membership changes during the 1970–75 period produced a change in the ideological composition of the committee (Ornstein and Rohde, 1977). The majority of new members joining the committee·in that time period were Democrats, partly as a result of the expansion of the committee in the Ninety-fourth Congress and partly because of the large influx of Democrats into Congress in 1975. At the same time, there was a loss of veteran Republican members of the committee. The result was a gradual movement of the committee membership toward the liberal end of the ideological continuum.

Despite the appearance of relative harmony between the parties in Price's analysis, issues that incite partisan and ideological conflict do fall within the committee's jurisdiction. As we noted in Chapter 2, the energy area incites both ideological and partisan conflict during the Ninety-third and Ninety-fourth Congresses. Liberal Democrats and conservative Republicans oppose one another on oil policy, energy conservation, synthetic fuels, and oil company reporting requirements. The ideological-partisan polarization we find in this committee is similar to that displayed by the Interior Committee and can be detected in the bipolarity of the committee's factional alignments (table 13).

Faction 1 reflects the agreement among conservative Republicans (ADA, $r = -.94$) and the strong opposition of liberal Democrats (John E. Moss [Calif.], Bob Eckhardt [Tex.], Ralph H. Metcalf [Ill.], and Brock Adams [Wash.]). The less liberal, but equally partisan (party unity, $r = .96$) Democrats—Fred B. Rooney (Pa.), Paul G. Rogers (Fla.), Harley O. Staggers (W.Va.) and Richardson Preyer (N.C.)—are the nominal leaders of Faction 2. The polarization within this committee is evident in the tight clustering of Democrats (upper-left quadrant) and Republicans (lower-right quadrant) in opposite quadrants in the two-dimensional representation of the committee's factional structure (figure 10). In the Commerce Committee, ideology also appears to cross-pressure Republican H. John Heinz III (Pa.); his liberalism pushes him away from the cluster of conservative Republicans (lower-right quadrant).

Our study reaches somewhat different conclusions from Price's studies. We agree that there is ideological divergence on the committee and that executive and clientele pressures do not have a significant impact on the decision-making environment. These findings, however, suggest a greater degree of partisanship than described by Price.

TABLE 13. Factions in the Interstate and Foreign Commerce Committee, 1973–1976

Committee Member	Factions 1	2	Explained Variation (%)
Clarence J. Brown (R-Ohio)	.81	(−.46)	87
Tim Lee Carter (R-Ky.)	.80		75
John Y. McCollister (R-Nebr.)	.80	−.50	89
Norman F. Lent (R-N.Y.)	.77		75
Joe Skubitz (R-Kans.)	.77	(−.43)	78
Louis Frey Jr. (R-Fla.)	.77	(−.44)	79
James T. Broyhill (R-N.C.)	.75	(−.48)	79
Samuel L. Devine (R-Ohio)	.70	−.60	84
David E. Satterfield III (D-Va.)	.68	−.51	72
H. John Heinz III (R-Pa.)	.63		43
James M. Collins (R-Tex.)	.63	−.66	84
John E. Moss (D-Calif.)	−.65	.56	73
Bob Eckhardt (D-Tex.)	−.64	.62	79
Ralph H. Metcalfe (D-Ill.)	−.60	.70	84
Brock Adams (D-Wash.)	−.54	.60	65
Fred B. Rooney (D-Pa.)		.83	70
Paul G. Rogers (D-Fla.)		.81	74
Harley O. Staggers (D-W.Va.)		.78	81
Richardson Preyer (D-N.C.)		.78	62
Charles J. Carney (D-Ohio)		.72	74
James W. Symington (D-Mo.)		.70	66
Lionel Van Deerlin (D-Calif.)	(−.48)	.58	56
John D. Dingell (D-Mich.)	(−.41)	.56	48

Correlates of Factional Alignments

Presidential support	.93*	−.92*
Conservative coalition	.90*	−.88*
Party unity	−.94*	.96*
ADA	−.94*	.87*
COPE	−.90*	.91*
NFU	−.92*	.95*
CCUS	.88*	−.93*
ACA	.89*	−.93*
Energy (I)	−.98*	.95*

Note: Doublet: Heinz (R-Pa.) and Lent (R-N.Y.). Pearson correlations marked with asterisks are significant at the .01 level.

Figure 10. Two-Dimensional Representation of Cleavages in the House Committee on Interstate and Foreign Commerce: 1973-1976.

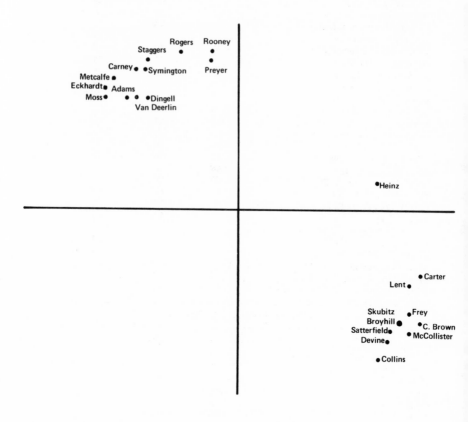

It may be that membership changes disrupted the ideological convergence between Democrats and Republicans on the committee; in the period studied by Price the Democrats on the committee were more conservative than the Democrats as a whole. The influx of more liberal Democrats, documented by Ornstein and Rohde (1977), may have led to a greater congruence between party and ideology on the part of Democrats. The appearance of issues that divided the committee along ideological and partisan lines and the greater ideological divergence between the parties could lead to the polarized configurations we uncover in the committee.

Judiciary

Recent studies of the Judiciary Committee by Lynette Perkins (1980, 1981) described the committee as being populated by members with mixed goals. Congressmen queried during the Ninety-third Congress cited three major reasons for joining the committee: reelection (47.3 percent), good public policy (34.2 percent), and higher office (15.8 percent) (Perkins, 1980, p. 375). The mixed motives for joining the committee also led to a variety of strategic premises pursued by the committee: avoiding lobbying of fellow members, obtaining voting cues from other members during full committee meetings, conducting meetings in a fair and orderly manner, and minimizing time spent on committee matters. Perkins describes the declining appeal of Judiciary membership, attributing it to the mxed goals held by members and the departure of Emanuel Celler as chairman in the Ninety-second Congress. "Reelection and higher office oriented members on Judiciary contributed less than policy oriented members to the committee's functioning and the committee became unpopular once Celler's departure lessened the attractiveness of the committee and left exposed its poor contribution to reelection" (Perkins, 1981, p. 364).

Under the liberal and policy-oriented leadership of Celler, the committee attained a high degree of status, which enhanced the attractiveness of the committee to more liberal members of the House. Further, the committee membership during the Ninety-second Congress tended to be "clustered at the center of the political spectrum" (Schuck, 1975, pp. 37–38).

From these descriptions, we would not expect this committee to display the same degree of ideological polarization as Interior or Commerce. Yet, because the committee deals with ideological issues such as busing, school prayer, the Equal Rights Amendment (ERA), and gun control, we do expect ideology to play a major role in the formation of factions. In addition, since the two parties stake out different policy positions on these issues, we would expect party to be a major influence in the committee. Although different interest groups are associated with the above-mentioned issues, such groups are not expected to create factions, because, like those on the Commerce Committee, these groups lack the scope necessary to create lasting cleavages. Single-issue groups that seek to influence the committee are not pervasive forces, given the large size of the committee's jurisdiction. "Although particular groups were influential in certain policy areas, none dominated the Judiciary Committee in all of its jurisdiction and few dominated even in one area" (Perkins, 1980, p. 376).

Our analysis of the substantive roll-call votes (impeachment votes are excluded from the analysis) illustrates the importance of party and ideology in the committee, and it uncovers a difference in effect of these two factors from the polarized committees discussed earlier in this chapter. While party and ideology are as important in the Judiciary Committee as they are in the Interior and Commerce committees, they promote a factional structure in Judiciary that differs from these two committees.

In the Judiciary Committee, the factional alignments are fragmented and appear to represent a broad range of ideological positions and policy cleavages (table 14). Democrats on the committee are dispersed over three factions (1, 3, and 4) with each Democratic faction representing a different level of ideological liberalism. Faction 1 represents the vote agreement among Democratic liberals (ADA, $r = .91$) and the intense opposition of conservative Republicans like Carlos J. Moorhead (Calif.), Edward Hutchinson (Mich.), M. Caldwell Butler (Va.), and Charles E. Wiggins (Calif.). The remaining Democratic factions capture the agreement among conservative (Faction 3) and moderately liberal (Faction 4) Democratic committee members. Despite the similarities in party affiliation, these three Democratic factions do not vote together with any degree of frequency: the moderately liberal Democrats (Faction 4) vote as frequently with their liberal Democratic colleagues (Faction 1, $r = .40$) as they

TABLE 14. Factions in the Judiciary Committee, 1973–1976

Committee Member	Factions 1	2	3	4	Explained Variation (%)
Herman Badillo (D-N.Y.)	.89				85
John Conyers, Jr. (D-Mich.)	.88				88
Don Edwards, Jr. (D-Calif.)	.88				86
Robert W. Kastenmeier (D-Wis.)	.86				77
Robert F. Drinan (D-Mass.)	.84				84
John F. Seiberling (D-Ohio)	.81				79
Elizabeth Holtzman (D-N.Y.)	.81				77
Peter W. Rodino (D-N.J.)	.73				67
Barbara C. Jordan (D-Tex.)	.61		.52		66
Carlos J. Moorhead (R-Calif.)	−.83				81
Edward Hutchinson (R-Mich.)	−.70	.50			87
M. Caldwell Butler (R-Va.)	−.54	.53			63
Charles E. Wiggins (R-Calif.)	−.51	.65			78
Henry J. Hyde (R-Ill.)	(−.48)	(.46)			47
William S. Cohen (R-Maine)		.80			75
Tom Railsback (R-Ill.)		.79			75
Hamilton Fish, Jr. (R-N.Y.)		.70			66
William J. Hughes (D-N.J.)		(.41)			29
William L. Hungate (D-Mo.)			.78		64
Jack Brooks (D-Tex.)			.75		59
Joshua Eilberg (D-Pa.)			.73	(.44)	79
Paul S. Sarbanes (D-Md.)			.66	.53	79
Walter Flowers (D-Ala.)			.64		59
Edward Mezvinsky (D-Iowa)			.56	(.46)	70
Edward W. Pattison (D-N.Y.)			.54		45
James R. Mann (D-S.C.)			.49		54
George E. Danielson (D-Calif.)				.75	67
Robert McClory (R-Ill.)		(.46)		−.68	69

Correlates of Factional Alignments

Presidential support	−.83*	.79*	−.37	−.64*
Conservative coalition	−.90*	.77*	−.15	−.57*
Party unity	.80*	−.76*	.33	.61*
ADA	.91*	−.72*	.20	.58*
COPE	.85*	−.76*	.33	.69*
NFU	.83*	−.69*	.37	.64*
CCUS	−.87*	.67*	−.23	−.63*
ACA	.87*	.64*	−.24	−.58*
Illegal Practices and Crime Control (I)	.63*	−.72*	.64*	.73*
Gun Control (II)	−.70*	.56*	.52*	.22

Note: Doublets: Sarbanes (D-Md.) and Hughes (D-N.Y.); Hyde (R-Ill.) and McClory (R-Ill.). Pearson correlations marked with asterisks are significant at the .01 level.

vote with their more conservative colleagues (Faction 3, $r = .39$), and Faction 1 rarely joins forces with Faction 3 (conservative Democrats). Ideology is not the only basis for the division between liberal (Faction 1) and conservative (Faction 3) committee Democrats; the liberal Democrats support gun control measures ($r = -.70$) that the conservative Democrats vigorously oppose ($r = .52$).

Faction 2 represents the alignment of conservative (ADA, $r = -.72$) and partisan Republicans (presidential support, $r = .79$). This Republican faction can be expected to support the conservative Democrats when the issue under consideration deals with gun control legislation (gun control, $r = .56$). Further fragmentation of the factional structure occurs as the result of the individualistic behavior of Henry J. Hyde (R-Ill.), Robert McClory (R-Ill.), and William J. Hughes (D-N.J.). None of these members displays a strong attachment to any of the committee factions; however, their behavior is not entirely unique, since they form doublets: Hughes tends to agree with Paul S. Sarbanes (D-Md.), and Hyde with McClory.

The two-dimensional graph of the vote agreement among committee members reflects this dispersion in ideological and partisan sympathies (figure 11).) Unlike polarized committees, committee members span the entire spectrum rather than clustering into distinct quadrants; the committee space is anchored by Democratic liberals (Herman Badillo [N.Y.], John Conyers, Jr. [Mich.], Don Edwards, Jr. [Calif.], Robert E. Drinan [Mass.], John F. Seiberling [Ohio], Robert W. Kastenmeier [Wis.], and Elizabeth Holtzman [N.Y.]) and Republican conservatives (Moorhead, Wiggins, Hutchinson, Hyde, and Butler) at the ends of the spectrum. The remaining committee members fall between these two poles, with the more conservative committee members located closer to the Republican end of the spectrum (lower-left quadrant) and more liberal members located nearer to the Democratic end of the space (upper-right quadrant). This representation of the factional structure confirms the saliency of party and ideology in the committee and also points to the particular importance of ideology in the creation of cleavages among Democrats in the Judiciary Committee.

Science and Technology

The ideological divisions among members of the Science and Technology Committee are even more complicated than those among

Figure 11. Two-Dimensional Representation of Cleavages in the House Committee on Judiciary: 1973-1976.

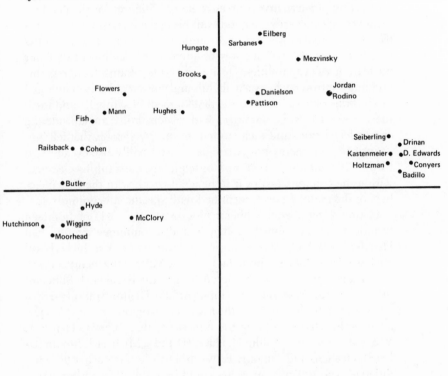

members of the Judiciary Committee. Issues related to the development of fossil and synthetic fuels, and the responsibilities of the newly created Department of Energy—Energy Research and Development Administration (ERDA)—create ideological and partisan divisions within the committee (table 15). The intertwining of ideological and partisan positions is evident in a variety of conflicts over the use and production of alternative sources of energy. Support for the development of nuclear energy is a good example of these divisions. Committee liberals generally support an antinuclear stance that contrasts with the conservatives' support of attempts to develop further our nuclear energy capabilities. During the Ninety-fourth Congress this ongoing controversy between liberals and conservatives is manifested in divisions over support for the development of synthetic and fossil fuels. Since two subcommittees had responsibility for considering energy legislation, and each favored the energy sources that fell into its jurisdiction, energy-policy conflicts are probably also excaberated by the subcommittee structure. Consequently, the resulting cleavages within the committee appear to be ideological, with the core members of the major factions identified with specific subcommittees.

Faction 1 represents a liberal bloc (ADA, $r = .81$) of freshmen Democrats (Ninety-fourth Congress) and a committee veteran, Ken Hechler (D-W.Va.), who favor the development of fossil fuels (Fossil Fuel Research and Development, $r = .73$). Most of the members with strong attachments to this faction belong to the Fossil Fuels Subcommittee (Energy Research, Development and Demonstration—Fossil Fuels) that actively promoted the fossil fuel programs in ERDA's legislative authorizations during the Ninety-fourth Congress: Henry A. Waxman (D-Calif.), Philllip H. Hayes (D-Ind.), Michael T. Blouin (D-Iowa), Hechler, and Timothy E. Wirth (D-Colo.). In earlier decades, differences in policy approaches could be resolved in authorization legislation by ensuring funding for all alternative programs. Such logrolling strategies for resolving conflict are probably less effective now because budgetary constraints have forced programs into competition with one another. This certainly appears to be the case in the energy area, where alternative fuel sources, such as coal and synthetic fuels, compete for program support and funding.

Competition for support is a possible explanation of the opposition of Faction 2 to fossil fuel programs (Fossil Fuel Research and Development, $r = -.63$). Faction 2 is a bipartisan alignment of

TABLE 15. Factions in the Science and Technology Committee, 1973–1976

Committee Member	Factions					Explained Variation (%)
	1	2	3	4	5	
Henry A. Waxman (D-Calif.)	.99					100
Richard L. Ottinger (D-N.Y.)	.92					94
Phillip H. Hayes (D-Ind.)	.88					85
Michael T. Blouin (D-Iowa)	.87					96
Ken Hechler (D-W.Va.)	.73					71
Tim L. Hall (D-Ill.)	.70	.56	(.42)			100
Timothy E. Wirth (D-Colo.)	.63			.51		91
Jerome A. Ambro (D-N.Y.)	.63				−.52	86
Alphonzo Bell (R-Calif.)	−.54	.79				100
Charles A. Mosher (R-Ohio)		.85				90
Louis Frey, Jr. (R-Fla.)		.84				84
Mike McCormack (D-Wash.)		.82				81
Don Fuqua (D-Fla.)		.76	(.49)			83
Jim Lloyd (D-Calif.)		.76				64
Dale Milford (D-Tex.)		.63	(.40)			87
Marilyn Lloyd (D-Tenn.)		.55	.59			78
Ray Thornton (D-Ark.)			.98			99
Olin E. Teague (D-Tex.)			.92			94
George E. Brown, Jr. (D-Calif.)			(.42)		−.50	58
Tom Harkin (D-Iowa)				.84		80
James H. Scheuer (D-N.Y.)	(.49)			.76		83
David Emery (R-Maine)				.66		74
Christopher J. Dodd (D-Conn.)	(.49)			.58		90
Gary Myers (R-Pa.)					.71	63
Larry Winn, Jr. (R-Kans.)					.71	77
Barry M. Goldwater, Jr. (R-Calif.)	(−.44)				.57	78

Correlates of Factional Alignments					
Presidential support	−.70*	.52*	.02	−.48*	.66*
Conservative coalition	−.79*	.51*	.23	−.58*	.55*
Party unity	.79*	−.45*	−.04	.53*	−.66*
ADA	.81*	−.58*	−.41	.57*	−.47*
COPE	.74*	−.44*	−.09	.45*	−.63*
NFU	.76*	−.52*	−.15	.48*	−.64*
CCUS	−.76*	.52*	.26	−.55*	.60*
ACA	−.79*	.51	.24	−.58*	.52*
Fossil Fuel Research and Development (I)	.73*	−.63*	−.51*	−.14	−.08
Synthetic Fuels Loans (II)	−.28	.47*	.37	−.91*	−.10
ERDA Funding (III)	.44*	−.29	.51*	.24	−.87*

Note: Doublets: Brown (D-Calif.) and J. Lloyd (D-Calif.); Myers (R-Pa.) and Winn (R-Kans.).
Pearson correlations marked with asterisks are significant at the .01 level.

generally conservative (ADA, $r = -.58$) Democrats (Mike McCormack, [Wash.], Don Fuqua [Fla.], Jim Lloyd [Calif.], and Dale Milford [Tex.] and Republicans (Alphonzo Bell [Calif.], Charles A. Mosher [Ohio], and Louis Frey, Jr. [Fla.]). A number of members of this bloc (McCormack, Fuqua, Bell, and Frey) are also members of the other energy subcommittee (Energy Research, Development, and Demonstration). This bloc's opposition to fossil fuel programs probably reflects both the jurisdictional responsibilities of the subcommittee and the ideological position that a greater emphasis should be placed on research into synthetic fuels rather than fossil fuels. This support of synthetic fuel research is evident in the strong support Faction 2 gives to financial incentives, in the form of loan guarantees, for the development of synthetic fuels (Synthetic Fuels Loan Guarantees, $r = .47$).

The members of Faction 3 appear to take a position similar to those of Faction 2 in opposing the strengthening of fossil fuel programs (Policy- Dimension I, Fossil Fuel Reserch and Development, $r = -.51$). While Factions 2 and 3 share a conservative ideological outlook and agree on the importance of research in the area of synthetic fuels, they do divide over the levels of funding in the Energy Research and Development Act. The southern Democratic members of Faction 3 join with their liberal colleagues from Faction 1 in opposing reductions in the ERDA appropriations that are advocated by the Republicans from Faction 5: Faction 1 ($r = .44$) and Faction 3 ($r = .51$) oppose reductions in energy research authorizations (ERDA funding). In contrast, the solid bloc of Republicans in Faction 5 strongly supports these budgetary reductions ($r = -.87$).

The remaining Democratic faction, Faction 4, represents the agreement among a largely liberal (ACA, $r = -.58$) bloc composed of Democrats Tom Harkin (Iowa), James H. Scheuer (N.Y.), Christopher J. Dodd (Conn.), and Wirth and of Republican David Emery (Maine), who votes frequently with this faction. Perhaps the most distinguishing characteristic of Faction 4 is its opposition to loan guarantees for the commercial development of synthetic fuels ($r = -.91$). The final committee bloc, Faction 5, represents the agreement among committee Republicans. As in other committees, the influence of party and ideology may obscure the impact of the executive branch in this committee. Caution, therefore, must be exercised in ignoring administration influences, especially when the establishment of responsibilities of a new agency are at issue within the committee.

The two-dimensional representation of the factional alignments within the committee reflects the same type of ideological and partisan dispersion that is found in the Judiciary Committee (figure 12): committee members span the entire spectrum with few definable clusters. Although it is difficult to identify the basis for the dispersion in partisan loyalties, the ideological nature of the major policy cleavages in the committee appears to be at least a contributing factor. Our interpretation of the factional organization of the Science and Technology Committee should be considered tentative, since these alignments are based on fewer than twenty votes, all of which are recorded for the Ninety-fourth Congress.

Public Works and Transportation

The Public Works and Transportation Committee's decision-making process has been described as displaying two contradictory trends, or faces—party cooperation and party conflict (Murphy, 1974). Party cooperation arises from the shared goal of most members, that of serving the constituency. James Murphy (1974) found from his interviews with members in the Ninetieth Congress that 60 percent of the members joined the committee because of the benefits they could provide to their districts, and another 19 percent joined because of the benefits they could provide to members of their state delegations. This orientation toward the committee stimulated cooperation between members of each party because it was needed to ensure that the benefits each member wanted would receive approval. To further this pursuit on the part of members, the committee made up allocation formulas to ensure fairness in the distribution of benefits. "The threat of partisan allocations has induced the congressional parties to adopt relatively rigid allocation rules such that neither party can make substantial gains at the polls at the expense of the other" (Murphy, 1974, p. 170).

Conflicts of an ideological and partisan nature, however, did enter the decision-making process. Because of the large number of bills handled by the committee, many bills did not have constituency demands attached to them, and still others benefited the districts of a minority of committee members. Regional allocation issues were

Figure 12. Two-Dimensional Representation of Cleavages in the House Committee on Science and Technology: 1973-1976.

particularly likely to generate partisan conflict, as were issues on which the parties took opposite stands. "Most committee legislation will engender party disputes because committee Democrats and Republicans cannot arrive at a consensus either on regional allocation issues (allocations benefiting a minority in each party) or on traditional party issues" (Murphy, 1974, p. 169). Ideological disagreements resulted from a basic disagreement over the role of the federal government in the economy.

From Murphy's description, we would expect to find party and ideology influential factors in the formation of factions, particularly because this analysis focuses on the areas of conflict in committee roll-call votes. For this same reason we would not expect to find constituency influences to be important; bills that provide benefits to a majority of members would be decided without much conflict through the use of allocation formulas.

Factions 1 and 2 (table 16) capture the partisan disagreement in the committee with Republicans aligning on Faction 1 and Democrats on Faction 2. In contrast, ideology is not as salient a factor in the committee as partisanship. The behavior of two members accounts for the ideological influences in the committee; Bella S. Abzug (D-N.Y.) and Gerry E. Studds (D-Mass.) form a voting doublet that conistently opposes the conservative Republicans in Faction 1 (ACA, r = .85).

The two-dimensional graph of the vote agreement among committee members demonstrates the significance of partisanship and ideology in the formation of factions in the Public Works Committee (figure 13). This representation isolates three clusters of committee members, which reflect the ideological differences between and within the parties—liberal Democrats, Democrats, and Republicans. Studds and Abzug anchor the liberal end of the spectrum, opposing the cluster of conservative Republicans like James Abdnor (S.D.), Thad Cochran (Miss.), and John P. Hammerschmidt (Ark.). Since the remaining committee Democrats are generally less liberal than Studds and Abzug, but steadfastly partisan (Faction 2, party unity, r = .66), they cluster somewhere between these polar ideological positions. Although both party and ideology appear to be influential in the organization of the committee's factional structure, party appears to be the more salient of the two environmental influences in the

111

TABLE 16. Factions in the Public Works and Transportation Committee, 1973–1976

Committee Member	Factions 1	Factions 2	Explained Variation (%)
Gene Taylor (R-Mo.)	.95		91
James Abdnor (R-S.D.)	.91		82
Thad Cochran (R-Miss.)	.89		81
John P. Hammerschmidt (R-Ark.)	.89		80
M.G. "Gene" Snyder (R-Ky.)	.86		74
James C. Cleveland (R-N.H.)	.81		65
William H. Harsha (R-Ohio)	.75		58
Don H. Clausen (R-Calif.)	.70		50
E. G. Shuster (R-Pa.)	.58		38
William F. Walsh (R-N.Y.)	.52		32
Dale Milford (D-Tex.)	.50		28
Bella S. Abzug (D-N.Y.)	−.89		81
Gerry E. Studds (D-Mass.)	−.88		82
Robert E. Jones (D-Ala.)		.95	91
Mike McCormack (D-Wash.)		.92	86
David N. Henderson (D-N.C.)		.90	83
John B. Breaux (D-La.)		.87	77
Robert A. Roe (D-N.J.)		.84	71
Ray Roberts (D-Tex.)		.78	62
James J. Howard (D-N.J.)		.77	71
Harold T. Johnson (D-Calif.)		.75	57
Ronald B. "Bo" Ginn (D-Ga.)		.75	57
Jim Wright (D-Tex.)		.70	49
Glenn M. Anderson (D-Calif.)		.69	63

Correlates of Factional Alignments		
Presidential support	.88*	−.60*
Conservative coalition	.87*	−.46*
Party unity	−.89*	.66*
ADA	−.85*	.36
COPE	−.84*	.66*
NFU	−.80*	.59*
CCUS	.79*	−.35
ACA	.85*	−.52*
Mass Transportation (I)	−.80*	.92*
Airport Regulation (II)	.54*	.22

Note: Doublet: Abzug (D-N.Y.) and Studds (D-Mass.). Pearson correlations marked with asterisks are significant at the .01 level.

Figure 13. Two-Dimensional Representation of Cleavages in the House Committee on Public Works and Transportation: 1973-1976.

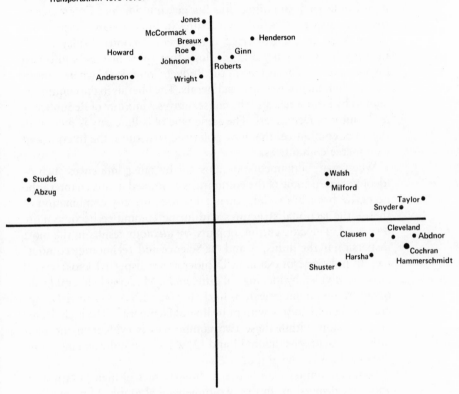

Public Works Committee. This finding appears to be consistent with Murphy's (1974) earlier findings.

The committees examined in this chapter span a continuum from highly polarized committees like Budget, Interior, and Commerce to the more dispersed factional structures in Judiciary and Science and Technology. In the polarized committees, factions display a collinearity between party and ideology that splits members into two distinct camps. This is true in the Budget Committee, where conservatives align themselves against liberals. The liberals in the committee tend to be Democrats and the conservatives a mixture of Republicans and southern Democrats. The same type of collinearity is present in the other committees that have polarized structures: the Interior and Commerce committees.

When party alignments are crosscut by other influences such as ideology (as in some of the committees examined in this chapter), the executive branch, or constituency interests (or any combination of these), the factional structures within the committee become more dispersed. The crosscutting of party *by ideology* results in the most dispersion in the Judiciary and the Science and Technology committees. In Judiciary, for example, Democrats are dispersed across several factions, divided by ideological differences. Moderately liberal Democrats in this committee are as likely to vote with conservative Democrats as they are to vote with more liberal Democrats. The high degree of dispersion within these two committees is evident in the two-dimensional graphs (figure 11 and 12) where committee members are dispersed across the graph.

Some committees fall between the extremes of high polarization and high dispersion. In the two-dimensional graphs of committees like Government Operations, House Administration, Rules, Standards, Public Works (figures 5, 6, 7, 8, and 13), while clustering of members is apparent, the clustering is not as tight as in committees like Interior and Commerce (figures 9 and 10). Ideology in these committees divides party members. The lack of a high degree of collinearity between party and ideology means that these committees will not be highly polarized. Hence, it is apparent that while all ten of the committees explored here can be grouped by the predominance of partisan and ideological influences on decision making, such influences do not create identical factional structures. These differences are apparent in both the factions and the two-dimensional graphs.

CHAPTER FOUR

The Executive Branch
and Cleavages

Executive influences on committees can come from two sources—the president and the bureaucracy. While the president and the bureaucracy may work in coordination with one another to ensure the passage of favorable legislation, they may also work independently or even in opposition. It is not unusual, for example, for the military services to work directly with Armed Services Committee members in both Houses to obtain research money for projects not explicitly endorsed by the administration, or for agencies to influence Appropriations Committee members to provide the agency with more funding than is contained in the president's budget. Hence, although the bureaucracy is under the nominal control of the president, it is often difficult for the president to exercise actual control over the actions of the bureaucracy. The development of "cozy" relationships between agencies and committee members makes it even more difficult for the president to ensure that the bureaucracy will act in a manner that he prescribes. Thus, when we speak of the influence of the exe600tive branch in this chapter, that influence may reflect the actions of the president or the actions of the bureaucracy or the actions of the two working in concert.

The president's arsenal is stocked with resources to persuade 115

Congress to follow his directives. As Richard Neustadt (1960) suggests, the power of the presidency rests not on the president's ability to command or demand but on the ability to persuade. This power to persuade results in part from the constitutional prescriptions and institutional arrangements attached to the presidency. Among the duties of the president outlined in the Constitution is the presentation of a State of the Union message to the Congress. Recently, presidents have used this function to present legislative programs they wish to pursue, thus assuming a major policy initiation role in legislative politics. Until recently the president's preeminence in the areas of military and foreign policy has gone unchallenged by either Congress or special-interest groups. The centralized, hierarchical structure of the executive branch, and the economic and budgetary expertise at his disposal also made the president nearly invincible in the area of budgeting until the congressional reforms of 1974. Despite the fact that the reforms were designed to curb presidential ascendancy in the areas of military and foreign policy and to strengthen the congressional voice in the setting of legislative priorities, the executive branch continues to be a significant influence on decision making in military policy (Armed Services), foreign policy (Foreign Affairs), appropriations (Appropriations), and taxing (Ways and Means).

The president's ability to persuade also depends on some less formal resources. With a broader constituency and greater access to the media, the president is better able to make appeals directly "to the people" than are individual congressmen. Ronald Reagan's successful exploitation of this resource to help persuade legislators to pass his budget recommendations in 1981 demonstrates how potent such appeals may be, and how great the fears on Capitol Hill of stirring the constituency. Another popular presidential technique is the extension of special attention to legislators who might be persuaded to support the president's position. In order to win the support of wavering or uncommitted members, the president may invite them to the White House to be "wined and dined." When the president's party also controls Congress, the president as the party leader adds another claim to his role as policy initiator. Finally, presidential control of information needed for policy making in military and foreign affairs is important to executive influence in these areas.

Control of information is also an important resource that is employed by bureaucrats when they try to influence committees. William Niskanen (1971, 1975) has described bureaucrats as monopolists who deal in the provision of information to decision makers. By manipulating the type of information that is presented, the bureaucrat is able to maximize the benefits he receives in the appropriations process. An auxiliary technique employed by bureaucrats is the provision of information and services to particular congressmen who serve on committees that are influential in that bureau's activities.

> In fact, Congress keeps program administrators on a short leash, first with single-year authorizations and then with single-year appropriations. Although in the short run bureaucrats are free to allocate benefits as they see fit, those who seek long-term budgetary security and growth must pay careful heed to congressmen's allocational preferences. If they expect Congress to approve their budget requests in subsequent years, they have little choice but to allocate benefits in a manner pleasing to at least a majority of congressmen (Arnold, 1979, pp. 208–209).

In addition, the provision of services by bureaus results in the growth of constituencies that benefit from those services. These agency constituents transfer their support to particular congressmen in exchange for the congressman's support for favorable legislation. The growth of such "cozy" (triangle) relationships has had a significant impact on congressional decision making.

Several factors may obscure the influence of the executive branch in our analysis. When the president's party controls both the houses of Congress, the influence of the executive branch may be highly collinear with party because the president presses his demands through the party leadership. When the opposition party controls Congress, it should be easier to detect executive influence, because the president is forced to seek the support of congressmen from the opposition party in order to ensure passage of his legislation. Executive influence should be particularly salient in committees like Appropriations and Ways and Means, which depend on policy initiation in the executive branch to perform their decision-making role. It is less likely to be seen in the Armed Services committee, where past studies suggest that the predominant executive-branch influence comes from the military bureaucracy rather than the president.

Another factor that tends to obscure the impact of the executive branch is ideology. If the committee has a large conservative Demo-

117

cratic membership, executive influence may be intertwined with ideology, because the opposition party members that a Republican president tries to win over are those who are closest to him ideologically. For instance, executive-branch influence in such a committee may appear as ideological divergence among Democrats; this seems to be the case in the Appropriations Committee in the 1973–76 period. Where executive influence is obscured but suspected, other evidence, such as the findings of past studies and the composition of the ideological faction, can be used to detect it.

In addition to executive-branch influences, the ubiquitous impact of party and ideology are also present in most of the committees examined in this chapter. The one exception is Foreign Affairs, where we find ideology and a high degree of bipartisanship. Further, when the same party controls the White House and the Congress, as the Democrats did from 1977 through 1980, we expect partisanship to become more marked in some of the committees.

Appropriations

The jurisdiction of the Appropriations Committee makes it one of the most influential committees in the House. Because it handles the funding decisions for programs authorized by the House, this committee has the potential of affecting every member and every district in the House. It is this potential for influence in the House which makes the Appropriations Committee so attractive to its members.

Fenno's (1962, 1966, 1973) extensive research on the committee identified two goals held by members. The primary goal of most members of the committee was the desire for influence and power in the House. A secondary goal mentioned by many members was serving the constituency, but this goal was clearly subordinate to the desire to attain influence in the House. There was also an agreement among members that the primary role of the committee was that of guardian of the treasury, protecting revenues from excessive demands from either their House colleagues or the executive branch.

A general consensus developed in the committee on how best to achieve the desired ends of the members; the first strategic premise was that executive-agency requests should be cut. Committee members realized, however, that the House depended on the committee to provide funding adequate enough to ensure that the authorized programs met the goals set by the House. Therefore a second strategic premise was agreed upon; adequate funding for executive programs must be provided. The two premises required a balance between cutting the budgets and providing what had been requested. The committee reconciled the differences between the two strategies by cutting the agency requests but at the same time providing more funding to the agency than it received in the previous year. Members used these strategic premises not only to attain the goal of House influence but also to allow the committee some policy independence from the forces operating within the committee's environment.

Three environmental influences were identified by Fenno (1973) as having either a direct or indirect influence on the committee. The degree of power that the House bestowed upon the committee to make funding decisions, including the privilege of bringing committee legislation to the floor under restrictive rules, required that members be responsive to the desires of individual members as well as to the "mood" of the House as a whole. As Fenno (1973) notes, however, such House-led policy coalitions influenced the committee infrequently.

> When the chamber speaks to a committee in terms of policy, it does so, we think, by way of an amorphous and evanescent policy mood. . . . Once in a while, for example, an "economy mood" in the House will affect Appropriations Committee behavior. Committee members should always apprise themselves of "the mood" or "the temper" or, in Sam Rayburn's phrase, "the rolling waves of sentiment" in the chamber. But House-led coalitions as the prime shapers or movers of external policy coalitions are strictly a sometime thing.   (Pp. 22–23)

The influence of House-led policy coalitions on committee decision making, therefore, could be expected to be indirect rather than direct in most instances and reflected in the directive that committee members be responsive to the House.

Parties exerted an indirect effect on the committee as well, acting more through assignment practices than through direct appeals to committee members by the party leadership. Although not totally absent from committee deliberations in the past (see Fenno, 1966, pp. 245–52, for a discussion of partisanship during the Eightieth Congress), the pursuit of extreme partisanship was seen as a hinderance to the achievement of influence in the House and the passage of committee bills on the floor. As a result, members tried to minimize partisanship on the committee.

> Its [Appropriations Committee] members have all the same incentives
> for nonpartisanship as Ways and Means. In pursuing their goal of
> House influence, they lean hard on executive budgets. But unless they
> can win House support for their decisions, neither the committee
> collectively nor the members individually will be influential. So Appropriations members become as concerned as Ways and Means members for their reputation and their success in the House. One requisite,
> they believe, is the curbing of internal partisanship, to the end that the
> Committee will come to the floor united (or, at least, apparently
> united) in support of its recommendations. Under such circumstances
> they will maximize the likelihood of winning on the floor. Unlike Ways
> and Means, however, Appropriations members face few external demands for partisanship so they try to minimize partisanship at the
> point of decision as well as at the deliberative stage.   (Fenno, 1973, pp.
> 87–88)

The influence that parties exerted on the committee resulted from careful screening of potential members; new members were chosen on the basis of their ability to work with their colleagues—"a responsible legislative style." "By attending to legislative style, House leaders screen in . . . Congressmen who value good working relationships with their colleagues, and they screen out Congressmen whose working style seems egregiously outside the established House modes" (Fenno, 1973, p. 21). By this process, the party ensured at least a minimum of responsiveness from the party members it assigned to the committee, and hence, the parties operated indirectly as an influence on the committee.

The executive branch was identified as the most important environmental constraint operating on the committee. Both the budget requests and legislative priorities (as reflected in the funding requests) with which the committee dealt were proposed by the executive branch.

> Decisions allocating federal money to the agencies and programs are
> the lifeblood concern to every executive official. The requests made of
> the Appropriations Committee originate in the executive branch, and
> come to the committee via the Chief Executive's budget. All the
> Committee's working documents are products of the executive
> branch.   (Fenno, 1973, p. 22)

In addition, clientele groups with an interest in the policy decisions of the committee tended to work through the executive agencies rather than acting directly to influence decision making.

Finally, in the time period that Fenno studied the committee (Eighty-fourth through the Eighty-ninth Congress), he noted that a degree of policy convergence existed on the committee. That is, the Republican members appointed to the committee tended to be less conservative than the typical House Republican, and the Democrats tended to be less liberal than Democrats as a whole. This was helpful in muting partisan conflict in the committee. According to his earlier description of the Appropriations Committee, the most important influence on the committee would be expected to be the executive branch, with party exerting an indirect influence on decision making. If the degree of ideological convergence within the committee declined, partisanship might become a more overt influence.

In our examination we find that like most House committees, factions within the Appropriations Committee reflect the influence of party and ideology (table 17); in addition, there is evidence of a bloc of executive-agency supporters. Two conservative factions appear in the committee: Faction 1 is a bloc of conservative (ADA, $r = -.78$) Republicans, and Faction 2 represents an alignment of conservative (ACA, $r = .65$) Democrats. These are not purely partisan factions, since Republicans J. Kenneth Robinson (Va.), Robert C. McEwen (N.Y.), and Mark Andrews (N.D.) vote with the conservative Democrats, whereas Democrats Daniel J. Flood (Pa.) and Robert L.F. Sikes (Fla.) vote with the conservative Republicans in Faction 1.

The correlates of Faction 3 are not very helpful in interpreting this faction; the only significant correlation indicates that this bloc is generally supportive of defense appropriations and opposed to attempts to restrict military spending (Restricting Military Expenditures, $r = .42$). There is another peculiar feature of this faction: the nominal leaders of this voting bloc are subcommittee chairmen with images as "pro-agency" supporters—John J. McFall (D-Calif.; Transportation), Jamie L. Whitten (D-Miss.; Agriculture), John M. Slack (D-W.Va.; State, Justice, and Judiciary), Flood (Labor-Health, Education, and Welfare), and Tom Steed (D-Okla.; Treasury, Postal, and General Government). Whitten, for example, has developed close ties with the Department of Agriculture, and Flood has established a record of support for the liberal economic programs promoted by the

TABLE 17. Factions in the Appropriations Committee, 1973–1976

Committee Member	Factions					Explained Variation (%)
	1	2	3	4	5	
Burt L. Talcott (R-Calif.)	1.00					100
Robert H. Michel (R-Ill.)	.98					100
John T. Myers (R-Ind.)	.97					100
Elford A. Cederberg (R-Mich.)	.90					87
Robert L.F. Sikes (D-Fla.)	.89					99
Jack Edwards (R-Ala.)	.85					87
J. Kenneth Robinson (R-Va.)	.83	.51				97
Garner E. Shriver (R-Kans.)	.82					93
Robert C. McEwen (R-N.Y.)	.73	.60				96
R. Lawrence Coughlin (R-Pa.)	.71	(−.48)				75
Mark Andrews (R-N.D.)	.64	.51				81
Daniel J. Flood (D-Pa.)	.53		.67			86
J. Edward Roush (D-Ind.)	−.79					86
Clarence D. Long (D-Md.)	−.65					59
Joseph P. Addabbo (D-N.Y.)	−.61			.54		74
Edward R. Roybal (D-Calif.)	−.69	−.51				83
George Mahon (D-Tex.)		.86				84
Tom Bevill (D-Ala.)		.69				83
Bill Chappell Jr. (D-Fla.)	(.47)	.67				88
K. Gunn McKay (D-Utah)		.60				50
Edward P. Boland (D-Mass.)		−.79				73
Silvio O. Conte (R-Mass.)		−.54		.69		100
John J. McFall (D-Calif.)			.89			96
Tom Steed (D-Okla.)			.86			87
Jamie L. Whitten (D-Miss.)			.79			74
John M. Slack (D-W.Va.)			.68			65
Edward J. Patten (D-N.J.)			.50			51
David R. Obey (D-Wis.)				.84		88
Sidney R. Yates (D-Ill.)				.83		96
Robert N. Giaimo (D-Conn.)				.70		90
George E. Shiple;y (D-Ill.)				−.56		69
Bill D. Burlison (D-Mo.)					.74	67
Clarence E. Miller (R-Ohio)					.65	67
Frank E. Evans (D-Colo.)					−.73	74
William H. Natcher (D-Ky.)[a]	—	—	—	—	—	—

Correlates of Factional Alignments					
Presidential support	.78*	.37	−.03	−.52*	.22
Conservative coalition	.74*	.65*	.07	−.75*	.28
Party unity	−.78*	−.49*	.04	.66*	−.23
ADA	−.78*	−.61*	−.14	.70*	−.24
COPE	−.70*	−.47*	.22	.55	−.29
NFU	−.78*	−.42*	−.03	.60*	−.35
CCUS	.71*	.62*	.03	−.68*	.27
ACA	.72*	.65*	.02	−.67*	.23
Restricting Military Expend. (I)	.65*	.73*	.42*	−.68*	.07
Budget Reductions (II)	−.66*	−.09	−.03	.19	.37

[a]Voted "no" on every vote.

Note: Pearson correlations marked with asterisks are significant at the .01 level.

executive agencies within his subcommittee's jurisdiction. Similarly, Steed has been accused of being too responsive to the White House's requests for funding: "Steed figures the President doesn't tell him how many secretaries he should hire and that he, as chairman, shouldn't dictate the number of secretaries the President has. This attitude keeps Steed well-liked by the Administration" (Nader, 1972, p. 4). Steed's support for White House appropriations was criticized, and the expenditure levels he supported were slashed on the House floor—an unusual experience for an Appropriations subcommittee chairman. McFall also ignored party orthodoxy by leading the fight in the House for the Republican-supported supersonic transport (SST) program, which most Democrats opposed. While Edward J. Patten (D-N.J.) is not a subcommittee leader, he is still quite supportive of agency appropriations because of the benefits they provide his district: "he lists substantial federal grants as his primary accomplishments for the district, citing his participation as a member of the Labor/HEW subcommittee as a key point in bringing home the money" (Nader, 1972, p. 4). These characteristics of the nominal leaders of Faction 3 suggest that this bloc reflects the influence of the executive-branch agencies on the formation of cleavages within the committee.

The power and influence of subcommittee chairmen in committee decision making make the leaders of these subcommittees primary targets for agency lobbying:

> Tradition grants to the subcommittee chairman impressive decision-making prerogatives. He is expected to allocate tasks to subcommittee members, set the timetable for subcommittee hearings, preside over the hearings, preside over subcommittee markup sessions, initiate action in those sessions, write (or oversee the writing of) the subcommittee report, present the subcommittee's recommendations to the full Committee, manage the floor debate on his subcommittee's bill, lead the House conferees in conference on the bill, and speak for the subcommittee to the agencies of the executive branch. (Fenno, 1966, p. 169)

With this impressive assortment of powers, it is understandable that "when agency officials concerned with their budget look toward the Congress, they see a picture of a subcommittee of the House of Representatives dominated by the figure of its chairman" (Fenno,

1966, p. 278). The agencies that fall into the subcommittee jurisdictions of the nominal leaders of Faction 3 appear to be remarkably successful in cultivating subcommittee chairmen. The evidence for this is the success these bureaus historically have had in securing appropriations relatively close to their budget requests (Fenno, 1966, p. 368). The friendly attitude of the subcommittee leaders toward the agencies within their purview and the norm of subcommittee reciprocity may promote the vote agreement among the members of this faction (Fenno, 1962).

Committee liberals (David R. Obey [D-Wis.], Sidney R. Yates [D-Ill.], Robert N. Giaimo [D-Conn.], Silvio O. Conte [R-Mass.], and Joseph P. Addabbo [D-N.Y.]) form Faction 4; the liberalism of this bloc (ADA, $r = .70$) is also reflected in its opposition to defense appropriations (Restricting Military Expenditures, $r = -.68$). The remaining committee faction is a bipartisan and moderately ideological doublet (Bill D. Burlison [D-Mo.] and Clarence E. Miller [R-Ohio]). The wide dispersion of partisan loyalties is illustrated in the two-dimensional representation of the committee's factional structure (figure 14).

Committee liberals Edward R. Roybal (D-Calif.), Addabbo, Yates, Clarence D. Long (D-Md.), J. Edward Roush (D-Ind.), Conte, and Edward P. Boland (D-Mass.) cluster in a quadrant (lower-left) opposite conservatives J. Kenneth Robinson (R-Va.), John T. Myers (R-Ind.), McEwen, Jack Edwards (R-Ala.), Andrews, Robert H. Michel (R-Ill.), Sikes, and Elford A. Cederberg (R-Mich.) (upper-right quadrant). These two groups anchor the ideological ends of the spectrum, and the remaining committee members fall somewhere between these two polar extremes. Clearly, ideology creates cleavages among the Democrats as well as between the parties.

In fact, the bipartisan composition of many of the factional alignments within this committee (Factions 1, 2, 4, and 5) suggests that ideology may have a greater impact than party on the formation of committee cleavages. This is similar to Fenno's finding that ideological convergence serves to restrain partisanship on the committee. Thus, while partisanship is a salient influence, it seems to be tempered by ideological divisions which encourage bipartisanship. These findings also clearly suggest that executive-branch agencies exert a strong influence on committee decision making.

Figure 14. Two-Dimensional Representation of Cleavages in the House Committee on Appropriations: 1973-1976.

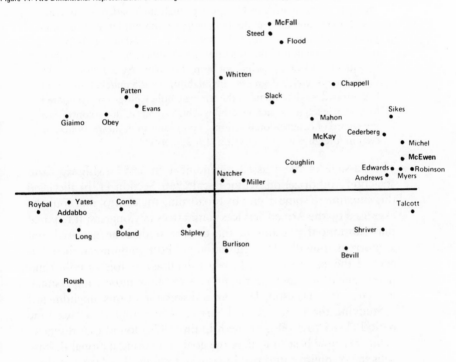

Armed Services.

Prior to 1959, there was very little opportunity for the Congress or the Armed Services Committee in either chamber to exert much influence over military policy.

> The important positive decisions about defense and strategy have therefore not been made by Congress, though anticipations of congressional opposition have no doubt operated as inhibitions against some policy choices. In a degree not paralleled in any other field of public policy, the position of the executive in this sphere has been definitely ascendant, and Congress has not been able to reverse that fact. . . . In the main, however, a degree of "inviolability"—as Samuel Huntington has phrased it—has attended the strategic policy proposals embodied in executive requests, an inviolability which stands in sharp contrast to the record of congressional action on programs in domestic policy, or even in foreign policy. (Dawson, 1962, p. 44)

The passage of the Russell amendment in 1959 (Military Construction Authorization Act for Fiscal 1960, Section 412b) alleviated this situation to some degree by broadening the control that could be exercised by the Armed Services committees in Congress. It required that substantial portions of the defense budget be reviewed and authorized annually. This legislation did little to diminish the influence of the executive branch, which retained its role as policy initiator, but it did open up the process to allow more congressional influence. (See Dawson, 1962 for a discussion of this amendment.)

Studying the House Armed Services Committee in a later time period (1965 to 1968), Kenneth Entin (1974) found that disagreement over how best to achieve the goal of a strong national defense split the committee into two bipartisan factions. The larger of these supported positions set forth by the committee's policy committee (composed of the five ranking members of each party and the chairman). This faction also supported a strong voice for the military in the committee. The second and smaller faction, made up of a handful of members (called "the fearless five"), offered alternatives to the majority faction's policy proposals on such controversial issues as the draft, Vietnam policy, the C5A transport plane, and the ABM program. It was the view of these dissidents that the policy alternatives offered by the majority faction were often too promilitary in tone.

Entin emphasized that the formation of the minority faction should not be interpreted as an attempt to introduce partisanship into the committee, since both factions were bipartisan in nature. Nor could the group be interpreted as antimilitary, because they tended to support the majority faction's proposals in other areas. It appeared that the minority faction's function was to introduce alternatives to the policy control exercised by the senior members of the committee.

Bruce Ray's (1980b) examination of the House and Senate Armed Services Committees between the Ninety-first and Ninety-fifth Congresses (1969–78) addressed the question of whether these committees were more promilitary than their parent bodies. By examining the group ratings of members' support for the military industrial complex, he found that committee assignment practices led to a promilitary bias in the committee: "The House panel has consistently drawn its new members from among those *already* the most supportive of the military industrial complex, and this tendency appears to have been growing even more true recently" (Ray, 1980b, p. 515). As Ray noted, however, the committee members' bias did not preclude the appearance of partisan differences. Despite the bipartisan consensus on the goal of a strong national defense, Democratic members of both the Senate and House committees tended to be far more "dovish" than their Republican counterparts.

Carol Goss's (1972) research on the committee illustrated that there were constituency benefits to be derived from committee membership. Unlike Goss's study, however, we do not find constituency pressures to be a salient influence in the committee's environment. Contrary to the operation of some House committees that distribute benefits, such as Agriculture and Banking, the distribution of particularistic benefits does not appear to create salient cleavages within the Armed Services Committee. This absence of conflict over constituency "pork" may result from equity in the distribution of Department of Defense (DOD) spending. For instance, most committee members in our analysis have in their districts at least one major military installation or businesses that are recipients of multimillion dollar defense contracts. In some cases, committee members have several major military installations in addition to businesses with multimillion dollar defense contracts. (G. William Whitehurst [R-Va.], Marjorie S. Holt [R-Md.], Charles E. Bennett [D-Fla.], William L. Dickinson [R-Ala.], and Charles H. Wilson [D-Calif.]).

Another reason for the lack of constituency influences in this committee is that similar to the situation in the Appropriations Committee, Armed Services' constituent groups tend to make their demands to the executive rather than directly to the committee. As a result committee factions do not appear to reflect divisions over the distribution of particularistic benefits. Previous studies of the committee and the data on members included in this analysis suggest that the major cleavages in Armed Services reflect the impact of the administration and ideological pressures.

Although Armed Services *cannot* be categorized as a partisan committee, the identifiable partisan core in every faction suggests that partisanship exists (table 18): Faction 1 represents a bloc of conservative (ADA, $r = -.78$) Republicans; Faction 2 is also a conservative (ADA, $r = -.60$) alignment but with a Democratic core; and Faction 3 is a less conservative group of southern (Robert H. Mollohan [D-W.Va.], G.V. "Sonny" Montgomery [D-Miss.], and Mendel J. Davis [D.-S.C.]) and western (Wilson and Floyd V. Hicks [D-Wash.]) Democrats. Factions 1 and 2 are bipartisan and hawkish: they both support measures to strengthen our military forces (Military Strength Reductions, $r = .76$ and $r = .63$, respectively), and they tend to vote together ($r = .42$) to form a conservative coalition.

The major difference between the two conservative factions (1 and 2) is that Faction 2 is more likely to support administration positions in defense policy, such as DOD procurements (Policy Dimension II, $r = .66$), than the conservative Republicans in Faction 1. The fact that Faction 2 champions the causes of the Defense Department policies (military procurement and strength) suggests that this bloc has a proadministration posture. Such support may be crucial during periods when there is disagreement between the programs and priorities of the president and those of the Department of Defense (Entin, 1974). Thus, administration supporters appear to organize to defend Defense Department policies from detractors and opponents.

The conservative skew of the committee's membership is illustrated by the two-dimensional representation of the factional alignments within the committee (figure 15): most committee members cluster into the upper-right quadrant, diagonally opposite a small bloc of committee liberals—Les Aspin (D-Wis.), Patricia Schroeder (D-Colo.), and Robert Leggett (D-Calif.). Is it any wonder that the policies that are favored by the committee tend to have a conservative bias to them?

TABLE 18. Factions in the Armed Services Committee,
1973–1976

Committee Member	Factions 1	Factions 2	Factions 3	Explained Variation (%)
Robin L. Beard, Jr. (R-Tenn.)	.90			98
G. William Whitehurst (R-Va.)	.81			84
Charles E. Bennett (D-Fla.)	.73			83
William L. Dickinson (R-Ala.)	.73			67
Marjorie S. Holt (R-Md.)	.67			59
Richard H. Ichord (D-Mo.)	.63		.51	66
Les Aspin (D-Wis.)	−.74			56
Robert W. Daniel, Jr. (R-Va.)	.60	.59		71
Floyd Spence (R-S.C.)	.54	.52	.60	93
F. Edward Hebert (D-La.)		.79		92
Melvin Price (D-Ill.)		.75		82
Bill Nichols (D-Ala.)		.71	.52	84
Bob Wilson (R-Calif.)	(.42)	.69		66
Samuel S. Stratton (D-N.Y.)		.63		44
W.C. "Dan" Daniel (D-Va.)		.53		53
Patricia Schroeder (D-Colo.)		−.77		72
Robert L. Leggett (D-Calif.)		−.54		32
Robert H. Mollohan (D-W.Va.)			.79	84
Charles H. Wilson (D-Calif.)			.71	52
G.V. "Sonny" Montgomery (D-Miss.)			.62	56
Mendel J. Davis (D-S.C.)			.58	50
Floyd V. Hicks (D-Wash.)			.56	41

Correlates of Factional Alignments			
Presidential support	.71*	.41	−.12
Conservative coalition	.75*	.41	.09
Party unity	−.75*	−.45	−.04
ADA	−.78*	−.60*	−.07
COPE	−.71*	−.32	.04
NFU	−.80*	−.34	.06
CCUS	.75*	.51*	.09
ACA	.74*	.42	.12
Military Strength Reductions (I)	.76*	.63*	.56*
Military Procurement Reductions (II)	−.15	.66*	−.23

Note: Doublet: Hicks (D-Wash.) and Davis (D-S.C.). Pearson correlations marked
with asterisks are significant at the .01 level.

Figure 15. Two-Dimensional Representation of Cleavages in the House Committee on Armed Services: 1973-1976.

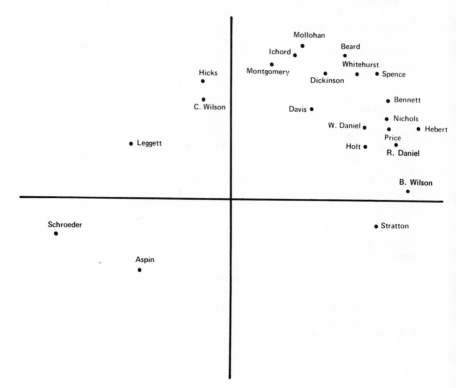

Our findings do not diverge significantly from those of previous studies. As suggested by these studies, our findings confirm the influence of the executive branch on committee cleavages. The small cluster in the two-dimensional graphs (figure 15) appear to be similar to earlier findings of Entin (1974) that a faction of members appears to offer alternatives to the dominant position in the committee. This analysis differs from Goss's (1972) in that we do not find that constituency interests influence committee cleavages. We have suggested several reasons for this difference. It appears that cleavages within the Armed Services Committee reflect administration and ideological pressures.

Foreign Affairs.

Similar to the Armed Services and Appropriations committees, members of the Foreign Affairs Committee work in a policy area dominated by the executive branch and more specifically by presidential initiatives and prerogatives. Relative to the chief executive, the Congress has little impact on the formulation or initiation of foreign policy; the major actions of Congress are concerned with the "legitimization" of executive actions.

> Congressional participation in foreign policy decisions is principally in the recommendation and prescription stages of the decision process. Recommendations of important measures frequently are initiated by the executive rather than the legislative branch. Thus, in the prescription stage Congress is legitimating, amending, or vetoing executive proposals. The scope of Congressional influence varies with the constitutional provisions governing the making and conduct of foreign relations. The Senate, with an advantage in confirming diplomatic appointments and approving treaties has not exploited the former and is finding the latter less and less an important instrument of policy. The House, with an advantage derived from its constitutional position with respect to appropriations, awaits the executive budget and reacts to it by legitimating or cutting it, but rarely by raising it. (Robinson, 1962, pp. 14–15)

Fenno's (1973) examination of the Foreign Affairs Committee revealed that members joined the committee to produce "good" public policy. Few members saw the committee assignment as an aid in serving their constituencies or in gaining influence in the House.

The analysis of the environmental constraints operating on the committee confirmed the predominance of executive-led coalitions in the committee's environment.

> The President's negotiating prerogatives and his Commander-in-Chief prerogatives give him the ability to initiate actions and create commitments that the Foreign Affairs Committee is virtually powerless to alter. Eisenhower's action in Lebanon, Kennedy's action in the missile crisis, and Johnson's action in the Dominican Republic are cases in point. We can expect, further, that once a presidential commitment is made, the President will summon up whatever personal and institutional resources are necessary to gain committee acceptance. (Fenno, 1973, p. 29)

The bipartisanship that characterized the committee was possible in part because of the ideological convergence of the members, much like the convergence that characterized the Appropriations Committee. "Committee Democrats and (especially) Committee Republicans have markedly more liberal leanings than their respective party colleagues in the House" (Fenno, 1973, p. 89). That is, both Democratic and Republican members were distinctly more liberal than their House counterparts, which made bipartisan decision making easier. Partisanship was also dampened in the period studied by Fenno because "all but two or three Democrats and a majority of Republicans have supported the foreign aid program" (Fenno, 1973, p. 89). Finally, high levels of partisanship are not conducive to the goal of making good public policy—the prime goal of Foreign Affairs members.

Both Fenno (1973, pp. 283–85) and Norman Ornstein and David Rohde (1977) found that the congressional reforms in the early 1970s and membership turnover during that period had a significant impact on the committee. The strengthening of the subcommittee system, the activist perspective of the new subcommittee chairmen, and the failure of the country's Vietnam policy all encouraged the committee to challenge the dominance of the executive in foreign policy.

> With an influx of liberal activists into subcommittee leadership positions, the challenge to executive-branch supremacy in foreign-policy making increased greatly in the 1970s. The institutional changes and the growth of the liberal activist wing in the committee and in the House both contributed to the substantial change in the committee's role in foreign policy. (Ornstein and Rohde, 1977, p. 253)

The passage of the War Powers Act was just another manifestation of this determination on the part of Congress to exert a greater role in foreign-policy making.

> To make Fenno's description of the committee applicable to the mid-70s, we do not have to alter the references to the executive branch's desire for legitimation, for this certainly has not changed. Nor do we have to revise to a great extent the subsequent description of the committee majority's willingness to respond to the executive branch's desires. What do have to change are the references to the lack of congressional challenge from the House and the lack of attempts by the House to influence the committee. (Ornstein and Rohde, 1977, p. 255)

The rejuvenated subcommittee system of the Foreign Affairs Committee provided a useful vehicle for expressing opposition and alternatives to White House policies. With increased independence from the committee chairmen, and with a legislative mandate to oversee those programs within the jurisdictions of its subcommittees, subcommittee chairmen gained considerable prominence in legislative-executive struggles. In addition, the reforms instituted by the Democratic Caucus that prohibit committee and subcommittee chairmen from simultaneously serving as subcommittee leaders on other committees, created a number of leadership vacancies within the subcommittee system that allowed many liberal Democrats to obtain subcommittee chairmanships. The combination of a more liberal set of subcommittee leaders and the increased autonomy of subcommittees created a more active subcommittee system (Fenno, 1973).

In the time period examined here, therefore, it is expected that party and interest groups will exert at best only a slight influence on the committee. Far more important should be the influence of the executive branch. The new proclivity to challenge executive proposals should be manifested by factions supportive and/or critical of the executive branch. Further, the push by the activist, liberal subcommittee chairmen should exacerbate ideological cleavages among pro-administration and antiadministration factions.

The antiadministration nature of Faction 3 (table 19) is reflected in the composition of this bloc: three Democratic liberal subcommittee leaders (Dante B. Fascell [Fla.], Donald M. Fraser [Minn.], and Lee H. Hamilton [Ind.]) and two maverick Republicans (Edward G. Biester, Jr. [Pa.], and John Buchanan [Ala.]). The subcommittee

133

TABLE 19. Factions in the Foreign Affairs Committee, 1973–1976

Committee Member	Explained Variation (%)	Factions 1	2	3	4	5	
Charles W. Whalen, Jr. (R-Ohio)	.88						79
Benjamin S. Rosenthal (D-N.Y.)	.77	(−.40)	(.44)				96
Jonathan B. Bingham (D-N.Y.)	.68	(−.46)					76
Donald M. Fraser (D-Minn.)	.56		.74				93
Michael J. Harrington (D-Mass.)	.55			(−.45)			72
Robert N.C. Nix (D-Pa.)	(.48)						49
Robert J. Lagomarsino (R-Calif.)	−.83			(.43)			100
Clement J. Zablocki (D-Wis.)	−.56	.71					82
Thomas E. Morgan (D-Pa.)		.84					83
L.H. Fountain (D-N.C.)		.82					73
Tennyson Guyer (R-Ohio)		.68	.53				86
Larry Winn, Jr. (R-Kans.)		.59	.59				86
William S. Broomfield (R-Mich.)	(−.49)	.51	.61				93
Dante B. Fascell (D-Fla.)			.85				84
Lee H. Hamilton (D-Ind.)			.84				75
Edward G. Beister, Jr. (R-Pa.)			.60		(.49)		71
Benjamin A. Gilman (R-N.Y.)				.87			82
John Buchanan (R-Ala.)			.61	.68			86
Pierre S. "Pete" Du Pont (R-Del.)					.84		74
Lester L. Wolff (D-N.Y.)	(.44)				.62		73

Correlates of Factional Alignments

Presidential support	−.71*	.49*	−.31	.78*	−.16
Conservative coalition	−.81*	.67*	−.46	.71*	−.20
Party unity	.71*	−.50*	.43	−.70*	.12
ADA	.80*	−.72*	.50*	−.69*	.13
COPE	.64*	−.36	.23	−.64*	.12
NFU	.77*	−.45	.44	−.52*	.13
CCUS	−.61*	.58*	−.22	.65*	−.24
ACA	−.75*	.61*	−.49*	.71*	−.30
Limits on Presidential Discretion (I)	−.48	.41	.19	.41	.42
Sanctions (II)	−.79*	.41	−.65*	.45	−.40
Military Assistance (III)	−.03	.54*	−.57*	.20	.05

Note: Pearson correlations marked with asterisks are significant at the .01 level.

leadership positions provide a forum for criticizing the policies of the executive branch; in fact, these subcommittee leaders have emerged as some of the most vigorous overseers of executive policies (Kaiser, 1977). Since Biester and Buchanan are notable party mavericks, it is not unusual to find them frequently voting with this bloc. In addition to their antiadministration stance, this liberal bloc (ADA, $r = .50$) supports the application of sanctions against countries that violate democratic principles, such as Rhodesia, South Vietnam, and South Korea (Sanctions, $r = -.65$), and of restrictions on U.S. foreign aid (Military Assistance, $r = -.57$). It seems likely that the alignment of committee members in Faction 3 reflects opposition to the control that the executive branch exercises over foreign-policy matters. Since the nominal leaders of this bloc are chairmen of subcommittees, the organization of this faction may represent tacit support of alternatives to administration policies.

The other factions within the Foreign Affairs Committee exhibit an unusual degree of bipartisanship (table 19). Faction 1 represents an alignment of committee liberals (ADA, $r = .80$) with nominal leaders Charles W. Whalen, Jr. (R-Ohio), Benjamin S. Rosenthal (D-N.Y.), and Jonathan B. Bingham (D-N.Y.). This faction supports the application of sanctions to foreign countries that are undemocratic (Sanctions, $r = -.79$) and generally votes with the members of Faction 3 ($r = .47$). Faction 2 is also a bipartisan faction of committee conservatives (ADA, $r = -.72$)—Democrats Thomas E. Morgan (Pa.), Clement J. Zablocki (Wis.), and L.H. Fountain (N.C.), and Republicans Tennyson Guyer (Ohio), Larry Winn, Jr. (Kans.), and William S. Broomfield (Mich.)—that opposes the placement of restrictions on military assistance to U.S. allies (Military Assistance, $r = .54$). Faction 4 is the only partisan bloc on the committee—an alignment of conservative (ACA, $r = .71$) Republicans. It is interesting to note that the only Republicans who vote *infrequently* with this faction are the less-conservative partisans (Whalen, Biester, and Pierre S. du Pont [Del.]). The final committee faction (Faction 5) appears to represent a bloc of moderates (du Pont, Lester L. Wolff [D-N.Y.]). The significance of the ideological cleavages within the committee demonstrates the relevance of ideology to the organization of committee factions. The existence of an antiadministration bloc, Faction 3, suggests that factions also form in response to the impact of the executive branch.

The two-dimensional representation of the committee's factional alignments (figure 16) illustrates the diffuse ideological nature of the Foreign Affairs Committee and makes it clear that party is not a very useful way to differentiate between committee members. The vote spectrum is anchored at either end by the ideological extremes within the committee: conservatives like Broomfield, Winn, Zablocki, Robert J. Lagomarsino (R-Calif.) and Fountain anchor the right-side of the spectrum and committee liberals like Bingham, Michael J. Harrington (D-Mass.), Whalen, and Rosenthal form a loose cluster in the opposite, upper-left, quadrant. The remaining committee members are located somewhere between the ideological poles. In conclusion, our findings are consistent with the findings of Fenno (1973) and Ornstein and Rohde (1977) on the impact of the rejuvenated subcommittee structure. Ideology and the influence of the executive branch are the major sources of committee cleavages. As in the Armed Services Committee, party is relatively unimportant as evidenced by the bipartisan composition of committee factions.

Post Office and Civil Service

The Post Office and Civil Service Committee was one of the few committees that showed a substantial change between Fenno's (1973) initial investigation and his later reexamination in the 1970–72 period. Prior to 1970, the committee was dominated by a clientele-led coalition of postal groups, composed primarily of postal employees and certain postal patrons. Each of these groups sought their own distinct benefits from committee members: unions representing postal employees worked to keep salaries high, while patrons worked to keep certain postal rates low. The willingness of committee members to meet these demands rested on the goal held by most committee members of serving their constituencies. A Post Office assignment offered little opportunity to gain influence in the House, but it did provide members who had a large number of postal workers in their districts a distinct advantage in courting their constituencies. In order to further this goal, the committee operated under a strategic premise that provided the largest benefits to the clientele groups: "to support maximum pay increases and improvements in benefits for employee groups and to oppose all rate increases for mail users" (Fenno, 1973, p. 64).

Figure 16. Two-Dimensional Representation of Cleavages in the House Committee on Foreign Affairs: 1973-1976.

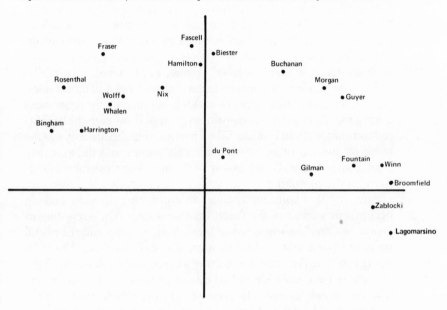

Yet, even in the pre-1970 period, clientele-group dominance did not go unchallenged. Most postal legislation originated in the executive branch, which operated under a different set of principles from the committee. Unlike the postal workers and patrons, the executive branch proposed legislation designed to keep postal rates high and salaries low. The goals of the executive branch served to temper the demands of the clientele groups and caused the introduction of a second strategic premise into the committee: "to accede to executive branch wishes when, in the judgement of committee members and employee groups, to do otherwise would net employee groups nothing in that Congress" (Fenno, 1973, p. 66).

According to Fenno, partisanship and ideology played minor roles, at best, in committee decision making because of the agreement among members to pursue constituency support through the benefits the committee could provide. When partisanship did arise, it was the result of direct conflict between clientele groups and the executive branch and of appeals for support by the president to members of his party on the committee.

After 1970, significant changes in committee decision making occurred as a result of the Postal Reorganization Act. According to Fenno, the pre-Christmas postal breakdown in 1966 and the postal strike of 1970 heightened public awareness of postal issues. The 1970 Reorganization Act removed the power to set postal salaries from the purview of the committee and vested this power in the postal service. This move both lessened the influence of the clientele groups in the committee and heightened executive influence; it also diminished the ability of committee members to provide substantial benefits to constituency groups.

Based on these observations, it is expected that the executive branch is a salient influence in the committee's environment. By contrast, clientele groups are not expected to be as influential as Fenno initially found them to be, partially as a result of postal reforms and partially as a result of the consensus among committee members on the benefits clientele groups should receive. Further, although clientele groups and the executive may continue to clash on occasion over issues before the committee, when this conflict is fought along party lines, the influence of constituency as well as the executive branch are likely to be obscured by partisanship.

The shadowing of constituency and executive-branch influences by

TABLE 20. Factions in the Post Office and Civil Service Committee, 1973–1976

Committee Member	Factions		Explained Variation (%)
	1	2	
James M. Hanley (D-N.Y.)	.92		84
Dominick V. Daniels (D-N.J.)	.89		80
Patricia Schroeder (D-Colo.)	.79		72
William "Bill" Clay (D-Mo.)	.72		59
William Lehman (D-Fla.)	.72		61
Charles H. Wilson (D-Calif.)	.70		49
John H. Rousselot (R-Calif.)	−.77	.53	86
Edward J. Derwinski (R-Ill.)		.84	84
Albert W. Johnson (R-Pa.)		.79	63
David N. Henderson (D-N.C.)		.71	50
Richard C. White (D-Tex.)	(.32)	−.59	45

Correlates of Factional Alignments			
Presidential support	−.85*	.77*	
Conservative coalition	−.86*	.59	
Party unity	.95*	−.73*	
ADA	.85*	−.71*	
COPE	.95*	−.76*	
NFU	.93*	−.69*	
CCUS	−.94*	.67*	
ACA	−.93*	.73*	
Limiting Presidential discretion	−.89*	.92*	
Federal Salaries (II)	.46	.25	
Postal Regulations (III)	.05	.06	

Note: Doublet: Wilson (D-Calif.) and Clay (D-Mo.). Pearson correlations marked with asterisks are significant at the .01 level.

partisanship may be the case during the Ninety-third and Ninety-fourth Congresses in the Post Office Committee: while there is hardly a trace of the impact of the executive branch on the factional alignments within the Post Office Committee, partisan and ideological factions are clearly visible (table 20). Faction 1 appears to represent the voting agreement among liberal (ACA, $r = -.93$), partisan (party unity, $r = .95$) Democrats; the other committee faction (2) represents a bloc of conservative (ACA, $r = .73$) Republicans. The committee chairman, Henderson, is the only Democrat to align with the Republican faction. As in several other House committees, partisan and ideological influences are impossible to disentangle since party unity scores are correlated above .9 with each of the ideological measures. The significance of party and ideology to the formation of committee cleavages is reflected in a graph of these factional alignments (figure 17): committee Democrats and Republicans occupy opposite segments of the two-dimensional space. The Democrats appear to cluster in the lower-right quadrant, across from a loose cluster of Republicans (area near upper-left quadrant); David Henderson (D-N.C.), the chairman of the committee, also is positioned near this bloc.

It should be noted that Henderson's behavior may not be as aberrant for a committee leader as it may first appear. He votes with the three highest ranking Republicans on the committee—Edward J. Derwinski (Ill.), Albert W. Johnson (Pa.), and John H. Rousselot (Calif.), which suggests that his faction could represent a relationship organized around agreement, compromise, and bargaining between the major leadership elements of the committee, the committee chairman (Henderson), and the ranking minority members of the committee. This faction could be instrumental in removing obstacles to the passage of legislative measures favored by the president. Despite their loss of power, committee chairmen are still influential leaders who retain a modicum of control over committee deliberations and outcomes. It is unlikely that Henderson's agreement with faction 2 is totally ideological, since conservative Democrat Richard C. White (Tex.) votes *against* this faction (Faction 2). This leads to the suspicion that there are more significant influences on the factional structure of this committee than merely party and ideology. The agreement among the major leadership elements of both parties suggests that Faction 2 may represent a bloc of committee members that are supportive of executive policy initiatives. At the very least, these committee leaders are likely to be involved in any compromise and bargain struck between the majority and minority parties.

Additional evidence makes it difficult to discount the influence of the executive branch on committee cleavages. One of the major dimensions of policy conflict within the committee (Limiting Presidential Discretion) concerns attempts to limit the discretion of the president in such matters as setting postal rates and executive-branch personnel decisions. Two other major policy dimensions, the level of federal salaries (Policy Dimension II) and regulating the postal serv-

Figure 17. Two-Dimensional Representation of Cleavages in the House Committee on Post Office and Civil Service: 1973-1976.

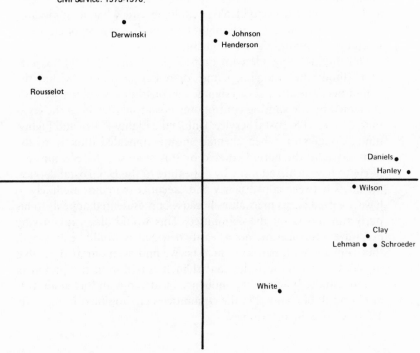

ice, are also policy areas where the issues are likely to have explicit administration positions attached. Since the major policy conflicts directly concern the president, it seems reasonable to expect the executive branch to have a noticeable influence on the factional alignments in the committee. Unfortunately, the most important policy dimension (Limiting Presidential Discretion) is highly collinear with party (party unity, $r = -.86$) and ideology (ACA, $r = .84$), and as a result, party and ideology could obscure whatever noticeable impact the executive branch might have on the creation of cleavages within the committee's environment.

Our findings coincide with Fenno's (1973, pp. 281–83) observations about the changing nature of policy coalitions within the committee. The absence of a significant constituency influence can be explained by the shifting control over postal salaries from the committee to the U.S. Postal Service. Unlike the Eighty-fourth and Eighty-ninth Congresses, when clientele groups appealed directly to the committee, in the period covered by this analysis, these groups are likely to have achieved more by appealing to the U.S. Postal Service. Conflicts between constituency and executive demands are likely to have involved partisan loyalties because of presidential appeals to his party's members on the committee. This would also explain why executive influences are not as easily detected as would be expected; they coincide with partisan interests. We find from our analysis that ideology is far more influential than it was during the period of Fenno's study. Whether the influence of ideology in this analysis is also a result of changes in the committee's environment in the early 1970s cannot be determined.

Ways and Means.

Three major studies of the Ways and Means Committee, by Fenno (1973) and John Manley (1965, 1970), provide a wealth of information about the committee during the 1960s. Similar to members of the Appropriations Committee, members of the Ways and Means Committee sought their assignments because of the influence they could gain in the House. The two committees are similar in other respects as well. Like Appropriations, the House granted the Ways and Means Committee privileges not extended to other committees, such as the closed rule for bringing legislation to the floor and the power to make committee assignments for House Democrats. In return, members were expected to be responsive to the desires of the House and to operate in a manner that would maintain the respect of their House colleagues. To meet these expectations, the committee developed the same hardworking style and reputation for expertise as the Appropriations Committee members. As an added check on the power granted to the committee, party leaders exercised the same careful scrutiny of potential members as they did in assigning members to the Appropriations Committee. Members were chosen for their cooperative legislative style, but unlike their counterparts on the Appropriations Committee, potential members had to display a degree of party orthodoxy. In both committees, the members selected tended to be those who had House experience and who had attained a degree of electoral security in their districts.

Electoral security seemed to be an important criterion, since most members interviewed by both Fenno and Manley agreed that membership on the committee did not offer any particular reelection benefits.

> Because Committee members must be reelected every two years, and because the Committee does permit them to serve some of the interests of their constituents, it might be thought that the members would see Ways and Means as an important electoral help. They do not. The overwhelming response of those who were asked if the Committee helps them get reelected, however, was that their Committee membership is of little value in their districts. (Manley, 1970, p. 82)

Like Appropriations, the executive branch appeared to be an important influence in the committee's environment, since the policies debated by Ways and Means were initiated and formulated in the executive branch:

> The basic, formative decisions on legislative program—to impose, extend, or alter a tax, to liberalize or contract trade policy, to change social security, welfare, or medical care policy—remain executive branch decisions. The policy proposals that structure the work of Ways and Means come from the executive branch. (Fenno, 1973, p. 23)

> Ceding initiation to the executive branch is important. During the summer of 1966, for example, there was much debate over whether a tax increase was needed to dampen inflationary pressures in the economy. Many economists argued in favor of raising taxes, others dis-

143

counted its importance, *but everyone waited to see what President Johnson would do, not what the Ways and Means Committee would do.* Congress was not irrelevant because in an election year a tax increase would not benefit the Democratic party, but clearly in this case, as in the case of almost every major bill reported by Ways and Means (under Democratic administrations), it is up to the president to move first. He sets the agenda for Congress . . . ; he determines, with important exceptions (e.g. tax reform in 1969), what major policy proposals Congress will look at, and when. (Manley, 1970, pp. 326–27)

One should not assume from these analyses that committee members saw themselves as subordinate to the executive branch; even when both the executive and legislative branches were under Democratic control, a basic antagonism between the two branches materialized.

Committee members . . . look upon themselves as "we" and upon executive department officials as "they." In many important cases the members, at least the Democratic members, identify with the president's program and tend to define the committee's job as getting the major administration bills through the Committee and House. But the members are also members of the Committee and they have a natural attachment to the Committee that orients them—to some degree—against the executive branch. They are people to be bargained with, not directed, and their political goals are respected. (Manley, 1970, p. 379)

The policy-initiator and the agenda-setting functions of the executive branch lead Fenno to characterize the committee as facing an environment in which executive-led policy coalitions play an important role.

Unlike his description of Appropriations, however, Fenno (1973) also points to the importance of party forces in the committee's environment. One important strategic premise under which Fenno describes the committee as operating was the agreement to "prosecute policy partisanship." The issues handled by the committee were perceived to be areas of fundamental disagreement between the parties and to have an important electoral impact.

A Ways and Means member commented, "We deal with things on which Republicans and Democrats are in fundamental disagreement." And these policy disagreements have traditionally provided much of the policy content for party identification and national partisan controversy. Party stands on trade, social security, taxation, medicare—such are believed to help influence voters and win elections. (Fenno, 1973, p. 24)

Yet, because of the ramifications and widespread impact of the policies that the committee dealt with, and the desire to gain influence in the House, it was also necessary for the members to practice what Manley describes as "restrained partisanship." The dual pressures on the committee toward both partisanship and nonpartisanship were described by Manley (1965):

> Ways and Means is neither racked by partisanship nor dominated by nonpartisanship; conflict and consensus coexist within the committee and the balance between them varies chiefly with the nature and intensity of the external demands which are made on the Committee. (P. 927)

Noting the stage at which members practice restrained partisanship and that at which they prosecute policy partisanship is crucial to understanding the seeming contradiction between these two directives. As Manley (1965) describes it, the norm of restrained partisanship prescribed that "members should not allow partisanship to interfere with a thorough study and complete understanding of the technical complexity of the bills they consider" (p. 929). Hence, during the deliberation stage of policy formation, attempts were made to limit the degree of partisanship that entered the process. Partisanship was very prevalent, however, in the decision stage of policy formation. As Fenno (1973) notes: "Ways and Means members limit the play of partisanship to the final stages of decision making and do most of their work in a nonpartisan atmosphere" (p. 84). Under this procedure, members were able to answer the demands of party leaders while maintaining influence and respect in the House.

Another important factor in promoting nonpartisanship was the leadership style of Chairman Wilbur Mills. Not only did Mills practice fairness in allowing all members to express opinions on the legislation being considered, but he placed a heavy emphasis on designing policy alternatives on which he could win a consensus in the committee. Further, Mills considered what would pass the House as well as what could pass the committee and thus moved the committee toward legislation on which they could win. Winning on the floor, in turn, enhanced the influence of committee members in the House;

therefore, an incentive existed for members to follow Mills's lead on legislation.

Along with partisanship, and in fact partially as a result of the partisan differences present on the committee, ideological divergence was evident among members:

> Ways and Means Republicans and Democrats are seen to exhibit a sharp ideological divergence. . . . It appears that this ideological divergence parallels a strong set of partisan predispositions—the strongest, overall, of any of our six committees. . . . it would appear that Ways and Means members are especially well disposed toward the prosecution of partisanship generally. (Fenno, 1973, p. 56)

Another contributing factor to the ideological divergence exhibited by the committee was the nature of the House membership and the ideological coalitions that existed in House voting. Since maintaining the prestige of the committee depended upon the passage of bills in the House, committee members had to be sensitive to the ideological divisions in the House and coalitions that formed in the House (such as the conservative coalition).

> That Ways and Means bills are not defeated by the conservative coalition does not mean the coalition is irrelevant to the Committee. Indeed, it suggests that the Committee, with southern Democrats always represented on it, shapes many bills along conservative lines and thereby prevents the coalition's appearance. Liberal Democrats in the House rarely have enough votes to pose a serious threat to Committee bills, but conservatives do. Hence decision making in Ways and Means has traditionally been oriented along conservative lines. (Manley, 1970, p. 162)

Interest groups were more prevalent in Ways and Means than they were in Appropriations, but as in Appropriations such groups were likely to appeal first to the executive branch and then to the committee if they could not secure their demands from the executive branch. Thus, such groups were not as important in the committee's environment as party and the executive.

> Party pressures, we believe, are more important in the environment of Ways and Means than of Appropriations. Should one party control both White House and Congress, the President or "the administration" would clearly be the dominant force in the Ways and Means policy environment. We think of policy coalitions, then, as *executive-plus*

party-led or *Administration-led* in Ways and Means and *executive-led* in Appropriations. (Fenno, 1973, p. 26)

Fenno's and Manley's descriptions of the Ways and Means Committee are based on data and observations collected prior to the House reforms of the early 1970s. The changes of the early 1970s, however, might be expected to produce some changes in the way the committee operated. This is particularly true of Ways and Means because many of the reforms of this period were designed to curb the powers of this committee. The Democratic Caucus, when it met in 1974, removed the power from Ways and Means to make Democratic committee appointments; increased membership on the committee from twenty-five to thirty-seven; modified the closed rule under which most Ways and Means legislation had been brought to the floor; and mandated a subcommittee system for the committee. Many of these reforms had a direct impact on the type of committee leadership that could be exercised. For instance, increasing the size of the membership also increased the size of the pro-tax reform contingent on the committee (Nader, 1975). The addition of subcommittees diffused the power of the chairman and, coupled with the increase in membership, made it more difficult for the chairman to enforce a consensual decision rule.

At the same time that the Caucus was acting to limit the powers of the chairman, Wilbur Mills retired from Congress. Although Mills's power had been waning for several years prior to his official retirement, the combination of the Caucus reforms and his retirement meant that the committee was likely to be operating under a significantly different leadership style. The impact of these changes would be likely to be manifested in the decision-making process in the committee. Even if the new chairman, Al Ullman (D-Oreg.) was inclined to practice the consensual style of Mills, it would be much more difficult to do so under the new system, which tended to decentralize power in the committee.

The acrimony and the ideological and partisan splits within the committee are also expected to be augmented by the opening of committee meetings.

When the Ways and Means Committee closes its doors to mark up a bill, thereby closing out the press and all other "outsiders," the rules of the game change. In public sessions there's more politics. Members play up witnesses and introduce them. . . . But in executive session politics is less. It's different . . . no gallery to play for, no publicity. (Manley, 1970, p. 76)

Therefore, we would expect to find differences between our analysis of the committee and analyses that were conducted before the early 1970s. Specifically, we would expect to see much less bipartisanship and more ideological divergence among committee members, especially during the deliberative stages. The committee was no longer working under the firm guiding hand of Wilbur Mills, directing members toward consensus. Further, because mark-up sessions are now more open to the public, actions are no longer easily hidden from public view, and members can be expected to practice more "politics" during such sessions. Ideological divergence should also be augmented by the addition of more pro-tax reform members, a group which previously was limited to a small minority of the membership.

Faction 1 captures the ideological conflicts within the committee (table 21): the opposition of liberals Charles A. Vanik (D-Ohio), Martha Keys (D-Kans.), William J. Green (D-Pa.), and Joseph L. Fisher (D-Va.) to a coalition of conservative (ACA, $r = .88$) southern Democrats and Republicans. The liberal Democrats, who so vigorously oppose Faction 1 on matters before the committee, help to form the second committee faction (Faction 2), which is both liberal (ACA, $r = -.90$) and partisan (party unity, $r = .88$) in nature. The remaining committee faction (Faction 3) represents a small bloc of conservative (ACA, $r = .70$) Republicans with Barber B. Conable, Jr. (N.Y.), and Herman T. Schneebeli (Pa.) serving as nominal leaders of the faction.

Ways and Means appears to possess all the characteristics of a polarized committee: the measures of party and ideology are highly intercorrelated (r) .90) and the two-dimensional configuration of the major cleavages within the committee fits the pattern of a partisan and ideologically polarized committee like Interior or Commerce (figure 18). We observe, for example, that the Republicans and their conservative Democratic coalition partners cluster into a quadrant (upper-left) that is diagonally opposite a cluster of Democrats (lower-right). Membership turnover and the expansion of the committee during the Ninety-fourth Congress have intensified the ideological polarization of the committee. The result of these actions has been the infusion of liberal Democrats (Bowler, 1976) into a committee for-

TABLE 21. Factions in the Ways and Means Committee, 1973–1976

Committee Member	Factions 1	Factions 2	Factions 3	Explained Variation (%)
Joe D. Waggonner (D-La.)	.90			84
Omar Burleson (D-Tex.)	.90			84
Phil M. Landrum (D-Ga.)	.90			81
Bill Archer (R-Tex.)	.71			76
Donald D. Clancy (R-Ohio)	.60		.51	67
John J. Duncan (R-Tenn.)	.54		.53	58
Charles A. Vanik (D-Ohio)	−.66	(.46)		75
Martha Keys (D-Kans.)	−.58	.55		69
William J. Green (D-Pa.)	−.51	.66		77
Joseph L. Fisher (D-Va.)	−.50	.60		64
Al Ullman (D-Oreg.)		.85		72
Dan Rostenkowski (D-Ill.)		.80		65
Joseph E. Karth (D-Minn.)	(−.45)	.70		70
James C. Corman (D-Calif.)	(−.46)	.61		61
Sam Gibbons (D-Fla.)	(−.43)	.52		47
James A. Burke (D-Mass.)		(.42)		30
Barber B. Conable, Jr. (R-N.Y.)			.87	76
Herman T. Schneebeli (R-Pa.)			.80	74
William A. Steiger (R-Wis.)			.60	47

Correlates of Factional Alignments

Presidential support	.73*	−.85*	.85*
Conservative coalition	.88*	−.88*	.71*
Party unity	−.82*	.88*	−.79*
ADA	−.81*	.83*	−.66*
COPE	−.79*	.87*	−.81*
NFU	−.79*	.86*	−.77*
CCUS	.89*	−.91*	.76*
ACA	.88*	−.90*	.70*
Individual and Corporate Taxes (I)	−.52*	.77*	−.90*
Oil and Gas Depletion (II)	−.66*	.50*	−.01

Note: Pearson correlations marked with asterisks are significant at the .01 level.

merly characterized as relatively conservative (Manley, 1970). In short, there is every reason to characterize the Ways and Means Committee as a committee dominated by partisan and ideological cleavages.

Nonetheless, we are apprehensive about identifying the committee's factional structure totally in partisan and ideological terms.

Figure 18. Two-Dimensional Representation of Cleavages in the House Committee on Ways and Means: 1973-1976.

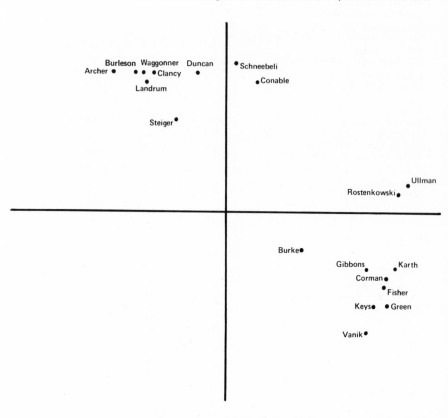

With the exception of Bill Archer (R-Tex.), all the Republican leaders included in the analysis form a separate faction (Faction 3). Further, the nominal leaders of this bloc—Conable and Schneebeli—are strong supporters of administration economic programs during the span of this part of the analysis (Ninety-third and Ninety-fourth Congresses). Thus, this Republican leadership faction represents a natural vehicle for articulating and promoting administration policies. Another reason to suspect that the executive branch could be a source of committee cleavages is that the policy proposals that create conflict and guide the committee's deliberations are primarily formulated within the executive branch, as Fenno noted.

Finally, as outlined previously, assignment to the committee depends in part on a demonstrated tendency to follow party positions. Republican party leadership rested in the White House during this period, which could explain the strong association between attachment to this faction and support for the president's policies (presidential support, $r = .85$) and positions on tax matters before the committee (Individual and Corporate Taxes, $r = -.90$). The presence on this policy dimension of both partisan (party unity, $r = .81$) and ideological (ACA, $r = -.72$) issues could obscure the impact of the executive branch on the formation of committee factions. Therefore, we suspect that while party and ideology appear to be dominant influences, executive-branch influences are also important factors in the formation of factions even though they are not as evident as party and ideology.

This analysis uncovers a greater degree of partisanship than have previous studies of the Ways and Means Committee. It has been suggested that the increase in partisanship stems from changes in membership and in the procedures governing committee deliberations that occurred in the interim between this study and earlier ones. The departure of Chairman Mills, who served as a force pushing the committee toward consensual, bipartisan decision making, could be an additional factor in the increase in partisanship. Similar to past research, this study finds that a significant degree of ideological divergence exists in the committee. While a high degree of ideological and partisan polarization is present in committee decision making, closer examination leads to evidence of executive-branch influences as well. This finding also is consistent with earlier research on the committee.

151

Similar to the committees examined in the last chapter, the five committees in which the influence of the executive branch is discernible also show a great deal of variation in the degree of dispersion among their members. The greatest amount of dispersion occurs in the Appropriations and Foreign Affairs committees. In these two committees, members are spread across the two-dimensional graphs, indicating a high degree of factionalization within the committee. In Appropriations, ideology creates splits within the parties as well as between them; the factions and the clusters on the graphs are bipartisan in nature. A similar phenomenon is apparent in the Foreign Affairs Committee, where the factions are also characterized by a high degree of bipartisanship. Executive influence in these committees manifests itself as a bloc of agency supporters in Appropriations and a bloc of administration opponents in Foreign Affairs.

In the Ways and Means and Post Office committees, we use several pieces of information to detect the influence of the executive branch. When the policy positions of the executive are highly intertwined with both party and ideology, as they are in Ways and Means, it is likely that executive influence will be obscured. This is particularly true if a member's assignment to the committee depends on a high degree of loyalty to the party and the party's ideological position, as it does in Ways and Means. Although the two-dimensional graph (figure 18) indicates a committee polarized by party and ideology similar to the Interior and Commerce committees, examined in the last chapter, additional information about the factions indicates that executive influence is also important in decision making in Ways and Means.

The use of additional information in the examination of the Post Office and Civil Service Committee leads to the same conclusions as it did in that of Ways and Means. The seemingly aberrant behavior of the committee's chair, Henderson, when contrasted with the behavior of his conservative Democratic colleague, White, leads us to conclude that the executive branch as well as party and ideology are influential in Post Office and Civil Service. Examination of the nature of the policies dividing the committee reinforces this conclusion. Policies that impinge upon the prerogatives of the executive, such as setting limits on the size of the White House staff, divide the committee along party and ideological lines as well as along proadministration and antiadministration lines.

Unlike Post Office and Ways and Means, where the intertwining of party and ideology divides the committee into two distinguishable camps, ideology seems to be most important in the divisions that arise in Armed Services. This committee occupies a midpoint in the degree of dispersion between the extremes of the Appropriations and Foreign Affairs committees, and the Post Office and Ways and Means committees. The conservative skew of the Armed Services membership indicates the importance of ideology. Closer examination of the two conservative factions helps to uncover the influence of the executive branch. Faction 2 shows a high degree of support for policies reflecting a proadministration sentiment.

CHAPTER FIVE

Constituency Interests
and Cleavages

Party and ideology play an important role in the formation of factions in each of the three committees described in this chapter just as they do in most of the other committees we have examined. In addition, however, there is evidence that constituency influences have an impact on the factional structures of each of the three. When examining the influence of constituency interests on government, one commonly thinks about groups promoting legislation favorable to their interests, and certainly promotion is one of the major functions of such groups. However, as David Truman (1951) points out, another important function of these groups is prevention—blocking the passage of legislation that might alter the gains already won by the group or that might have an unfavorable impact on the group.

Several features of the political system favor both defensive and offensive actions on the part of the constituency groups. Multiple layers of government provide many access points for influencing legislation. Pressure may be applied at the subcommittee, full committee, or floor level of either or both chambers of Congress. Alternatively, groups can influence legislation by appealing to the executive branch or by working through the parties. Failing at all these points, they still have the opportunity to appeal unfavorable legislation in the courts.

As well as using multiple access points, interest groups employ a variety of techniques by which they seek to promote or prevent certain legislative actions. One of the most important of these is the provision of information. The information provided by such groups is timely and accurate, and it generally is constructed in a manner that promotes the group's point of view. Whether the information is provided directly to members of Congress or presented in hearings before the relevant committees, the purpose is always to provide support for the interest group's position.

Groups may promote their interests indirectly through the mobilization and manipulation of public opinion. In these instances, instead of appealing directly to members of Congress through their Washington representatives, interest groups will conduct grass-roots campaigns, hoping to stir enough public interest that individual citizens will pressure members of Congress to consider legislation favorable to the group. Letter-writing campaigns by group members are variants of this technique that are particularly well suited to large and/or well-organized groups.

Financial contributions are another source of influence exploited by interest groups. Contributions may be made either directly to the election campaigns of supportive politicians or may be furnished to the political parties to disburse. Another popular form of contribution, the honorarium, offers groups the opportunity to reward supportive legislators whenever the need arises rather than only during election periods. Further, since money earned by speaking to organizations is considered as earnings rather than contributions, members of Congress are free to spend such funds as they please.

A final effective technique used by interest groups is the alliance between several interests. Such an alliance may take the form of a quid pro quo relationship: "If you help me on an issue of interest to me, I will help you on an issue of interest to you." Or it may represent an alliance between groups with complementary interests on the issue. In the area of housing, for instance, commercial banks and mortgage institutions often join together to ensure that any federal subsidies are distributed through existing financial institutions, even though these two groups are often at odds over legislation to regulate financial institutions.

The choice of techniques depends in part on the resources of the groups involved. Groups with large membership often use letter-writing campaigns, because this technique is well suited to the strength of their organization—membership. Small groups without large reservoirs of public support but with large monetary resources, such as business lobbies, tend to emphasize techniques conducive to the strengths of their organizations—monetary benefits. E.E. Shatt-schneider (1960) suggests that the decision to "go to the public" may also be determined by whether the group expects to win or lose without doing so. Publicizing or "socializing" the conflict usually is undertaken if the group involved fears it may lose on the issue; by taking such action it seeks to bring more people into the conflict in hopes of swinging the decision to its side.

Whether a group seeks to influence policies at the committee deliberation stage or during the floor consideration appears to depend on the nature of the policy and the size of the group involved (Bacheller, 1977). Issues can be categorized as being either campaign defined or group defined, and as being either controversial or non-controversial. Campaign-defined issues emerge during electoral contests and as a result are relatively well recognized by the electorate. By contrast, group-defined issues emerge on the agenda of Congress or the bureaucracy without first having been defined in the electoral arena. These issues are less visible to the general public, because they have not been well publicized. John Bacheller (1977) finds that small groups tend to deal mainly in the less visible, group-defined issues, while large groups tend to concentrate on campaign-defined issues. Group-defined issues are pressed at the committee level, because the smaller number of members in committees than on the floor often makes it easier to get favorable legislation inserted in the committee. Further, since group-defined issues are less visible to the public, and committee actions are less visible than floor actions, it is possible to press group-defined issues in committee without arousing significant opposition in the public. Lobbying on campaign-defined issues, which by their nature are more visible to the public, occurs most frequently on the floor level, although pressure may also be applied at the committee level.

In this study, we find only three committees in which the impact of constituency can be identified in the factional structure of the committee—Agriculture; Banking, Finance, and Urban Affairs; and Education and Labor. Issues vital to three major interests in the American economic system—agriculture, labor, and business (financial institutions)—fall within the jurisdictions of these committees. Our finding should not suggest that constituency or interest groups do not influence other committees, but it does suggest that such group pressures may not be sustained or pervasive enough in other committees to create factions. Alternatively, in other committees, constituency interests may be so intertwined with party or ideology that they are subsumed by partisan or ideological cleavages. We suggest, for instance, that the collinearity between party, ideology, and environmentalist and commercial users interests on the Interior Committee obscures the impact of these groups on committee decision making.

Another explanation of the lack of constituent group influence is that a consensus has developed on the distribution of benefits to particular constituencies or groups, and thus constituency interests do not cause cleavages in decision making on those issues. This appears to be the case in the Public Works Committee, where allocation formulas determine the distribution of a large amount of the benefits disbursed by the committee. In this instance, cleavages do not occur, because conflict rarely centers on which constituents should receive benefits.

A third explanation is that groups operating in the environment of the committee concentrate on narrow issues. When these issues arise, constituency groups seek to influence decision making; however, these same groups will not seek to influence decision making on other issues in the committee's jurisdiction. As a consequence, they will not be pervasive enough in the committee's environment to create factions. This appears to be true of the Judiciary Committee, where there are several groups which seek influence on particular issues, such as gun control or immigration, but do not actively seek to influence the committee on other issues. The impact of these groups is transient and depends on whether an issue relevant to the group is being debated.

Finally, interest groups may seek access to other levels of government, such as the executive branch, or may act through the party to secure the legislation they desire. For example, many groups press their claims on the budget through the bureaucracy rather than seeking access directly through the Appropriations Committee. Similarly, business interests often work through the Republican party, and labor interests, through the Democrats. The impact of these groups would then be closely tied to the partisan conflict within the committee.

In the three committees in which we discover the influence of constituency interests, the groups pressuring the committee are interested in many issues falling within the committee's jurisdiction and therefore tend to be sustained and pervasive forces within the committee's environment. In the Banking Committee the different financial interests vie with one another over financial regulation, but they share an interest in housing legislation. Labor interests exert influence over a substantial portion of the Education and Labor Committee's jurisdiction as well as working through the Democratic party and the executive branch. Agricultural interests seek to influence a large proportion of the legislation falling within the Agriculture Committee's jurisdiction, and they wield substantial influence over how agricultural programs will be administered.

The nature of governmental structures designed to administer federal programs in the areas of agriculture, labor, and business also aids these groups in their lobbying efforts. Theodore Lowi (1969) describes how the organization and goals of the Department of Agriculture assist farm interests:

> Due to the special intimacy between federal agriculture programs and private agriculture, each administrative organization becomes a potent political instrumentality. Each of the self-governing local units becomes one important point in a definable political system which both administers a program and maintains the autonomy of that program in face of all other political forces. . . . The politics of each of these self-governing programs is comprised of a triangular trading pattern with each point complementing and supporting the other two. The three points are: the central agency, a congressional committee or subcommittee, and the local or district farmer committees. The latter are also usually the grass roots element of a national interest group. (pp. 110–11)

Lowi contends that both business and labor maintain the same type of special governmental relationships as does agriculture.

> Merged or separate, however, the entire history of Commerce and Labor [departments] attests to their special character and function in the governmental scheme. . . . Both were charged with any and all research and statistical work necessary to make certain that the prob-

lems and needs of their "clients" were known at every turn. . . . While the pattern of development has not been the same in the two departments, neither has departed from its original responsibility for being an official collectivity of unofficial economic interests. (p. 116)

Each of these interests has governmental structures that assist them in pressing their claims by providing information and official sanctions for their actions.

As mentioned previously, it is difficult to separate the influence of organized interest groups from that of unorganized constituency interests existing in the individual representative's district. John Kingdon's (1973) argument, however, is persuasive. He contends that the effectiveness of organized groups depends on a link between the interests of these groups and the interests of the member's constituency. It is assumed in this chapter, therefore, that the impact of constituency interests represents the mutual impact of both important organized groups and unorganized constituency groups within the member's district. No attempt will be made to separate the two, but in instances where the links between organized and unorganized groups are apparent, they are noted. In the Agriculture Committee, for example, both organized interest groups and unorganized constituency interests push certain members to support certain commodities. The more important those commodities are to the representative's constituents, the more effective are the organized interest groups' appeals for the passage of favorable legislation. Further, the designations "constituency interests" and "interest group" will be used interchangeably to represent this hybrid of constituency and organized group interests.

Agriculture

When Charles O. Jones (1961) investigated the Agriculture Committee, he found it to be dominated by members who were elected from rural, farming districts. At that time, only one member of the committee came from an urban district. Further, the rural members were heavily influenced by the primary commodity grown in their district, and these commodity interests coincided with the member's party affiliation. Thirteen of the nineteen Democrats on the committee represented districts where the major commodities were tobacco, cotton, peanuts, and rice. Republican members represented districts where corn, hogs, small grains, and wheat were major commodities. The conflicts in the committee revolved around the allocation of subsidies to each of these commodities, with midwestern Republicans, who represented one set (corn, hogs, etc.), squaring off against southern Democrats, who represented another set of commodities (cotton, tobacco, etc.). Which crops were emphasized in the subsidy programs depended upon which party controlled the committee.

Representation of commodity interests was facilitated by the organization of the subcommittee system in the committee and by subcommittee assignment practices. First, subcommittees were established to deal with currently critical commodity problems. Second, members were assigned to commodity subcommittees on the basis of their constituency interests (Jones, 1961, p. 363). Therefore, members were able to press their commodity demands through the subcommittee on which they served. In the absence of overt constituency demands, members followed party cues in voting. Support for party positions generally increased as bills moved past the formulation stage and toward the final vote, with more partisan voting being displayed at the final vote than at the formulation stage. From Jones's description of the committee, we can speculate that members joined the Agriculture Committee because of reelection goals, since membership provided district benefits that could be used for such purposes.

Two studies (Ornstein and Rohde, 1977; Ralph Nader Congress Project, 1975) of the Agriculture Committee describe the operation of the committee in the early 1970s (Ornstein and Rohde studied the years 1970–75; the Ralph Nader Congress Project covered 1971–1974). Each notes many of the changes in the committee that occurred as the result of the House reforms and changes in society. Using these studies, we can delineate three types of changes that have had an impact on the committee: changes in membership on the committee; changes in society that have led to changes in the number and type of member going to committee; and changes in attitudes toward farm policy.

In their examination of membership changes, Norman Ornstein and David Rohde (1977) note a sharp decline in the percentage of southern Democrats on the committee; in 1970, 74 percent of the Democrats represented southern districts, whereas in 1975, only 37 percent of the Democrats were from the south. While the membership remained conservative, membership turnover resulted in a greater liberal tendency on the committee than in the past. This conservatism was reflected in the antiurban, antiliberal, and antilabor bias of the predominantly rural representatives. By 1975, urban membership had increased to five members from the one member noted in Jones's study: Frederick Richmond (D-N.Y.), Matthew McHugh (D-N.Y.), Norman d'Amours (D-N.H.), Margaret Heckler (R-Mass.), and Peter Peyser (R-N.Y.).

The decline in southern Democratic membership also meant the decline of the dominance of cotton interests in the committee. Describing the committee in 1975, Alan Ehrenhalt (1975) reported the following:

> "Cotton has basically run that committee up until now," said a senior Republican. "Poage's [the chairman until 1975] number one interest has been cotton. But cotton is slipping in the South." It is also slipping in the committee. For years the Cotton Subcommittee was the most popular choice among freshmen. This year, it ranked eight out of 10. "Cotton will be recognized as a legitimate part of the discussion," said Bergland (D-Minn.), "but as you can see, it is no longer dominant." (p. 383)

As the number of Democratic members elected from traditionally Republican areas of the Midwest increased, there was a shift in the coincidence of party and commodity interests.

At the same time that membership changes on the committee were occurring, the Ralph Nader Congress Project (1975) reported societal changes that affected the ability of the committee to ensure passage of its farm bills. The declining size of the farm population between 1940 and 1970 resulted in fewer members who represented predominantly farming districts. In the 1940s farmers constituted 25 percent of the population; however, by 1970 they were a mere 5 percent of the population. The result of this change was that farming interests had far less influence in the House in the 1970s than they had previously, and it was harder for such interests to get favorable legislation passed.

The changing attitude toward farm legislation resulted from other factors as well as the declining size of the farm population. Rising food prices in the early 1970s sparked the formation of a consumer movement that lobbied for lower food prices and displayed hostility toward subsidy programs that drove prices up. In addition, a growing concern for poverty in the 1960s and 1970s led to the adoption of the Food Stamp Program that fell into the Agriculture Committee's juris-

161

diction. The inclusion of this program encouraged liberal-urban representatives to seek positions on the committee and created a great deal of conflict between conservative members with antiwelfare sentiments and more moderate members who sought to expand the program. As we noted in Chapter 2, a major policy area that caused divisions in the committee during the 1970s is food stamp legislation.

Finally, there has been a growing hostility toward farm subsidies because of the recognition that much of the subsidy money goes to richer rather than to poorer farmers. This made it harder for the committee to win floor support for its subsidy programs and shifted the nature of commodity conflict within the committee. Where previously commodity interests fought over how large a share each commodity would get, they now fight over which commodities will be supported and which will not be supported.

> The obsolete term "farm bloc" implied uniformity of interests that now misrepresents the complexity and turmoil of farm politics. In fact, the farm committees preside over a free-for-all among commodity groups for shares of the farm budget. . . . Gains for one commodity in one region are often won at the expense of another commodity in another region. (Ralph Nader Congress Project, 1975)

Thus, commodity interests are still very influential in the committee, but they no longer strictly follow party lines nor are the alignments between commodities as clear-cut as previously.

For this study, the foregoing studies suggest that party, ideology, and constituent interests will be important environmental influences in the committee. Partisanship is important becuase of the differing policies pursued by each party: Democrats favor high price supports with rigid controls; Republicans on the other hand, prefer smaller programs with fewer controls. The influx of more moderate and liberal members to the committee, and the increasing influence of social welfare and urban interests suggest that ideology will also be important in explaining factional alignments in the committee. The importance of constituency influences has remained stable over all the committee studies, and we do not expect that to change in this study. Members still come from mainly rural districts that are dependent on particular commodities. Further, members still appear to be seeking to represent these interests on the committee in order to fulfill commodity group demands.

TABLE 22. Factions in the Agriculture Committee, 1973–1976

Committee Member	Factions				Explained Variation (%)
	1	2	3	4	
Jerry Litton (D-Mo.)	.88				88
Thomas S. Foley (D-Wash.)	.85				81
Joseph P. Vigorito (D-Pa.)	.79				71
Bob Bergland (D-Minn.)	.76				78
George E. Brown, Jr. (D-Calif.)	.54	(−.48)			67
Steven D. Symms (R-Idaho)	−.59	.50			81
Charles Thone (R-Nebr.)		.83			75
Edward R. Madigan (R-Ill.)		.70			69
William C. Wampler (R-Va.)		.67			70
James T. Johnson (R-Colo.)	(−.47)	.63			62
Keith B. Sebelius (R-Kans.)		.57	(.49)		68
W.R. Poage (D-Tex.)			.84		76
Walter B. Jones (D-N.C.)			.81		75
Dawson Mathis (D-Ga.)			.64		62
David R. Bowen (D-Miss.)			.51	(.45)	65
Ed Jones (D-Tenn.)				.83	76
John Melcher (D-Mont.)	(.48)			.73	86
Paul Findley (R-Ill.)		(.43)		−.62	63

Correlates of Factional Alignments

Presidential support	−.81*	.79*	.45	−.72*	
Conservative coalition	−.80*	.73*	.78*	−.37	
Party unity	.88*	−.85*	−.63*	.54*	
ADA	.74*	−.69*	−.82*	.36	
COPE	.89*	−.87*	−.47	.65*	
NFU	.89*	−.82*	−.66*	.59*	
CCUS	−.83*	.75*	.70*	−.49	
ACA	−.85*	.71*	.78*	−.38	
Food Stamps (I)	.83*	−.83*	−.69*	.57*	
Assistance to Farmers (II)	.44	−.32	.25	.46	

Note: Pearson correlations marked with asterisks significant at the .01 level.

Four factions appear to account for the types of cleavages that exist within the House Agriculture Committee (table 22): committee Democrats divide into northern (Faction 1) and southern (Faction 3) blocs and committee Republicans form the other major faction (2); the remaining committee members—Ed Jones (D-Tenn.) and John Melcher (D-Mont.)—form a factional doublet (Faction 4) that tends to vote with the northern Democrats ($r = .49$). These factions reflect the salience of party and ideology in the formation of committee cleavages. Faction 1 is a liberal (ACA, $r = -.85$) and partisan (party unity, $r = .88$) bloc of Democrats. The Conservative members divide into a faction of conservative (ADA, $r = -.82$) Democrats (Faction 3) and a bloc of conservative (ACA, $r = .71$) Republicans (Faction 2). Faction 4 represents a bloc of fairly supportive Democrats (presidential support, $r = -.72$). Even the major policy dimension—food stamps—is strongly correlated with party (party unity, $r = .89$) and ideology (ACA, $r = -.89$).

The ideological and partisan polarization of the Agriculture Committee is evident in the two-dimensional representation of the major committee cleavages (figure 19). Southern Democrats (with the exception of David R. Bowen [Miss.]) and Republicans (Steven D. Symms [Ida.], William C. Wampler [Va.], Keith B. Sebelius [Kans.], Charles Thone [Nebr.], Edward R. Madigan [Ill.], James T. Johnson [Colo.], and Paul Findley [Ill.]) form a conservative coalition that clusters in the upper-left quadrant of the graph opposite committee Democrats (Joseph P. Vigorito [Pa.], Jerry Litton [Mo.], Thomas S. Foley [Wash.], John Melcher [Mont.], Bob Bergland [Minn.], and George E. Brown, Jr. [Calif.]). Party and ideology are impossible to disentangle because they are highly interrelated ($r \rangle .90$); these characteristics are similar to those exhibited by congressional committees that are dominated by partisan and ideological cleavages.

A closer examination of the bloc of southern Democrats suggests that constituency interests may also influence the formation of factions within the Agriculture Committee. The nominal leaders of Faction 3 are chairmen of the committee's commodity subcommittees: W.R. Poage (D-Tex.; Livestock and Grains), Dawson Mathis (D-Ga.; Oilseeds and Rice), Walter B. Jones (D-N.C.; Tobacco), and David R. Bowen (D-Miss.; Cotton). Sebelius is the ranking Republican on Poage's subcommittee in the Ninety-fourth Congress. These commodities are important to the constituencies of the subcommittee leaders, as well as to the interest groups that represent these commodity products. The formation of this faction appears to reflect attempts to further or to protect constituency (commodity) interests.

The formation of a bloc of commodity supporters may be necessary, since the particularistic benefits that flow from these programs (e.g., subsidies) no longer go unchallenged. Therefore, there is some rationale for cleavages to form over the distribution of farm benefits and

Figure 19. Two-Dimensional Representation of Cleavages in the House Committee on Agriculture: 1973-1976.

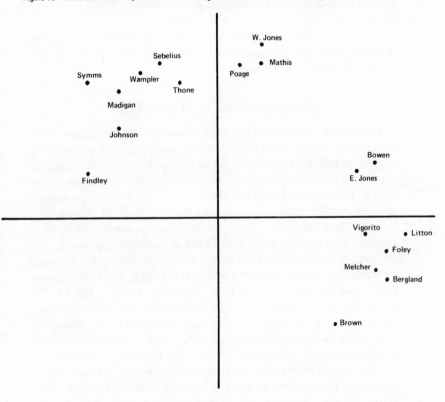

for the emergence of a faction suppoftive of commodity interests. In addition, Faction 3 represents the basis of the coalition that Poage created on farm legislation during his chairmanship: "conservative southern and southwestern congressmen from cotton, tobacco, peanut, and rice districts have traditionally provided his base of support" (Engeke, 1975, p. 156).

Thus, consistent with past research, we find that constituency interests, ideology, and party are important environmental influences on the Agriculture Committee.

Banking, Finance, and Urban Affairs

The jurisdiction of the Banking, Finance, and Urban Affairs Committee helps to explain why interest groups play a particularly important role in its operation. While committee decisions are important to the health of the entire economy, including their indirect effect on the inflation and unemployment rates, the jurisdiction can be divided roughly into two major areas—regulation of the banking industry and the formulation of urban development and housing policies. Three major areas of the banking industry regulated by the committee are particularly pertinent to understanding the factional structure in this committee: commercial banks, mortgage institutions, and the insurance industry (including pension funds). The rivalry between commercial banks and savings and loan institutions for an individual's savings is readily apparent in their advertising and their offers made to potential customers; it is also readily apparent in the divisions that split the members of the Banking Committee.

Even though both commercial banks and savings and loan institutions have managed to divide the banking industry between themselves and each has been able to maintain its portion of the market with little encroachment, they still fight to engrandize their portion and maintain their share intact. To do so requires them to be vigilant about the regulations and policies debated in this committee. In the past, the savings and loan institutions could be sure of the support of the Banking Committee's chairman Wright Patman, but as a result of the Democratic reforms in the Congress, these institutions lost their edge in committee decision making with the ouster of Patman by vote of the Democratic Caucus (Parker, 1979). It is expected, therefore, that disputes between these two interests will be divisive of the committee membership, especially in view of the stakes each has in ensuring that regulations passed by the committee treat them in a favorable manner.

Financial institutions also have a stake in the second major legislative area handled by the committee, urban development and housing. Joining the banking interests are other interest groups that stand to benefit or lose as a consequence of legislation governing housing policy and urban development debated by the committee. For example, the building industry, urban lobbies and representatives, and suburban and rural interests join the banking lobbies in bringing their appeals to the Banking Committee. The banking industry seeks to ensure that any federal help or subsidies are funneled through private financial institutions. Urban representatives, including mayors and congressmen, want to see federal money funneled directly to local governments. Rural and suburban interests want to stem the flow of federal funds to urban districts, or at least see that the programs are written in a manner that will include their constituents in a share of the benefits. The building industry supports federal assistance for housing but would like to see legislation that emphasizes new construction rather than the renovation of existing structures. Thus, the Banking Committee is buffeted by a multitude of private interests that must be satisfied in drafting legislation.

These lobbying groups use four weapons in pressing their claims on the committee. The first is information; in the area of banking legislation particularly, the committee is dependent on information provided by the institutions they seek to regulate, because the committee does not have the resources to amass by itself the information it needs nor does it even have access to some of it. The second weapon is money. These lobbying groups provide large amounts of money to congressional campaigns in general and to Banking Committee members in particular. The third is the ability of these interests, with their efficient organizations, to launch effective grass roots campaigns to sway wavering members. Finally, these groups generally employ full-time liaison staffs to be sure that members are aware of their positions on any legislation that comes before the committee.

When the committee was investigated in the early 1970s, it was found that committee membership was biased in favor of urban representatives and members with large banking interests in their districts: 19.1 percent of the members were from rural districts and

81 percent were from urban districts (Salaman, 1975). The urban members found a Banking assignment attractive because they could use it to provide direct, tangible benefits to their constituents. Other members, however, found fewer benefits to be derived from membership.

While Salaman (1975) found the committee membership to be more liberal than the House as a whole in the early 1970s, the liberal edge was small and could be disrupted by the shifting of a few key "swing" votes. As a result of the various pressures operating on the committee, liberal-conservative divisions were unstable.

> While the House Banking Committee is hardly a well-integrated, harmonious team, however, neither is it a complete free-for-all; for the cleavages that divide the members do not all overlap neatly, as we have already seen. Enemies on one issue are frequently allies on another, so that all feel some constraint about pushing issues to the limit. On issues like distribution of control over committee staff or matters on which the White House has established a clear partisan position, the committee splits along party lines, particularly since Patman tends to be a strongly partisan chairman. On traditional social-welfare issues like public housing, traditional party lines break and the conservative coalition of southern Democrats and small-town Republicans makes its appearance. (Salaman, 1975, p. 57)

In the period examined in this analysis, we expect to find the same influences on committee decision making that Salaman finds—party, ideology, and interest groups.

The impact of these three influences can be identified in the factions that form in the House Banking Committee (table 23). Faction 1 represents a bloc of mostly liberal (ACA, $r = -.71$)—with the possible exception of Hanley—and partisan (party unity, $r = .75$) Democrats: James M. Hanley (N.Y.), Joseph G. Minish (N.J.), Fernand J. St. Germain (R.I.), and Frank Annunzio (Ill.). There is reason to believe that this Democratic bloc is supportive of policies favoring noncommercial banking concerns, such as the establishment of banking and economic policies ($r = .61$). While all types of financial institutions oppose government loans and subsidy programs that deplete their potential banking clientele, divisions between commercial and noncommercial banking interests (savings and loans, mortgage bankers) can become intense. Symptomatic of the differences between commercial and noncommercial bankers is the disagreement over the

TABLE 23. Factions in the Banking, Finance and Urban
Affairs Committee, 1973–1976

Committee Member	Factions 1	2	3	4	Explained Variation (%)
James M. Hanley (D-N.Y.)	.80				69
Joseph G. Minish (D-N.J.)	.79				73
Fernand J. St. Germain (D-R.I.)	.77				71
Frank Annunzio (D-Ill.)	.75				69
J. William Stanton (R-Ohio)		.83			74
Albert W. Johnson (R-Pa.)		.81			82
Chalmers P. Wylie (R-Ohio)		.64			47
Robert G. Stephens, Jr. (D-Ga.)		.56			57
Garry Brown (R-Mich.)		.63	−.57		77
Corinne C. Boggs (D-La.)			.78		68
Parren J. Mitchell (D-Md.)			.54		64
Thomas M. Rees (D-Calif.)	(.45)		.51		49
Henry S. Reuss (D-Wis.)			.57	.56	73
William A. Barrett (D-Pa.)				.89	88
Wright Patman (D-Tex.)				.71	78

Correlates of Factional Alignments

Presidential support	−.78*	.89*	−.70*	−.56**
Conservative coalition	−.66*	.93*	−.66*	−.63*
Party unity	.75*	−.93*	.65*	.51*
ADA	.63*	−.87*	.55	.32*
COPE	.82*	−.95*	.72*	.71*
NFU	.73*	−.93*	.58*	.73*
CCUS	−.74*	.98*	−.66*	−.67*
ACA	−.71*	.92*	−.66*	−.77*
Banking and Economic Policy (I)	.61*	−.88*	.42	.67*
Limitations on Housing and Urban Programs (II)	.44	−.36	.67*	.16

Note: Pearson correlations marked with asterisks are significant at the .01 level.

extent to which "the government should intervene to assist mortgage lenders to compete for funds, and, if so, how" (Salaman, 1975, p. 201). The cleavage between these two banking interests results from the extent to which they rely on mortgage lending as a source of assets: commercial banks invest few of their assets in residential mortgages; both savings and loan associations and mortgage bankers deal most exclusively in real estate mortgages. Noncommercial banking interests favor government intervention in assisting mortgage

169

lenders, whereas commercial banking interests are unsympathetic to such federal intrusion. In short, we can expect cleavages to appear over issues that involve the intervention of the federal government in the affairs of commercial or noncommercial banking interests. There is some rationale for the support given by Faction 1 to the interests of savings and loan associations and mortgage bankers, since the nominal leaders of this bloc receive financial support from savings and loan (St. Germain, Thomas M. Rees [Calif.]), and mortgage banking (Hanley, Minish) interests. Annunzio's agreement with this faction may be a consequence of his specialization; he is a member of St. Germain's subcommittee on Bank Supervision and Insurance.

Faction 2 (table 23) also appears to represent the influences of party, ideology, and constituency interests: the bloc reflects the vote agreement among conservative (ACA, $r = .92$) and partisan Republicans (party unity, $r = -.93$). Southern Democrat Robert G. Stephens, Jr. (Ga.), also votes with this bloc, which tends to champion the causes of commercial banking interests (Banking and Economic Policy, $r = -.88$). The remaining committee factions can also be described in partisan and ideological terms: Faction 3 is another group of liberal (ACA, $r = -.66$) and partisan Democrats (party unity, $r = .65$); Faction 4 represents a bloc of leadership Democrats—Henry S. Reuss (Wis.), William A. Barrett (Pa.), and Patman, the three top-ranking Democrats on the committee—that is both liberal (ACA, $r = -.77$) and somewhat partisan (presidential support, $r = -.56$). This faction of leadership Democrats, like Faction 1, opposes the interests of commercial banking groups ($r = .67$).

Members of the committee who represent urban districts see membership on the committee as an opportunity to improve local conditions with urban grants and housing programs. Although many committee members represent metropolitan areas, there is partisan (Republican) and ideological (conservative) opposition to the government's role in housing and urban policies. Conflict between central city and suburban interests often become intertwined with issues relating to housing programs. Thus, a second set of constituency interests may also be influential in the organization of committee factions: The four nominal leaders of Faction 3 (Corinne C. Boggs [D-La.], Parren J. Mitchell [D-Md.], Rees, and Reuss) represent urban areas and tend to support the legislative interests associated with these constituencies, such as housing programs (Limitations on Housing and Urban Programs, $r = .67$). The urban nature of their districts and the support they provide for urban programs suggest that constituency interests may underlie attachments to this faction.

The coalition structure of this committee is a familiar one: Democrats and Republicans cluster in quadrants directly opposite each other (figure 20). Since southern Democrat Stephens is pulled in different directions by his partisan and ideological persuasions, as are many southern Democrats, he occupies a position almost directly between the partisan and ideological clusters of Democrats (lower-right quadrant) and Republicans (upper-left quadrant). Clearly, party, ideology, and constituency interests are important sources of committee cleavages in the Banking Committee.

Education and Labor

Like the Banking Committee, the Education and Labor Committee offers few constituency benefits that *all* members can exploit to gain reelection. The only members who could serve their constituencies by committee membership are those from northern, urban districts. The one feature that committee membership appears to offer and that has been cited by members in other studies is the opportunity to make "good" public policy (Fenno, 1973).

The eclectic nature of the influences operating in the committee is indicative of the wide collection of groups that take an interest in the issues that fall into the committee's jurisdiction. Fenno (1973, pp. 30–31) identified executive, party, clientele, and House members as part of the committee's environment. The influence that predominated in Education and Labor, however, was the party-led policy coalitions. The issues that fall into the Education and Labor Committee's jurisdiction tend to be the type that arouse partisan sentiments; they include federal aid to education, social welfare, and labor policy. Members are divided ideologically on these issues as well. What results is a committee in which intense partisan-ideological conflict is a normal part of decision making.

> The subjects of labor, education, and poverty pose issues over which Democrats and Republicans have tended to divide and which have often been the major points of domestic disagreement in Presidential and Congressional campaigns. Each subject propounds ideologically inflammable questions of government involvement in the society. In the

Figure 20. Two-Dimensional Representation of Cleavages in the House Committee on Banking, Finance, and Urban Affairs: 1973-1976.

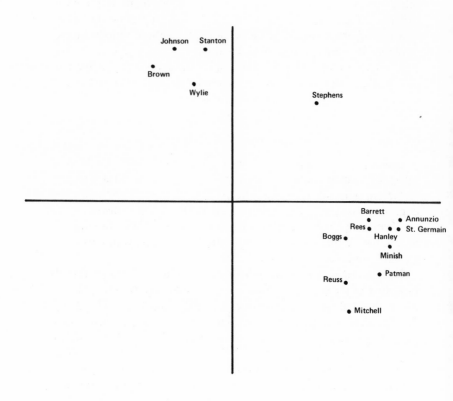

1950's and 1960's Democrats tended to give liberal (more involvement) answers and Republicans tended to give conservative (less involvement) answers. (Fenno, 1973, p. 32)

Reflecting the influence of party on the committee, a strategic premise under which the committee operated was to "prosecute policy partisanship." Members of the committee tended to follow their party leaders: if the party controlled the White House, members would follow the president's lead; if not, they followed the party leadership in the House. Given these observations by Fenno (1973), it is not surprising that he found that policy conflict in the committee tended to fall along partisan-ideological lines. The committee was not just divided by party and ideology; the willingness of members to pursue their own policy goals even when they conflicted with those of the parties created more divisiveness in decision making. As Fenno (1973) notes: "The basic alignments are still Democratic-Republican, but policy individualism introduces important extrapartisan nuances" (p. 77).

One of the most important constituency groups operating in the committee's environment was organized labor. The ability of labor unions to achieve their policy goals was tied to their ability to influence committee decision making, as one AFL-CIO member described to Fenno (1973): "We have to control the labor committee. It's our lifeblood" (p. 31). One indication of the influence of labor in the committee was the degree to which it was consulted by Democratic party leaders in appointing members to the committee. One labor official related how the chairman would use lists of acceptable members provided by the labor union in selecting new committee members (Fenno, 1973). In return for this influence, labor provided money, manpower, and organization to the political campaigns of party candidates who supported labor. One result of this practice of consulting labor on appointments was an underrepresentation of southern Democrats on the committee (Fenno, 1973). Based on these observations by Fenno, we would expect to find that party, ideology, and constituent groups are salient influences on committee decision making.

The Education and Labor Committee divides into three factions that reflect the impact of party, ideology, and constituency interests on the formation of committee cleavages. Faction 1 (table 24) represents a bloc of conservative (ACA, $r = .89$) Republicans who strongly

TABLE 24. Factions in the Education and Labor Committee, 1973–1976

Committee Member	Factions 1	2	3	Explained Variation (%)
Alphonzo Bell (R-Calif.)	.89			85
Ronald A. Sarison (R-Conn.)	.89			85
Marvin L. Esch (R-Mich.)	.82			71
John N. Erlenborn (R-Ill.)	.82			90
Albert H. Quie (R-Minn.)	.80			82
Edwin D. Eshleman (R-Pa.)	.72			74
Augustus F. Hawkins (D-Calif.)	−.57		.59	84
Lloyd Meeds (D-Wash.)	−.50		(.46)	53
William Lehman (D-Fla.)	−.52	.60		67
Dominick V. Daniels (D-N.J.)		.87		89
Joseph M. Gaydos (D-Pa.)		.85		84
John H. Dent (D-Pa.)		.84		82
Frank Thompson, Jr. (D-N.J.)		.80		84
Carl D. Perkins (D-Ky.)		.76		66
Mario Biaggi (D-N.Y.)		.69		66
John Brademas (D-Ind.)		.69	.52	77
William "Bill" Clay (D-Mo.)			.86	88
Patsy T. Mink (D-Hawaii)			.73	86
William D. Ford (D-Mich.)			.69	69
Shirley Chisholm (D-N.Y.)	(−.46)		.66	70
James G. O'Hara (D-Mich.)			.65	69
Philip Burton (D-Calif.)	(−.43)		.60	64

Correlates of Factional Alignments

	1	2	3
Presidential support	.82*	−.73*	−.83*
Conservative coalition	.88*	−.61*	−.91*
Party unity	−.93*	.77*	.84*
ADA	−.86*	.60*	.77*
COPE	−.89*	.84*	.81*
NFU	−.86*	.78*	.83*
CCUS	.86*	−.75*	−.86*
ACA	.89*	−.73*	−.84*
Labor and Education (I)	−.96*	.86*	−.86*

Note: Doublet: Ford (D-Mich.) and O'Hara (D-Mich.). Pearson correlations marked with asterisks are significant at the .01 level.

oppose legislation benefiting labor and education interests ($r = -.96$). The bipolar nature of this faction reflects the saliency of partisan and ideological cleavages between committee Republicans and Democrats. The conflict is probably exacerbated by committee assignment practices that tend to place intensely partisan and ideological members on this committee (Fenno, 1973).

Faction 2 represents a bloc of labor Democrats (COPE, $r = .84$) that is also liberal (ACA, $r = -.73$) and partisan (party unity, $r = .77$) in its voting behavior. The labor orientation of this faction is demonstrated by its sizable correlation with COPE ratings (the group rating with the largest correlation with this faction), and the fact that the chairmen of the labor subcommittees (1973–76) have the strongest attachments to this faction (Frank Thompson, Jr. [D-N.J.], John H. Dent [D-Pa.], and Dominick V. Daniels [D-N.J.]). This faction generally joins with the remaining liberal (ACA, $r = -.84$) Democrats (Faction 3) to form a coalition supportive of Democratic programs in the areas of labor and education policy ($r = .56$).

As the two-dimensional representation of the major committee cleavages illustrates (figure 21), the Education and Labor Committee is polarized along partisan and ideological lines: Democrats on the committee form a tight cluster (upper-right quadrant) that is located diagonally opposite a similarly tight cluster of Republicans (lower-left quadrant). This configuration fits the pattern of other polarized committees. In conclusion, factions in the Education and Labor Committee reflect the impact of party, ideology, and constituency interests (labor). This analysis is consistent with Fenno's description of the forces operating in the environment of this committee.

In Agriculture and in Education and Labor, subcommittee chairmen supportive of particular interests that fall within the committee's jurisdictions align with one another on separate factions. Members heading subcommittees concerned with specific commodities join Faction 3 in the Agriculture Committee. This finding is similar to the findings of Jones (1961) in his earlier examination of the Agriculture Committee. Similarly, committee leaders supportive of organized labor align themselves with Faction 2 in the Education and Labor committee. This is also similar to the findings of Fenno's (1973) examination of this committee.

The Banking Committee membership is influenced by the com-

175

Figure 21. Two-Dimensional Representation of Cleavages in the House Committee on Education and Labor: 1973-1976.

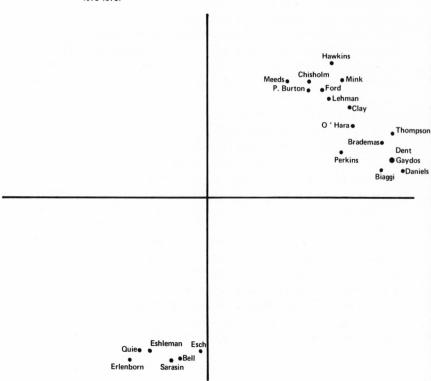

mercial and noncommercial banking interests which they oversee. In this committee we find two factions in support of noncommercial interests such as savings and loans and mortgage banks, and these factions are opposed by members who support commercial banking interests. The split between these interests in the committee also seems to coincide with the division between the liberals and conservatives on the committee. Finally, the significant association between Faction 3 and restrictions on housing and urban problems (Policy Dimension II) suggests that issues concerning urban development may also generate a core of strong supporters, although the evidence of such support is not as clear as that for the differing banking interests.

Taking stock of the committees examined in the Ninety-third and Ninety-fourth Congresses, we should note that party and ideology create divisions in most of the committees examined (except Armed Services, Standards, and Foreign Affairs, where we find bipartisanship and ideology). The nature of the divisions created by these two forces differs from committee to committee. In some committees ideology and party are highly intertwined and result in highly polarized alignments. This is true of Budget, Interior, Commerce, Ways and Means, and Education and Labor.

In other committees ideology creates divisions within the parties (Agriculture, Appropriations, Banking, Government Operations, House Administration, Judiciary, Rules, and Science and Technology). For instance, Republican and Democratic members of the Government Operations Committee are divided not only along partisan lines but also ideologically within their party clusters. In House Administration, committee Democrats are divided ideologically, while Republicans are not. Finally, in some committees ideology divides members into bipartisan factions such as in Standards, Armed Services, and Foreign Affairs.

We have also noted that interests other than ideology and party can divide committee membership. In five of the committees, there is evidence of executive influence as a salient factor in committee divisions: Appropriations, Armed Services, Foreign Affairs, Post Office and Civil Service, and Ways and Means. These committees have factions that can be characterized by the degree of support they display for the administration or particular executive agencies. Finally, three committees show signs of constituency influences: Agriculture, Banking, and Education.

Having examined the committees in one time period (1973–76) we can now move to the second stage of this study, an analysis of the stability of the factional alignments in another time period (1977–80). This section of the analysis will allow a longitudinal comparison of the factional structures of each committee, as well as an investigation of the effect of partisan control of the White House on the alignments within the committees. During the Ninety-third and Ninety-fourth Congresses, Republicans controlled the executive branch; in the second time period, control of the executive branch passed to the Democrats, leaving them in control of both the executive and legislative branches.

CHAPTER SIX

Stability and Change
in Cleavages

In the previous three chapters, we delineated the factions that arise in committee decision making in the four-year period, 1973–76. We found party and ideology to be pervasive influences on decision making in committees. We also found that committees can be categorized by the degree to which other influences affect the formation of factions. During that four-year period, however, control of the government was divided between the Democrats and Republicans, and this division defines in part the environment in which the committees operate. Under a Republican president and a Democratic Congress, an adversarial relationship exists between the president and the congressional leadership. Divided control can stimulate intense partisan and ideological conflict, particularly when the president is distinctly more conservative than the congressional leadership as was the case with Richard Nixon and the Democratic leadership in the House.

If divided control is an important factor in the formation of committee factions, then factions could have changed significantly when the Democrats won the presidency in 1976 and control of the government was no longer divided. Extending the analysis to a second four-year period, 1977 through 1980, provides the opportunity to assess both the impact of divided control on committee decision making and the stability of the factions that have already been uncovered. This part of the analysis allows us to explore three basic questions: How stable are the uncovered factions and cleavages within the committee? What impact does control of the White House have on committee conflict structures? If change is detected, what are the causes of that change?

In analyzing the stability of factions, we are answering the related question of how reliable are the cleavages uncovered in our earlier analysis. It may be that the development of factions depends solely on the nature of the issues discussed in the time period. If this were the case, factions would tend to be idiosyncratic, and significant changes might occur from one time period to the next. The factional structure within the committee might change significantly, indicating that the cleavages underlying these factions had also changed. Alternatively, the factional structures might remain the same while the correlates of these factions changed. This would suggest that although the cleavages underlying decision making still create analogous factions, the nature of the conflict in the committee had changed.

Stability would be indicated by evidence that the same types of cleavages lead to the formation of analogous factional structures within each committee in the two time periods. There are several reasons to suspect that the factional structures we have uncovered will display a high degree of stability. The jurisdictions of committees have remained reasonably stable over time; this means that the committees deal with the same types of issues in each time period. This, of course, does not preclude the introduction of new issues into committee decision making. For instance, when the problem of energy emerged as a national issue in the 1970s, it was added to the agendas of several committees in the House. The addition of this issue, however, followed certain jurisdictional guidelines; the development of synthetic fuels was sent to the Science and Technology Committee; the development of a windfall profits tax was sent to the Ways and Means Committee; the discussions of electrical rates and a distribution plan for oil were sent to the Commerce Committee. Hence, although new issues arise, they tend to be assigned to committees according to jurisdictional guidelines that display a great deal of stability. Because the types of issues sent to each committee have remained stable, we would suspect that the cleavages that the issues produce in the committees have remained relatively stable as well.

The second reason to suspect that factions will remain relatively stable is suggested by Fenno's (1973) analyses. Members seek membership on committees because they want to attain certain goals. In addition, members with similar goals tend to choose similar committee assignments. If the types of members being elected to the House changed, for example, the types of members going to the committee would also change. The issues handled by the committee might attract a new type of member because the policies have grown in national prominence or the nature of the conflicts over the issues have changed. For instance, a Government Operations Committee member suggested to Ornstein and Rohde (1977) that the investigation of the Nixon White House had attracted several more activist members to the committee. In the Agriculture Committee, the growth in importance of the issue of urban poverty has attracted more urban members to the committee than previously. Thus, while there is always the possibility of change, committee assignment practices tend to promote stability in the type of members assigned to the committees.

Finally, the policy dimensions examined in Chapter 2 display a high degree of stability. This suggests that the types of issues that divide the committees tend to remain fairly constant over time. In the few committees where the policy dimensions did change, examination of the factional structures in the second time period allows us to determine if these changes affected the committees' factional structures. Changes in the policy dimensions may be linked to the changing nature of the issues handled by the committee. For instance, an issue area such as energy which before the 1970s was not very prominent might become more important and alter the cleavage patterns in the committee. We expect that although some of the committees may display change, the majority of the factional structures will remain stable in the second time period.

The switch from divided to unified control of the government also could affect several aspects of committee decision making. Unified control might exacerbate partisan cleavages within the committees. In contrast, divided control may foster a high degree of bipartisanship because both parties realize they must compromise with one another in order to gain any benefits for their districts and to ensure approval by both Congress and the president. Unified control offers little incentive for such partisan cooperation; the party in control has no need to compromise with the minority party. If the party maintains a majority in the Congress and is in control of the White House, its legislation stands a good chance of passage both on the floor and by the president.

Unified control may also promote greater ideological and partisan polarization within the committees. Under divided control, southern Democratic members are strongly cross-pressured because of their partisan and ideological loyalties. They make a perfect target for a conservative Republican president trying to secure enough support to pass his legislative program. On several committees examined in the earlier time period, southern Democrats joined conservative Republicans in opposing Democrats on the committee. Under a president of their own party, the southern Democrats' partisan loyalties may weigh heavier in their decision making than their conservative ideologies. In this case, these members would vote with their Democratic colleagues and strengthen the degree of partisanship displayed by the committee. Examination of the behavior of southern Democrats, therefore, is an important element in detecting changes caused by shifting control of the White House.

A more general question that needs to be investigated is the impact of shifting control of the White House and Congress on the influence of ideology. It may be that unified control makes ideology far less important than partisanship in committees. Alternatively, it may be that partisanship is no more important but that the other influences such as ideology and/or the influence of the presidency become far more collinear with partisanship. If this is the case, we expect that committee factional structures will become more polarized. Finally, if party becomes more collinear with the other influences in the second time period, it may be more difficult to detect the influence of the administration on committee decision making.

The committees are categorized in this chapter as they were in the previous three chapters—those displaying simply party and ideology, those where in addition to party and ideology the administration influences decision making, and those where constituency groups as well as party and ideology influence decision making. The two-dimensional graphs can be used to identify changes in the clustering of members from the earlier time period. While committee membership changes in the two time periods, the factional structures can be compared by determining if the same type of cleavages form. By using members who were present in the earlier analysis as guides, it is possible to determine the manner in which new members align with previously uncovered factions.

STABILITY AND CHANGE IN PARTISAN AND IDEOLOGICAL PRESSURES

During the Ninety-third and Ninety-fourth Congresses, the Armed Services, Foreign Affairs, and Standards committees are the only committees where partisan conflict lacks saliency. In all the other committees in the House, partisan and ideological cleavages are ubiquitous features of committee conflict. Even in committees with jurisdictions that evoke partisan acrimony (Budget, Government Operations, House Administration, and Rules), ideological conflict is present, making it impossible to disentangle liberalism from Democratic support, or conservatism from Republican opposition. The existence of policy conflicts of an ideological nature adds an ideological color to the partisan divisions within these committees. In other committees (Interior and Insular Affairs, Interstate and Foreign Commerce, Judiciary, Public Works and Transportation, and Science and Technology), issues that are likely to create ideological divisions fall into their jurisdictions, generating committee conflict of an ideological nature: The close association between party and ideology during the Ninety-third and Ninety-fourth Congresses adds a partisan component to these ideological cleavages.

In the Ninety-fifth and Ninety-sixth Congresses, membership changes and committee assignment practices have intensified some of these cleavages. Yet, party and ideology continue to shape the major dimensions of conflict in these committees. The small number of roll-call votes in the Foreign Affairs and Standards committees prohibits examination of these committees in the Ninety-fifth and Ninety-sixth Congresses and prevents any discussion of the changes in their factional structures.

Budget

Membership turnover in the Budget Committee, unlike other committees, is mandated by House rules: no member may serve on the committee for more than four years during a ten-year period. As a result, the core membership shrinks from twenty-five members during the 1973–76 period to fourteen members during the 1977–80 period. This reduction in the size of the core membership in the Ninety-fifth and Ninety-sixth Congresses has no noticeable impact on divisions within the committee; the cleavages continue to reflect ideological and partisan differences among Budget Committee members.

Faction 1 (table 25) represents the agreement among conservative committee Republicans (James T. Broyhill [N.C.], Delbert L. Latta [Ohio], Marjorie S. Holt [Md.], Barber B. Conable [N.Y.], and Ralph S. Regula [Ohio]), and the opposition of liberal committee Democrats (Louis Stokes [Ohio], Paul Simon [Ill.], Elizabeth Holtzman [N.Y.] and David R. Obey [Wis.]); this is the same intense partisan-ideological polarization that existed within the committee during the earlier analysis period (1973–76). The remaining voting bloc (Faction 2) can be characterized as an alignment of partisan (party unity, $r = .74$) and basically liberal (ACA, $r = -.71$) Democrats that includes the majority leader, Jim Wright (D-Tex.), and the committee's chairman, Robert N. Giaimo (D-Conn.). The composition of these factions differs little from that of the major groups that initiated the budgetary reforms and instituted the present Budget Committee in the Ninety-fourth Congress—spending liberals and fiscal conservatives (LeLoup, 1979, p. 232).

The graphic representations of the major cleavages within the committee during the two time periods (figures 22a and 22b) reveal similar patterns of partisan and ideological polarization: Democratic liberals tend to cluster in a quadrant (upper-left) that is diagonally opposite the cluster of committee Republicans (lower-right quadrant). The spatial continuity between 1973–76 and 1977–80 is also evident in the location of conservative Democrat Jim Mattox (Tex.) between these two ideological and partisan clusters; this is the same position that southern Democrats like Butler Derrick (S.C.) and Harold Runnels (N.Mex.) held during the 1973–76 analysis (figure 22a). Thus, cleavages within the Budget Committee continue to

TABLE 25. Factions in the Budget Committee, 1977–1980

Committee Member	Factions		Explained Variation (%)
	1	2	
James T. Broyhill (R-N.C.)[a]	.94		93
Delbert L. Latta (R-Ohio)[a]	.90		86
Marjorie S. Holt (R-Md.)[a]	.87		83
Barber B. Conable (R-N.Y.)[a]	.85		75
Ralph S. Regula (R-Ohio)	.81		70
David R. Obey (D-Wis.)	−.68		58
Elizabeth Holtzman (D-N.Y.)[a]	−.78		63
Paul Simon (D-Ill.)	−.83		72
Louis Stokes (D-Ohio)[a]	−.86		85
Jim Wright (D-Tex.)[a]		.90	83
Robert N. Giaimo (D-Conn.)[a]		.89	81
Thomas L. Ashley (D-Ohio)[a]		.88	83
Norman Y. Mineta (D-Calif.)		.69	71
Jim Mattox (D-Tex.)[b]			1

Correlates of Factional Alignments		
Presidential support	−.84*	.80*
Conservative coalition	.97*	−.68*
Party unity	−.92*	.74*
ADA	−.88*	.50
COPE	−.96*	.75*
CCUS	.83*	−.61*
ACA	.96*	−.71*
Reductions in Nondefense Expenditures (I)	−.81*	.89*
Reductions in Defense Expenditures (II)	.58*	.19

Note: Pearson correlations marked with asterisks are significant at the .01 level.
[a]Core committee member during 1973–76 committee analysis.
[b]Does not exhibit an attachment to any of the committee factions.

follow ideological and partisan divisions among committee members.

Government Operations

The factional structure of the Government Operations Committee also remains quite stable during the span of our analysis: party and ideology continue to shape the factional attachments of committee

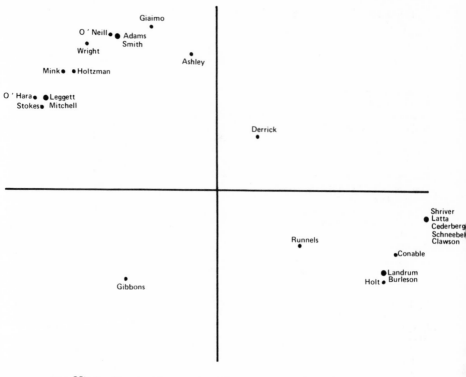

Figure 22a. Two-Dimensional Representation of Cleavages in the House Committee on Budget: 1973-1976.

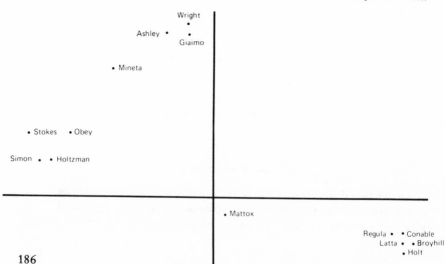

Figure 22b. Two-Dimensional Representation of Cleavages in the House Committee on Budget: 1977–1980.

186

TABLE 26. Factions in the Government Operations
Committee, 1977–1980

| Committee Member | Factions | | | Explained |
	1	2	3	Variation (%)
John Conyers, Jr. (D-Mich.)[a]	.85			79
Fernand J. St. Germain (D-R.I.)[a]	.84			77
Benjamin S. Rosenthal (D-N.Y.)[a]	.84			72
Peter H. Kostmayer (D-Pa.)	.83			70
Andrew Maguire (D-N.J.)	.81			74
Ted Weiss (D-N.Y.)	.75			63
Robert F. Drinan (D-Mass.)	.73			66
Cardiss Collins (D-Ill.)	.71			55
Dante B. Fascell (D-Fla.)[a]	.68			63
Henry A. Waxman (D-Calif.)	.67			56
William S. Moorhead (D-Pa.)[a]	.60			58
Anthony "Toby" Moffett (D-Conn.)	.53	−.50		63
Frank Horton (R-N.Y.)[a]	.50			34
John L. Burton (D-Calif.)	.50	−.63		64
Robert Walker (R-Pa.)	−.50	(.46)		48
Arlan Strangeland (R-Minn.)	−.53	.53		66
John N. Erlenborn (R-Ill.)[a]	−.66	.65		86
Paul N. McCloskey, Jr. (R-Calif.)[a]		.80		64
Clarence J. Brown (R-Ohio)[a]	(−.49)	.70		79
John W. Wydler (R-N.Y.)[a]		.69		54
Thomas N. Kindness (R-Ohio)		.51		43
Floyd J. Fithian (D-Ind.)			.72	55
Glenn English (D-Okla.)			.59	50
Elliott H. Levitas (D-Ga.)			.58	43
Don Fuqua (D-Fla.)[a]			.57	47
Jack Brooks (D-Tex.)[a]			.55	55
Richardson Preyer (D-N.C.)			.53	48
David W. Evans (D-Ind.)			.52	32
L.H. Fountain (D-N.C.)[a]			(.44)	21
Correlates of Factional Alignments				
Presidential support	.71*	−.64*	.33	
Conservative coalition	−.88*	.60*	.27	
Party unity	.85*	−.77*	.26	
ADA	.88*	−.59*	−.18	
COPE	.92*	−.74*	−.05	
CCUS	−.76*	.58*	.08	
ACA	−.87*	.69*	−.13	
Agency Regulation and Fiscal Assistance (I)	.77*	−.77*	.44*	
Revenue Sharing (II)	−.57*	.09	.77*	

Note: Doublets: English (D-Okla.) and Kindness (R-Ohio); Evans (D-Ind.) and Fountain (D-N.C.). Pearson correlations marked with asterisks are significant at the .01 level.
[a]Core member during 1973–76 committee analysis.

members. Faction 1 (table 26) represents the vote agreement among liberal Democrats (ADA, $r = .88$) on the committee (John Conyers, Jr. [Mich.], Fernand St. Germain [R.I.], Benjamin S. Rosenthal [N.Y.], Peter H. Kostmayer [Pa.], Andrew Maguire [N.J.], Ted Weiss [N.Y.], Robert F. Drinan [Mass.], Cardiss Collins [Ill.] and Henry A. Waxman [Calif.]); this faction is also intensely partisan (party unity, $r = .85$). The remaining committee Democrats form a more conservative faction (Faction 3), composed largely of southern Democrats (table 26). Ideology is not the only source of disagreement among these two Democratic voting blocs. Revenue sharing is also a source of dissension: Democratic liberals (Faction 1) favor increases in revenue-sharing programs (Revenue Sharing, $r = -.57$), while the members of Faction 3 (Floyd J. Fithian [Ind.], Glenn English [Okla.], Elliott H. Levitas [Ga.], Don Fuqua [Fla.], Jack Brooks [Tex.], Richardson Preyer [N.C.], David W. Evans [Ind.] and L.H. Fountain [N.C.]) favor fiscal restraint in the funding of these programs (Revenue Sharing, $r = .77$). These two Democratic factions do share the same attitude toward the administration's countercyclical economic aid programs (Agency Regulation and Fiscal Assistance), though Faction 3 is somewhat less supportive of these programs than is Faction 1. The infusion of southern Democrats into the committee during the Ninety-fifth and Ninety-sixth Congresses has strengthened the influence of Faction 3.

The partisan and ideological cleavages within the committee are exemplified by the voting behavior of committee Republicans (Faction 2). This bloc is strongly partisan (party unity, $r = -.77$) and conservative (ACA, $r = .69$); it also frequently opposes the positions favored by liberal Democrats (table 26). Thus, the partisan and ideological forces that promoted committee cleavages continue to divide committee members during the Ninety-fifth and Ninety-sixth Congresses.

The two-dimensional representations of the major cleavages within the committee between 1973 and 1980 reveal similar patterns of partisan-ideological conflict: liberal Democrats and conservative Republicans cluster in diagonally opposite quadrants of the space (figures 23a and 23b). In the Ninety-fifth and Ninety-sixth Congresses two southern Democrats, Levitas and English, are similarly cross-pressured by partisan and ideological loyalties (figure 23b); hence, like Fountain and Fuqua, their voting behavior places them between

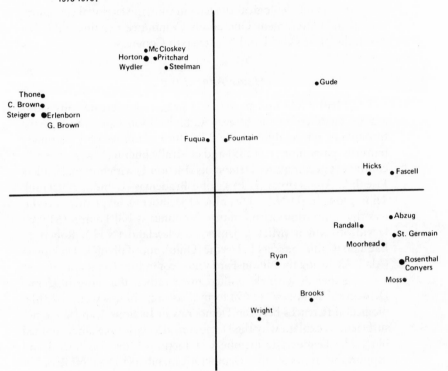

Figure 23a. Two-Dimensional Representation of Cleavages in the House Committee on Government Operations: 1973-1976.

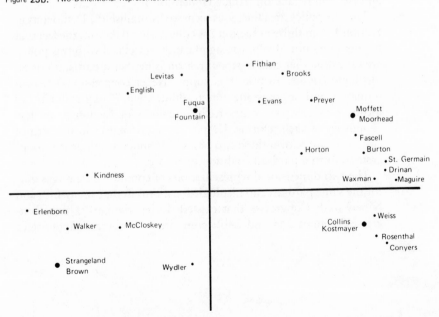

Figure 23b. Two-Dimensional Representation of Cleavages in the House Committee on Government Operations: 1977–1980.

the partisan and ideological clusters. In sum, the factional configuration of the Government Operations Committee remains stable between the Ninety-third and Ninety-sixth Congresses.

House Administration

The ideological and partisan cleavages that created divisions among members of the House Administration Committee persist throughout our analysis (table 27). Once again, we find a strongly partisan (party unity, $r = .89$) and generally liberal (ACA, $r = -.77$) contingent of committee Democrats (Faction 1) with nominal leaders Joseph S. Ammerman (D-Pa.), John Brademas (D-Ind.), and Frank Thompson, Jr. (D-N.J.). This bloc of Democrats frequently encounters the opposition of committee Republicans Bill Frenzel (Minn.), David Stockman (Mich.), James C. Cleveland (N.H.), Robert E. Badham (Calif.), Samuel L. Devine (Ohio), and William L. Dickinson (Ala.). As during the Nixon-Ford years, committee Democrats do not vote together as a single unified bloc; rather, the more moderate Democrats (ACA, $r = -.67$) form a separate bloc—Faction 2. Ideological differences between Democrats in Factions 1 and 2 are not sufficient to explain why the Democrats do not form a single unified bloc. The Democratic members of Faction 2 are also liberal and support the efforts of other Democratic members to fend off Republican initiatives in the ideological (ACA, $r = -.83$) area of campaign and election regulation (Policy Dimension I).

The one policy area that does seem to distinguish the Democrats in Faction 1 from those in Faction 2 is congressional reform; the fact that neither party nor ideology is significantly correlated with this policy area suggests that congressional reform is neither a partisan nor an ideological issue. Faction 1 is supportive of congressional reform initiatives and opposes attempts to dilute them (Congressional Reforms, $r = .58$); in contrast, the members of Faction 2 are less supportive of such reforms. Despite these differences in the area of congressional reform these two blocs of Democrats frequently cooperate to form a partisan coalition ($r = .56$).

The two-dimensional representations of committee cleavages mirror the same partisan and ideological patterns in the Ninety-fifth and Ninety-sixth Congresses that existed during the earlier two Congresses (Figures 24a and 24b): committee Democrats (upper-right

TABLE 27. Factions in the House Administration Committee, 1977–1980

Committee Member	Factions		Explained Variation (%)
	1	2	
Joseph S. Ammerman (D-Pa.)	.96		98
John Brademas (D-Ind.)[a]	.95		98
Frank Thompson, Jr. (D-N.J.)[a]	.92		95
Charlie Rose (D-N.C.)	.92		90
Ed Jones (D-Tenn.)[a]	.88		87
Augustus F. Hawkins (D-Calif.)[a]	.88		91
John L. Burton (D-Calif.)	.87		87
Lionel Van Deerlin (D-Calif.)	.82		70
John H. Dent (D-Pa.)[a]	.81	(.46)	87
Edward W. Pattison (D-N.Y.)	.74		55
Joseph M. Gaydos (D-Pa.)[a]	.57	.78	94
Leon E. Panetta (D-Calif.)	.54		32
Bill Frenzel (R-Minn.)[a]	−.57	−.60	69
David Stockman (R-Mich.)	−.63	−.57	72
James C. Cleveland (R-N.H.)[a]	−.78		70
Robert E. Badham (R-Calif.)	−.88		86
Samuel L. Devine (R-Ohio)[a]	−.94		90
William L. Dickinson (R-Ala.)[a]	−.98		100
Frank Annunzio (R-Ill.)[a]		.85	84
Joseph G. Minish (D-N.J.)[a]		.83	82
Robert H. Mollohan (D-W.Va.)[a]		.79	65
Lucien Nedzi (D-Mich.)[a]		.72	59
Mendel J. Davis (D-S.C.)		.55	39

Correlates of Factional Alignment		
Presidential support	.84*	.67*
Conservative coalition	−.75*	−.58*
Party unity	.89*	.77*
ADA	.72*	.50*
COPE	.87*	.80*
CCUS	−.58*	−.38
ACA	−.77*	−.67*
Regulation of Campaigns (I)	.80*	.90*
Congressional Reforms (II)	.58*	−.27

Note: Doublet: Pattison (D-N.Y.) and Panetta (D-Calif.). Pearson correlations marked with asterisks are significant at the .01 level.
[a]Core committee member during 1973–76 committee analysis.

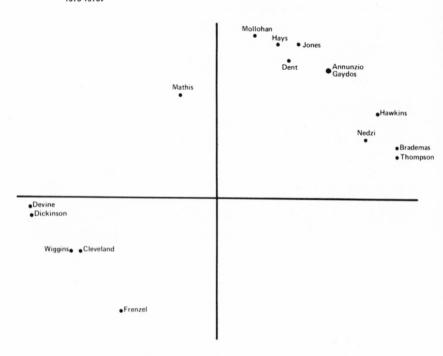

Figure 24a. Two-Dimensional Representation of Cleavages in the House Committee on House Administration: 1973-1976.

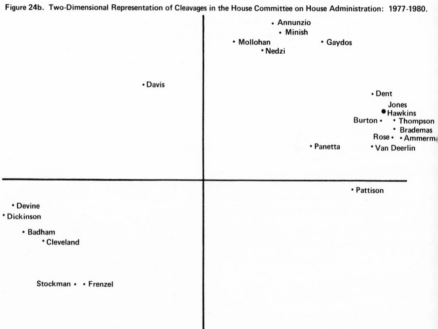

Figure 24b. Two-Dimensional Representation of Cleavages in the House Committee on House Administration: 1977-1980.

quadrant) and Republicans (lower-left quadrant) continue to cluster in diagonally opposite quadrants. Further, the ideological gulf between Democrats continues to create dispersion in the loyalties of Democratic committee members (upper-right quadrant) in the Ninety-fifth and Ninety-sixth Congresses. As in the Ninety-third and Ninety-fourth Congresses, these partisan and ideological pressures create cross-pressures on committee members. In the earlier Congresses, southern Democrat Dawson Mathis (Ga.) appears to be cross-pressured by the partisan and ideological cleavages within the committee (figure 24a); during the Carter presidency, another southern Democrat, Mendel Davis (S.C.), is faced with a similar set of cross-pressures, and his response to the countervailing pressures of ideology and party is the same as Mathis's. Thus, Davis's voting places him between the clusters of Democrats and Republicans (figure 24b). In short, party and ideology continue to create salient cleavages within the House Administration Committee.

Rules

While membership turnover on the Rules Committee has resulted in the replacement of conservative Democrats (John Young [Tex.], B.F. Sisk [Calif.], and James J. Delaney [N.Y.]) with more liberal ones (Shirley Chisholm [N.Y.], Christopher J. Dodd [Conn.], and Joe Moakley [Mass.]), the cleavages within the committee continue to follow ideological and partisan divisions. The bipolarity of Faction 1 (table 28) during the Carter presidency reflects the same partisan-ideological conflict that we observe in the committee during the Ninety-third and Ninety-fourth Congresses. Committee members with positive attachments to Faction 1 (Gillis W. Long [D-La.], Morgan F. Murphy [D-Ill.], Richard Bolling [D-Mo.], Claude Pepper [D-Fla.], and Moakley) are very supportive of the policies of the Democratic president (presidential support, $r = .91$) and the Democratic party (party unity, $r = .88$), while those with negative associations—committee Republicans Trent Lott (Miss.), Delbert L. Latta (Ohio), and James H. Quillen (Tenn.)—oppose these same policies. In the Ninety-third and Ninety-fourth Congresses, the other major committee faction represents a small bloc of relatively conservative Democrats; the replacement of conservative Democrats by liberal ones in the Ninety-fifth and Ninety-sixth Congresses appears to shift

TABLE 28. Factions in the Rules Committee, 1977–1980

Committee Member	Factions 1	Factions 2	Explained Variation (%)
Gillis W. Long (D-La.)[a]	.84		71
Morgan F. Murphy (D-Ill.)[a]	.82		70
Richard Bolling (D-Mo.)[a]	.77	(.46)	80
Claude Pepper (D-Fla.)[a]	.76		69
Joe Moakley (D-Mass.)	.73	.57	86
Trent Lott (R-Miss.)	−.65	−.51	68
Delbert L. Latta (R-Ohio)[a]	−.66	−.58	77
James H. Quillen (R-Tenn.)[a]	−.70		61
Christopher J. Dodd (D-Conn.)		.80	73
Shirley Chisholm (D-N.Y.)		.78	62

Correlates of Factional Alignments

Presidential support	.91*	.80*	
Conservative coalition	−.84*	−.95*	
Party unity	.88*	.37*	
ADA	.64	.92*	
COPE	.86*	.90*	
CCUS	−.17	−.69*	
ACA	−88*	−.87*	
Modification of Rules (I)	.77*	.93*	
Internal House Procedures (II)	.63	−.05	

Note: Pearson correlations marked with asterisks are significant at the .01 level.
[a]Core committee member during 1973–76 committee analysis.

committee Democrats to the left and also to enhance the prospects for partisan coalition building: the correlation between Factions 1 and 2 is $r = .66$.

The two-dimensional representation of committee cleavages for the 1977–80 period (figure 25b) reveals the same dominant partisan and ideological cleavages that created divisions within the committee during the Nixon-Ford period (figure 25a). Once again, committee Democrats (upper-right quadrant) and Republicans (lower-left quadrant) cluster into diagonally opposite quadrants of the space. New members Dodd and Chisholm appear to "pull" the committee Democrats to a more liberal position in the Ninety-fifth and Ninety-sixth Congresses in the same way that conservative Democrats pulled the committee to the right in the earlier Congresses. In sum, party and

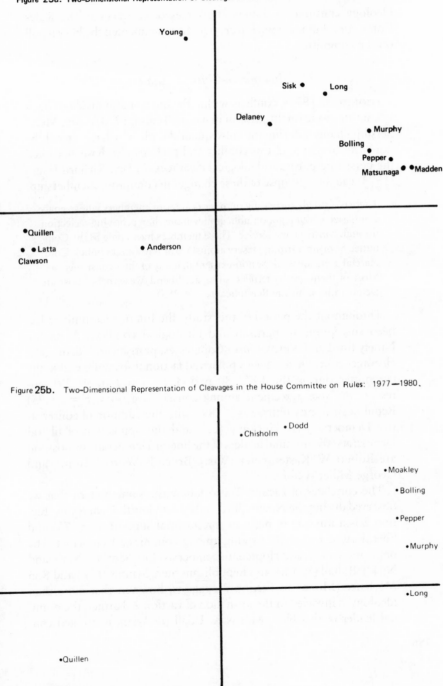

Figure 25a. Two-Dimensional Representation of Cleavages in the House Committee on Rules: 1973-1976.

Figure 25b. Two-Dimensional Representation of Cleavages in the House Committee on Rules: 1977—1980.

ideology continue as dominant sources of cleavages in the Rules Committee, but membership changes have augmented the liberal pull on the committee.

Interior and Insular Affairs

Prior to the 1970s, conflicts within the Interior and Insular Affairs Committee were rarely partisan in nature (Fenno, 1973, p. 59). Membership changes during the subsequent decade may have altered the nonpartisan nature of this conflict and perhaps also have generated the persisting partisan-ideological cleavages. In fact, Richard Fenno (1973) caught a glimpse of these changes in committee membership:

> There is a slowly increasing number of Interior members whose goals emphasize making good public policy more than achieving reelection through constituency service. These members have come to the Committee favoring a strong preservationist natural resources policy. Commercial users are weak or non-existent in many of their constituencies. Most of them are Easterners, some are liberal Westerners; most are Democratic, some are Republicans. (P. 285)

Throughout the period of this study, the Interior Committee has been susceptible to partisan and ideological conflicts. As in the Ninety-third and Ninety-fourth Congresses, partisan and ideological cleavages continue to create a polarized factional structure within the committee during the 1977–80 period. Faction 1 (table 29) represents the vote agreement among conservative (ADA, $r = -.95$) Republicans (party unity, $r = -.89$), with the addition of conservative Democrat Jerry Huckaby (La.) and the opposition of liberal Democrats; the nominal leaders of the liberal-Democratic opposition are Robert W. Kastenmeier (Wis.), Bruce F. Vento (Minn.), and George Miller (Calif.).

The correlates of Faction 2 also follow the same pattern that we observed during the Ninety-third and Ninety-fourth Congresses: Faction 2 is a mixture of partisan (presidential support, $r = .75$) and liberal (ACA, $r = -.69$) voting among committee Democrats. The opposition of prodevelopment Democrats Jim Santini (Nev.) and Nick J. Rahall (W.Va.), and Republicans Steve Symms (Ida.) and Ron Marlenee (Mont.) to Faction 2 suggests, however, that more than ideology is involved in the formation of Faction 2. Further, the nominal leader of this bloc, Morris K. Udall (D-Ariz.), is a noted con-

TABLE 29. Factions in the Interior and Insular Affairs
Committee, 1977–1980

Committee Member	Factions 1	Factions 2	Explained Variation (%)
Don Young (R-Alaska)[a]	.93	(−.41)	100
Robert J. Lagomarsino (R-Calif.)	.90		80
Manuel Lujan (R-N.Mex.)[a]	.89		80
Keith G. Sebelius (R-Kans.)[a]	.83		71
Don H. Clausen (R-Calif.)[a]	.82		79
Steve Symms (R-Idaho)[a]	.81	(−.44)	85
Dan Marriott (R-Utah)	.81		75
Mickey Edwards (R-Okla.)	.75	(−.46)	77
Abraham Kazen, Jr. (D-Tex.)	.72		58
James P. Johnson (R-Colo.)[a]	.69		55
Jerry Huckaby (D-La.)	.59		45
Ron Marlenee (R-Mont.)	.50	−.77	84
Bob Eckhardt (D-Tex.)	(−.48)		36
James J. Florio (D-N.J.)	−.57		40
Jonathan B. Bingham (D-N.Y.)[a]	−.72	.56	82
Phillip Burton (D-Calif.)[a]	−.76	.50	83
Edward J. Markey (D-Mass.)	−.78	.56	92
Peter H. Kostmayer (D-Pa.)	−.78	(.43)	80
Bob Carr (D-Mich.)	−.83		77
James Weaver (D-Oreg.)	−.84		70
John F. Seiberling (D-Ohio)[a]	−.84		79
George Miller (D-Calif.)	−.87		81
Bruce F. Vento (D-Minn.)	−.91		92
Robert W. Kastenmeier (D-Wis.)[a]	−.92		91
Jim Santini (D-Nev.)		−.74	69
Nick J. Rahall (D-W.Va.)		−.66	54
Morris K. Udall (D-Ariz.)[a]		.75	80
Philip Sharp (D-Ind.)		.72	72
Lamar Gudger (D-N.C.)		(.44)	36
Austin J. Murphy (D-Pa.)[b]			3
Correlates of Factional Alignments			
Presidential support	−.89*	.75*	
Conservative coalition	.93*	−.64*	
Party unity	−.89*	.71*	
ADA	−.95*	.64*	
COPE	−.88*	.58*	
CCUS	.68*	−.36	
ACA	.85*	−.69*	
Land Use and Water Use Regulation (I)	.98*	−.79*	

Note: Doublet: Rahall (D-W.Va.) and Murphy (D-Ha.). Pearson correlations marked
with asterisks are significant at the .01 level.
[a]Core committee member during 1973–76 committee analysis.
[b]Does not exhibit an attachment to any of the committee factions.

servationist and a staunch ally of wilderness, wildlife, and environmental protection groups. In short, Faction 2 appears to capture the same type of cleavages that divided members during the 1960s—the conflicts between conservationists and users over the commercial development of federal lands.

> Committee members want all conflicts—particularly intraconstituency or intraregional ones—to be solved before proposals are made to the Committee. But sometimes conflict outside, and cleavage inside, the Committee cannot be avoided. Quite often, as indicated earlier, such conflicts find Western-oriented clientele groups (such as users of natural resources, beneficiaries of reclamation) plus their Committee spokesmen aligned against Eastern-oriented clientele groups (such as preservationists, non-beneficiaries of reclamation) plus their Committee spokesmen. (Fenno, 1973, p. 59)

This characterization seems equally applicable in this analysis: Faction 2 (table 29) appears to reflect the disagreement between eastern conservationists and western users over mineral mining, wilderness protection, and reclamation reform (Land-Use and Water-Use Regulation). These are the types of issues that incite action by constituency groups, thereby creating constituency-interest cleavages among committee members. Since this policy conflict is intertwined with partisan (party unity, $r = -.87$) and ideological (conservative coalition, $r = .92$) loyalties, it is largely obscured by the operation of these forces. Since there is little evidence that this cleavage was salient during the Ninety-third and Ninety-fourth Congresses, it appears that the intrusion of issues related to constituency interests on the agenda of the Interior Committee has created *additional* pressures on committee members. Thus, we can add constituency interests to party and ideology as significant sources of committee cleavages in the Interior Committee. The introduction of constituency pressures into committee decision making represents an element of change in the salient cleavages within this committee that will be explored in a later section of this book.

Despite these changes, the continuity in the partisan and ideological cleavages within the committee should not be overlooked. The two-dimensional graphs (figures 26a and 26b) reveal the same patterns of partisan and ideological polarization: liberal Democrats cluster in the upper-left quadrant, while conservative Democrats (Santini, Rahall, and Huckaby in figure 26b) and Republicans oc-

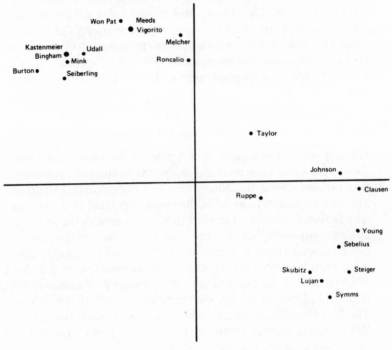

Figure 26a. Two-Dimensional Representation of Cleavages in the House Committee on Interior and Insular Affairs: 1973-1976.

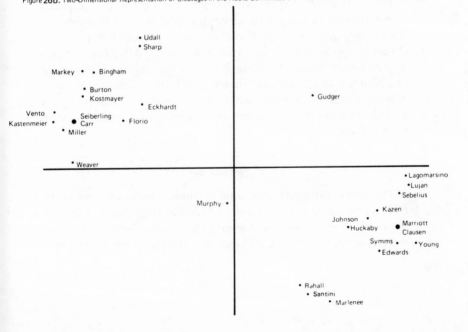

Figure 26b. Two-Dimensional Representation of Cleavages in the House Committee on Interior and Insular Affairs: 1977-1980.

cupy the lower-right quadrant. This pattern tends to characterize committees in which partisan and ideological conflicts are quite intense. While party and ideology continue as sources of cleavages among Interior Committee members, the introduction of constituency-interest pressures on committee members suggests there are other sources of potential fragmentation within the committee's environment.

Interstate and Foreign Commerce

The partisan-ideological polarization of Interstate and Foreign Commerce Committee members during the Nixon-Ford administration persists during the Ninety-fifth and Ninety-sixth Congresses. This polarization is reflected in the strong bipolarity of the committee's factional structure. Faction 1 (table 30) captures the agreement among conservative Republicans (ADA, $r = -.96$) and the conservative Democrat David E. Satterfield III (Va.), and the equally strong opposition from liberal Democrats with nominal leaders Edward J. Markey (Mass.), Andrew Maguire (N.J.), Henry A. Waxman (Calif.), Richard L. Ottinger (N.Y.), and Anthony "Toby" Moffett (Conn.). The less liberal committee Democrats join Harley Staggers (D-W.Va.), the committee chairman, to form the equally partisan block of Democrats (party unity, $r = .92$) in Faction 2.

The partisan-ideological polarization is evident in the graphical representation of committee cleavages: conservative Republicans (lower-right quadrant) and liberal Democrats (upper-left quadrant) cluster in opposite quadrants of the graph (figure 27b). These cleavage patterns are similar to those that existed during the Ninety-third and Ninety-fourth Congresses (figure 27a). Hence, there is a great deal of continuity in the cleavages within the Commerce Committee: party and ideology continue to create conflict among Commerce Committee members.

Judiciary

The dominant sources of conflict among Judiciary Committee Democrats continue to be party and ideology: Faction 1 (table 31) represents the vote agreement among Democratic liberals (conservative coalition, $r = -.89$), and Faction 2 represents the alignment of

TABLE 30. Factions in the Interstate and Foreign Commerce
Committee, 1977–1980

Committee Member	Factions		Explained Variation (%)
	1	2	
Clarence J. Brown (R-Ohio)[a]	.91		89
Samuel L. Devine (R-Ohio)[a]	.88		89
Carlos J. Moorhead (R-Calif.)	.86		77
James T. Broyhill (R-N.C.)[a]	.85		80
David E. Satterfield III (D-Va.)[a]	.85		81
David Stockman (R-Mich.)	.84		85
James M. Collins (R-Tex.)[a]	.84		86
Norman F. Lent (R-N.Y.)[a]	.79		64
Edward R. Madigan (R-Ill.)	.74		59
Tim Lee Carter (R-Ky.)[a]	.63		40
Marc L. Marks (R-Pa.)	.51		27
Albert Gore, Jr. (D-Tenn.)	−.52	.51	53
Barbara A. Mikulski (D-Md.)	−.55	.60	67
Doug Walgren (D-Va.)	−.68	(.44)	66
James J. Florio (D-N.J.)	−.73	(.44)	73
Bob Eckhardt (D-Tex.)[a]	−.75		71
Anthony "Toby" Moffett (D-Conn.)	−.80	(.42)	82
Richard L. Ottinger (D-N.Y.)	−.80	(.49)	88
Henry A. Waxman (D-Calif.)	−.82		77
Andrew Maguire (D-N.J.)	−.84		77
Edward J. Markey (D-Mass.)	−.86		85
Harley O. Staggers (D-W. Va.)[a]		.84	76
Richardson Preyer (D-N.C.)[a]		.67	45
Lionel Van Deerlin (D-Calif.)[a]		.62	47
John D. Dingell (D-Mich.)[a]		.53	30
Thomas A. Luken (D-Ohio)		.51	45
Timothy E. Wirth (D-Colo.)		(.41)	32
Philip Sharp (D-Ind.)		(.39)	19

Correlates of Factional Alignments		
Presidential support	−.89*	.88*
Conservative coalition	.95*	−.79*
Party unity	−.94*	.92*
ADA	−.96*	.76*
COPE	−.93*	.89*
CCUS	.67*	−.51*
ACA	.93*	−.90*
Energy and Health Care Costs (I)	−.91*	.93*

Note: Pearson correlations marked with asterisks are significant at the .01 level.
[a]Core committee member during 1973–76 committee analysis.

Figure 27a. Two-Dimensional Representation of Cleavages in the House Committee on Interstate and Foreign Commerce: 1973-1976.

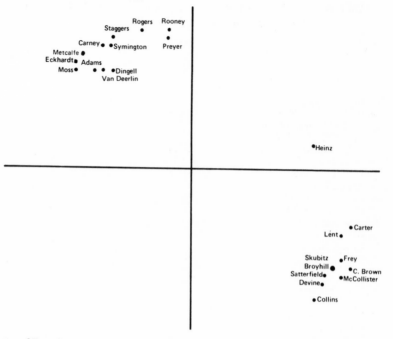

Figure 27b. Two-Dimensional Representation of Cleavages in the House Committee on Interstate and Foreign Commerce: 1977-1980.

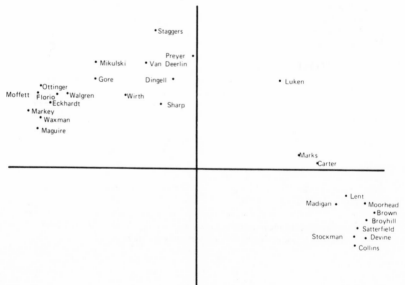

TABLE 31. Factions in the Judiciary Committee, 1977–1980

Committee Member	Factions			Explained Variation (%)
	1	2	3	
Elizabeth Holtzman (D-N.Y.)[a]	.88			82
Robert F. Dirnan (D-Mass.)[a]	.87			76
Herbert E. Harris II (D-Va.)	.83			69
Don Edwards (D-Calif.)[a]	.80			74
John F. Seiberling (D-Ohio)[a]	.73			73
John Conyers, Jr. (D-Mich.)[a]	.72			72
George E. Danielson (D-Calif.)[a]	.71			51
Peter W. Rodino, Jr. (D-N.J.)[a]	.70			74
Robert W. Kastenmeier (D-Wis.)[a]	.69			63
Carlos J. Moorhead (R-Calif.)[a]	−.50	.68		73
M. Caldwell Butler (R-Va.)[a]	−.53	.63		72
John M. Ashbrook (R-Ohio)	−.64	.59		81
Harold S. Sawyer (R-Mich.)		.82		68
Henry J. Hyde (R-Ill.)[a]		.80		74
Hamilton Fish, Jr. (R-N.Y.)[a]		.77		62
Tom Railsback (R-Ill.)[a]		.73		56
Robert McClory (R-Ill.)[a]		.59		58
Thomas N. Kindness (R-Ohio)		.50		43
Lamar Gudger (D-N.C.)			.60	36
Sam B. Hall, Jr. (D-Tex.)			.57	45
Jack Brooks (D-Tex.)[a]			.54	31
William J. Hughes (D-N.J.)[a]			.52	31
Romano L. Mazzoli (D-Ky.)			(.44)	20
Harold L. Volkmer (D-Mo.)[b]				2

Correlates of Factional Alignments			
Presidential support	.70*	−.59*	.06
Conservative coalition	−.89*	.74*	.06
Party unity	.79*	−.83*	.19
ADA	.86*	−.70*	−.08
COPE	.89*	−.83*	.01
CCUS	−.60*	.61*	.17
ACA	−.82*	.84*	−.15
Ethics in Government (I)	.67*	−.83*	.25
Additional Judges (II)	−.14	−.30	.87*
Individual's Rights	.41	−.37	.01

Note: Doublets: Brooks (D-Tex.) and Hall (D-Tex.); Mazzoli (D-Ky.) and Volkmer (D-Mo.). Pearson correlations marked with asterisks are significant at the .01 level.
[a]Core committee member during 1973–76 committee analysis.
[b]Does not exhibit an attachment to any of the committee factions.

conservative (ACA, $r = .84$) Republicans. The nominal leaders of the liberal supporters in Faction 1 are Elizabeth Holtzman (D-N.Y.), Robert F. Drinan (D-Mass.), Herbert E. Harris II (D-Va.), and Don Edwards (D-Calif.); Faction 2 is led by conservative Republicans Carlos J. Moorhead (Calif.) and M. Caldwell Butler (Va.). The remaining voting bloc, Faction 3, represents the rather unique voting behavior of two doublets (Jack Brooks [D-Tex.] and Sam B. Hall, Sr. [D-Tex.]; Romano L. Mazzoli [D-Ky.] and Harold L. Volkmer [D-Mo.]); the only distinguishing correlate of this faction is its opposition to Republican attempts to obtain federal judgeships for their states and congressional districts (Additional Judges, $r = .87$). We find that there is less diffusion in the loyalties of committee Democrats during the Carter years than during the 1973–76 period.

Some of the conflict between committee Democrats dissipates with the disappearance of gun control as a salient source of policy conflict and the election of a Democratic president during the Ninety-fifth and Ninety-sixth Congresses. The result is a far greater partisan and ideological polarization in the loyalties of committee Democrats during the Ninety-fifth and Ninety-sixth Congresses than in the Ninety-third and Ninety-fourth Congresses. This increased polarization is evident in the two-dimensional representations of the major committee cleavages between 1973 and 1980. In the Ninety-third and Ninety-fourth Congresses (figure 28a), there was a great deal of dispersion in the ideological and partisan sympathies of committee members, especially committee Democrats. The tight clustering of committee Democrats (figure 28b) in the lower-right quadrant, diagonally opposite committee Republicans, suggests that Democratic loyalties have become more polarized during the Ninety-fifth and Ninety-sixth Congresses. Although party and ideology persist as sources of cleavages in the Judiciary Committee, there is evidence that the factional structure may have become more polarized during the Ninety-fifth and Ninety-sixth Congresses.

Merchant Marine and Fisheries

Too few roll-call votes in the Merchant Marine and Fisheries Committee during the Ninety-third and Ninety-fourth Congresses prohibit examination of the cleavages within the committee during the 1973–76 period; however, the increase in votes taken during the

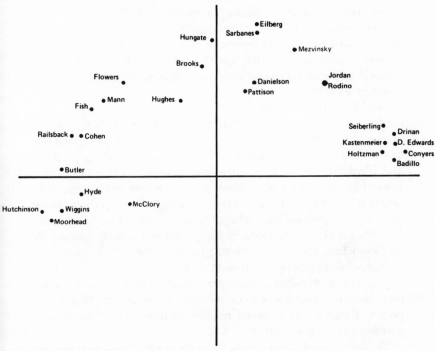

Figure 28a. Two-Dimensional Representation of Cleavages in the House Committee on Judiciary: 1973-1976.

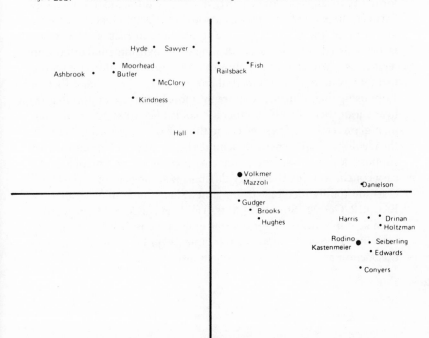

Figure 28b. Two-Dimensional Representation of Cleavages in the House Committee on Judiciary: 1977-1980.

committee's deliberations in the Ninety-fifth and Ninety-sixth Congresses permit analysis of its factional structure during this latter period. Therefore, our discussion of cleavages within the Merchant Marine Committee will concentrate on describing these cleavages, rather than discussing the continuity and change in the dimensions of committee conflict.

The Merchant Marine Committee is similar to other constituency-oriented committees in that there seems to be some disagreement among committee members about the treatment that constituencies and groups receive. Committee members also divide along partisan and ideological lines. Committee partisanship is captured by the strong bipolarity of Faction 1 (table 32): committee Democrats, with nominal leader James L. Oberstar (D-Minn.), are frequently opposed by an equally partisan bloc of Republicans, led by David F. Emery (R-Maine) and Thomas B. Evans (R-Del.). Faction 1 is fairly partisan in its Democratic loyalties as reflected by its support of the president (presidential support, $r = .54$) and the Democratic party (party unity, $r = .63$) on matters before the committee. This bloc also follows the party line in opposing attacks on the administration's Panama Canal policy (Panama Canal Treaty Implementation, $r = .58$)—a very partisan issue (party unity, $r = .81$).

The failure of Faction 1 to vote with other Democrats (Faction 2) to form a partisan coalition is partly due to the differences in ideology between these two Democratic factions. The Democrats in Faction 2 are far more liberal (ADA, $r = .72$) than those in Faction 1. The two factions also divide over issues dealing with environmental protection regulations, with Faction 2 supporting measures to protect environmental resources (Environmental Protection, $r = -.68$) and Faction 1 opposing them. Further, some of the more liberal committee Republicans join their liberal Democratic colleagues to support environmental protections. These facts and the lack of a relationship between the ideological differences of members (ACA, ADA) and opposition (or support) for environmental concerns prevent the acceptance of the easy conclusion that the policy differences among committee Democrats are totally ideological in nature. Since the nominal leaders of Faction 2, Gerry E. Studds (D-Mass.) and Les AuCoin (D-Oreg.), have been actively involved in promoting environmental protection issues, and since Faction 2 supports environmental policies, we characterize this faction as a bloc of environmentalists.

TABLE 32. Factions in the Merchant Marine and Fisheries
Committee, 1977–1980

Committee Member	Factions		Explained
	1	*2*	*Variation (%)*
James L. Oberstar (D-Minn.)	.87		76
Daniel K. Akaka (D-Hawaii)	.81		67
John M. Murphy (D-N.Y.)	.81		67
Glenn M. Anderson (D-Calif.)	.79		63
David R. Bowen (D-Miss.)	.79		64
Mario Biaggi (D-N.Y.)	.74		56
John D. Dingell (D-Mich.)	.60		37
John B. Breaux (D-La.)	(.40)		16
Don Young (R-Alaska)	(−.44)		32
Paul N. McCloskey (R-Calif.)	(−.44)		21
Paul S. Trible (R-Va.)	−.54		30
Joel Pritchard (R-Wash.)	−.55		34
Norman F. Lent (R-N.Y.)	−.56	−.57	64
Thomas B. Evans (R-Del.)	−.83		69
David F. Emery (R-Maine)	−.89		82
Carroll Hubbard, Jr. (D-Ky.)		(−.44)	31
Edwin B. Forsythe (R-N.J.)		−.69	57
Gerry E. Studds (D-Mass.)		.89	86
Les AuCoin (D-Oreg.)		.85	73
Barbara A. Mikulski (D-Md.)		.83	72
David E. Bonior (D-Mich.)		.82	67
Norman E. D'Amours (D-N.H.)		.55	30
William J. Hughes (D-N.J.)		(.45)	20

Correlates of Factional Alignment		
Presidential support	.54*	.76*
Conservative coalition	−.37	−.67*
Party unity	.63*	.71*
ADA	.12	.72*
COPE	.60*	.49*
CCUS	−.36	−.58*
ACA	−.64*	−.65*
Panama Canal Treaty Implementation (I)	.58*	.63*
Environmental Protection (II)	.62*	−.68*
Shipping U.S. Oil Imports on U.S. Flagships (III)	.41	.24

Note: Doublet: D'Amours (D-N.H.) and Hughes (D-N.J.). Pearson correlations
marked with asterisks are significant at the .01 level.

The two-dimensional representation of committee cleavages reveals the partisan splits between Democrats and Republicans, and the ideological and policy division among Democrats; the ideological conflict results in diffuse clusters of Democrats and Republicans (Figure 29). The less-liberal Democrats like John M. Murphy (N.Y.), Glenn M. Anderson (Calif.), and David R. Bowen (Miss.) are located at the end of the horizontal axis (right side of graph), while environmentalist Democrats (Studds, David E. Bonior [Mich.], AuCoin, and Barbara A. Mikulski [Md.]) form an independent cluster at the top of the vertical axis. Committee Republicans are spread across the lower-left quadrant, indicating some potential cracks in Republican cohesion. This factional configuration closely resembles the partisan and ideological cleavages on the Public Works Committee, where ideological differences also create divisions among Democrats. Party, ideology, and constituency interests appear to be the major sources of cleavages among members of the Merchant Marine and Fisheries Committee.

Public Works and Transportation

During the Ninety-third and Ninety-fourth Congresses, cleavages within the Public Works Committee were largely partisan in nature; however, we suggested that some ideological voting may also be present. In the Ninety-fifth and Ninety-sixth Congresses, party remains a dominant source of committee cleavages, but ideological conflict is far more salient. Faction 1 represents a bloc of partisan (party unity, $r = .68$) Democrats, and Faction 2 reflects the organization of committee Republicans (table 33). Democrats and Republicans divide over a traditional partisan issue—the role and authority of the federal government. Democrats (Faction 1) tend to support federal involvement in setting transportation policy (Transportation Policy, $r = .88$) while Republicans (Faction 2) oppose such involvement (Transportation Policy, $r = -.87$). This is a very partisan issue within the committee (party unity, $r = .83$), and it is the same policy cleavage that James Murphy (1974) had observed in his study of the Public Works Committee during the 1960s.

Membership changes in the committee—the addition of several liberal Democrats (David E. Bonior [Mich.], Robert W. Edgar [Pa.], Norman Y. Mineta [Calif.], Henry J. Nowak [N.Y.], and Jerome A.

Figure 29 Two-Dimensional Representation of Cleavages in the House Committee on Merchant Marine and Fisheries: 1977-1980.

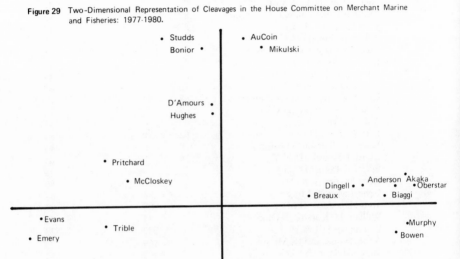

TABLE 33. Factions in the Public Works and Transportation Committee, 1977–1980

Committee Member	Factions			Explained Variation (%)
	1	2	3	
Harold T. Johnson (D-Calif.)[a]	.91			88
Nick J. Rahall (D-W.Va.)	.88			82
Marilyn Lloyd Bouquard (D-Tenn.)	.87			82
John B. Breaux (D-La.)[a]	.87			84
Robert A. Roe (D-N.J.)[a]	.87			85
Mike McCormack (D-Wash.)[a]	.87			85
James J. Howard (D-N.J.)[a]	.82			68
Robert A. Young (D-Mo.)	.80			75
Ray Roberts (D-Tex.)[a]	.72			67
Glenn M. Anderson (D-Calif.)[a]	.68	−.55		77
Douglas Applegate (D-Ohio)	.67			48
Allen E. Ertel (D-Pa.)	.67			55
John G. Fary (D-Ill.)	.62	−.50		64
James L. Oberstar (D-Minn.)	.58			44
Henry J. Nowak (D-N.Y.)	.54		−.58	68
Billy Lee Evans (D-Ga.)	(.47)			38
Gene Snyder (R-Ky.)[a]		.90		83
Gene Taylor (R-Mo.)[a]		.86		85
Tom Hagedorn (R-Minn.)		.85		85
William H. Harsha (R-Ohio)[a]		.85		75
Bud Shuster (R-Pa.)[a]		.82		73
Arlan Stangeland (R-Minn.)		.64	.57	73
James Abdnor (R-S.D.)[a]		.63	(.46)	61
Barry M. Goldwater, Jr. (R-Calif.)		.62		57
Bob Livingston (R-La.)		.56	.51	58
David E. Bonior (D-Mich.)			−.93	96
Robert W. Edgar (D-Pa.)			−.87	82
Norman Y. Mineta (D-Calif.)			−.74	76
Jerome A. Ambro (D-N.Y.)			−.67	75
Elliot H. Levitas (D-Ga.)	(.34)	(−.36)	(−.35)	37
John P. Hammerschmidt (R-Ark.)[a]			.78	76
Don H. Clausen (R-Calif.)[a]			.57	65
Ronnie G. Flippo (D-Ala.)			.56	43

Correlates of Factional Alignments			
Presidential support	.63*	−.85*	−.67*
Conservative coalition	−.48*	.77*	.72*
Party unity	.68*	−.87*	−.64*
ADA	.43*	−.72*	−.70*
COPE	.68*	−.79*	−.69*
CCUS	−.45*	.65*	.61*
ACA	−.66*	.82*	.62*
Transportation Policy (I)	.88*	−.87*	−.54*
Regulation (II)	−.34	−.35	−.62*

Note: Doublet: Applegate (D-Ohio) and Evans (D-Ga.). Pearson correlations marked with asterisks are significant at the .01 level.

[a] Core committee member during 1973–76 committee analysis.

Ambro [N.Y.])—have intensified liberal-conservative antagonisms between committee Democrats. This bloc of liberals frequently opposes the positions of conservative Republicans (conservative coalition, $r = .72$) with nominal leader John P. Hammerschmidt (R-Ark.); this pattern produces the bipolarity in Faction 3. The conservatives aligned with Faction 3 are also strong opponents of federal regulations (Regulation, $r = -.62$), whereas committee liberals support such federal prohibitions.

The impact that this influx of liberal Democrats has had on committee cleavages is evident in a comparison of the cleavages during the 1973–80 period. In the Ninety-third and Ninety-fourth Congresses, a liberal doublet (Bella Abzug [N.Y.] and Studds) anchored the left end of the horizontal axis, and the conservative Republicans clustered at the right-end of the same axis (figure 30a); the remaining Democrats clustered between these polar ideological positions. The influx of liberal Democrats into the committee during the Ninety-fifth and Ninety-sixth Congresses reduces the cohesiveness of committee Democrats; hence, there is less clustering of Democrats during the latter two Congresses (figure 30b) than in the earlier two (figure 30a). The sympathies of committee Democrats are now spread across the entire upper-left quadrant (figure 30b). It seems reasonable to attribute the diffusion of Democratic loyalties to the impact of ideology, because the addition of several liberal Democrats has intensified ideological conflicts by strengthening liberal influence in committee decision making. As a result, ideological differences among committee members are far more salient in the Ninety-fifth and Ninety-sixth Congresses.

Science and Technology

During the Ninety-third and Ninety-fourth Congresses, partisan and ideological cleavages characterized the policy conflicts within the Science and Technology Committee. The major controversy between Democrats and Republicans, and among Democrats, dealt with the relative emphasis that the Department of Energy should place on research into synthetic and fossil fuels. Committee liberals favored fossil fuel programs, and conservatives supported synthetic fuel research and production. In the Ninety-fifth and Ninety-sixth Congresses, a closely related ideological issue surfaces—the development

211

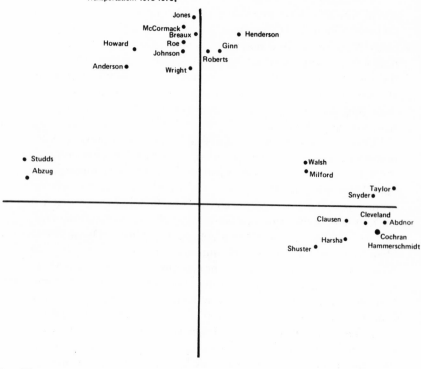

Figure 30a. Two-Dimensional Representation of Cleavages in the House Committee on Public Works and Transportation: 1973-1976.

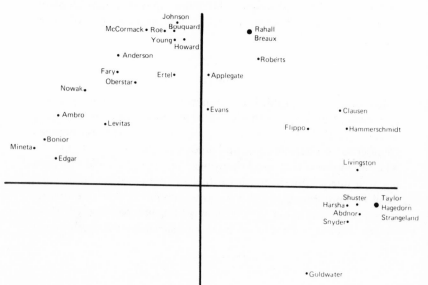

Figure 30b. Two-Dimensional Representation of Cleavages in the House Committee on Public Works and Transportation: 1977–1980.

and production of nuclear energy—which replaces the controversy over synthetic and fossil fuel research as the most divisive issue within the committee. The opposition of liberal Democrats to the attempts of conservatives to expand our nuclear energy capabilities (nuclear research) creates divisions among committee Democrats.

The conservative (ACA, $r = .85$) Republicans in Faction 1 (table 34) find supporters among two Democratic factions in fending off liberal attempts to curtail nuclear energy programs and policies: Factions 2 (Nuclear Research, $r = .48$) and 3 (Nuclear Research, $r = .74$) support Republican efforts to advance nuclear energy research. Most of the Democratic opposition to Faction 1 comes from liberal members of the Energy Development and Applications Subcommittee (Richard L. Ottinger [N.Y.], James J. Blanchard [Mich.], Doug Walgren [Pa.], and Dan Glickman [Kans.]); the nominal leaders of the Republican opposition to Faction 1 are the minority members of the same subcommittee (Robert K. Dornan [Calif.], Robert S. Walker [Pa.], and John W. Wydler [N.Y.]). This subcommittee has generally supported the development of energy alternatives to nuclear power.

Factions 2 and 3 are also supportive of nuclear energy research, but Faction 2 is less intense in its emphasis on such research. In addition, the members of Faction 2 (Wes Watkins [D-Okla.], Jim Lloyd [D-Calif.], Albert Gore, Jr. [D-Tenn.], and Jerome A. Ambro [D-N.Y.]) generally support the development of other sources of fuel and energy (Alternative Technologies Research, $r = -.77$)—programs opposed by most committee Republicans (Faction 1, Alternative Technologies Research, $r = .66$). The members of Faction 3, with nominal leaders Mike McCormack (D-Wash.), Harold C. Hollenbeck (R-N.J.), and Marilyn Lloyd Bouquard (D-Tenn.), are more supportive of nuclear energy research, and most are members of the energy subcommittee with jurisdiction over nuclear energy programs—Energy Research and Production Subcommittee; this bloc frequently votes with the conservative Republicans in Faction 1 ($r = .54$).

In the Ninety-third and Ninety-fourth Congresses, such energy-policy conflicts were exacerbated by the jurisdictions of the energy subcommittees, as each subcommittee leader (Ken Hechler [D-W.Va.] and McCormack) mobilized support for specific energy programs to solve our energy needs. This pattern appears to continue during the Carter years, as subcommittee leaders Ottinger and McCormack take up the fight over the development of nuclear energy.

TABLE 34. Factions in the Science and Technology Committee, 1977–1980

Committee Member	Factions 1	2	3	4	Explained Variation (%)
Robert K. Dornan (R-Calif.)	.95				99
Robert S. Walker (R-Pa.)	.91				87
John W. Wydler (R-N.Y.)	.85				88
Barry M. Goldwater, Jr. (R-Calif.)[a]	.78				70
Manuel Lujan (R-N.Mex.)	.77				72
Edwin B. Forsythe (R-N.J.)	.73		.57		93
Larry Winn (R-Kans.)	.72				74
Harold C. Hollenbeck (R-N.J.)	.59		.71		90
James J. Blanchard (D-Mich.)	−.55			.62	80
Dan Glickman (D-Kans.)	−.62				56
George E. Brown, Jr. (D-Calif.)[a]	−.84				73
Tom Harkin (D-Iowa)[a]	−.89				89
Richard L. Ottinger (D-N.Y.)[a]	−.93				87
Doug Walgren (D-Pa.)	−1.00				100
Wes Watkins (D-Okla.)		.90			92
Jim Lloyd (D-Calif.)[a]		.83			78
Albert Gore, Jr. (D-Tenn.)		.72	.59		87
Jerome A. Ambro (D-N.Y.)[a]		.65			54
Mike McCormack (D-Wash.)[a]		(.44)	.73		75
Marilyn Lloyd Bouquard (D-Tenn.)[a]			.68		86
Don Fuqua (D-Fla.)[a]				.83	73
Ronnie G. Flippo (D-Ala.)				.81	84
Hamilton Fish (R-N.Y.)		−.60		.60	88

Correlates of Factional Alignments

	1	2	3	4
Presidential support	−.86*	.32	−.23	.15
Conservative coalition	.73*	.13	.26	.13
Party unity	−.86*	.36	−.19	.17
ADA	−.77*	−.11	−.30	−.10
COPE	−.71*	.20	.00	.04
CCUS	.67*	−.18	.11	−.01
ACA	.85*	−.25	.22	−.17
Nuclear Research (I)	.71*	.48*	.74*	−.12
Alternative Technologies Research (II)	.66*	−.77*	.06	−.21

Note: Pearson correlations marked with asterisks are significant at the .01 level.
[a]Core committee member during 1973–76 committee analysis.

The remaining faction (Faction 4) is a minor bloc led by conservative southern Democrats Don Fuqua (D-Fla.) and Ronnie G. Flippo (D-Ala.).

The ideological and partisan dispersion in the commitments of committee members that we observed in the Ninety-third and Ninety-fourth Congresses continues during the Carter years, as committee members appear to span the entire ideological and partisan spectrum (figure 31b). The ideological nature of the major policy cleavages in the committee—nuclear power—may be partially responsible for the dispersion in partisan loyalties. This could explain the positioning (figure 31b) of southern Democrats Flippo, Fuqua, Watkins, Gore, and Bouquard between the clusters of liberal Democrats (left end of horizontal axis) and conservative Republicans (right end of horizontal axis). The location of these conservative Democrats may reflect the conflicting pressures of ideology and party that frequently cross-pressure southern Democrats and liberal Republicans (congressmen with partisan and ideological loyalties that are atypical of the majority of their party colleagues).

STABILITY AND CHANGE IN EXECUTIVE-BRANCH PRESSURES

During the Ninety-third and Ninety-fourth Congresses, the executive branch is a major source of cleavages in five committees: Appropriations, Armed Services, Foreign Affairs, Post Office and Civil Service, and Ways and Means. These committees exhibit factions that result from the interest of the president and/or the executive agencies in the policies handled by the committee. In most instances, the interest of the president is predictable, since these committees have historically dealt with important executive functions (foreign affairs, national defense, taxes, agency expenditures). That is, the jurisdictional responsibilities of these committees touch upon important executive-branch prerogatives, and therefore, they elicit the interest and the pressures of the president and the executive agencies. Occasionally a committee that does not normally deal with issues that attract the attention of the president will find itself the target of executive-branch pressures because issues important to the president

215

Figure 31a. Two-Dimensional Representation of Cleavages in the House Committee on Science and Technology: 1973-1976.

Figure 31b. Two-Dimensional Representation of Cleavages in the House Committee on Science and Technology: 1977-1980.

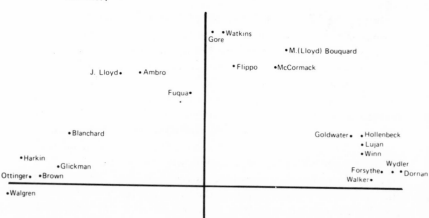

become matters requiring committee decisions. This explains the influence of the executive branch in the formation of cleavages in the Post Office Committee in the Ninety-third and Ninety-fourth Congresses. Since the chief executive continues to maintain interest in the policies handled by the Appropriations, Armed Services, Post Office, and Ways and Means committees, executive-branch pressures persist in these committees. (Too few votes were taken in the Foreign Affairs Committee to allow analysis during this period.)

Appropriations

Cleavages within the Appropriations Committee are stable throughout the period of our study: partisan, ideological, and executive-branch pressures continue to create divisions within the committee. Faction 1 (table 35) represents the vote agreement among liberal (conservative coalition, $r = -.88$), partisan (party unity, $r = .83$) Democrats with nominal leaders Sidney R. Yates (Ill.), David R. Obey (Wis.), and Robert N. Giaimo (Conn.); this bloc is frequently opposed by conservative Democrats (Tom Bevill [Ala.] and Bill Chappell, Jr. [Fla.]) and Republicans, with J. Kenneth Robinson (Va.) as the nominal leader of the opposition. Faction 2 represents a more moderate bloc of Republicans: Ralph S. Regula (Ohio), Lawrence Coughlin (Pa.), George M. O'Brien (Ill.), Jack Edwards (Ala.), and Silvio O. Conte (Mass.). The composition of these two factions mirrors the partisan and ideological pressures that operate on committee members.

The influence of the executive branch on committee cleavages is captured in the formation of blocs of administration and agency supporters. Faction 3 (table 35) represents a bloc that supports the administration's position on the Defense budget (Reducing Military Procurements, $r = .36$); this faction has the support of the leaders of the two subcommittees that deal with defense-related expenditures— Joseph P. Addabbo (D-N.Y.; Defense) and K. Gunn McKay (D-Utah; Military Construction).

Faction 4 represents an alignment of agency supporters, most of whom are also subcommittee leaders: Tom Bevill (D-Ala.; Energy and Water Development), John J. McFall (D-Calif.; Transportation), Clarence D. Long (D-Md.; Foreign Operations), Tom Steed (D-Okla.; Treasury-Postal Service-General Government), Jamie L. Whit-

TABLE 35. Factions in the Appropriations Committee, 1977–1980

Committee Member	Factions 1	2	3	4	5	Explained Variation (%)
Sidney R. Yates (D-Ill.)[a]	.98					98
David R. Obey (D-Wis.)[a]	.97					96
Robert N. Giaimo (D-Conn.)[a]	.97					100
Louis Stokes (D-Ohio)	.91					87
Frank E. Evans (D-Colo.)[a]	.77					77
Edward J. Patten (D-N.J.)[a]	.75		(−.45)			82
Edward P. Boland (D-Mass.)[a]	.69					75
Bob Traxler (D-Mich.)	.69					72
George H. Mahon (D-Tex.)[a]	.55					78
Joseph D. Early (D-Mass.)	.50				.62	68
Tom Bevill (D-Ala.)[a]	(−.48)			(.43)		65
Elford A. Cederberg (R-Mich.)[a]	−.68	.62				96
Robert H. Michel (R-Ill.)[a]	−.78					80
Bill Chappell, Jr. (D-Fla.)[a]	−.79					73
Clarence E. Miller (R-Ohio)[a]	−.80					82
Jack R. Kemp (R-N.Y.)	−.85					98
Clair W. Burgener (R-Calif.)	−.90					92
John T. Myers (R-Ind.)[a]	−.92					87
Virginia Smith (R-Nebr.)	−.93					92
C.W. Bill Young (R-Fla.)	−.94					93
J. Kenneth Robinson (R-Va.)[a]	−.97					96
Edward R. Roybal (D-Calif.)[a]		−.58		(.45)		81
Ralph S. Regula (R-Ohio)		.74				65
Lawrence Coughlin (R-Pa.)[a]		.68				48
George M. O'Brien (R-Ill.)		.57				75
Jack Edwards (R-Ala.)[a]		.55				40
Silvio O. Conte (R-Mass.)[a]	(.48)	.55				63
Charles Wilson (D-Tex.)		(.41)	−.77			81
K. Gunn McKay (D-Utah)[a]		.67				53
Joseph M. McDade (R-Pa.)		(.44)	.64			69
Joseph P. Addabbo (D-N.Y.)[a]			.59			40
Bill Alexander (D-Ark.)			(.47)			39
John J. McFall (D-Calif.)[a]				.86		78
Norman D. Dicks (D-Wash.)				.68		79
Clarence D. Long (D-Md.)[a]				.64		62
Corrine Boggs (D-La.)				.62		80
Tom Steed (D-Okla.)[a]				.55		33
Jamie L. Whitten (D-Miss.)[a]				.51		67
William H. Natcher (D-Ky.)[a]				(.49)	(.49)	63
Robert Duncan (D-Oreg.)					−.54	55
Bill D. Burlison (D-Mo.)[a]					.80	67
Adam Benjamin, Jr. (D-Ind.)					(.45)	37

TABLE 35. Continued

Committee Member	Factions					Explained
	1	2	3	4	5	Variation (%)

Correlates of Factional Alignments

Committee Member	1	2	3	4	5	
Presidential support	.85*	−.41*	−.01	.37*	.31	
Conservative coalition	−.88*	.36*	−.17	−.19	−.13	
Party unity	.83*	−.52*	.02	.36*	.31	
ADA	.79*	−.33	.18	.22	.20	
COPE	.78*	−.43*	.14	.23	.18	
CCUS	−.72*	.37*	−.03	−.23	−.20	
ACA	−.83*	.46*	−.12	−.34*	.28	
Reducing Military Procurements (I)	.59*	.19	.36*	−.53*	.16	
Reducing Agency Appropriatrions (II)	.61*	−.75*	.10	.57*	.25	

Note: Doublets: Whitten (D-Miss.) and Bevill (D-Ala.); Benjamin (D-Ind.) and Duncan (D-Oreg.); Steed (D-Okla.) and Edwards (R-Ala.). Pearson correlations marked with asterisks are significant at the .01 level.
[a]Core committee member during 1973–76 committee analysis.

ten (D-Miss.; Agriculture, Rural Development, and Related Agencies), and William H. Natcher (D-Ky.; Labor and Health, Education, and Welfare). The norm of "subcommittee reciprocity" may be the vehicle by which these subcommittee leaders generate support for their favorite agencies—that is, those agencies within the jurisdiction of their individual subcommittees. For whatever reason, the members of this faction mobilize to defend agency appropriations (Reducing Agency Appropriations, $r = .57$), especially from Republican attacks (Faction 2, Reducing Agency Appropriations, $r = −.75$). The persistence of factions composed of subcommittee leaders provides evidence of the stability of executive-branch pressures on committee members. The remaining faction (Faction 5) is a moderate bloc of Democrats (Bill D. Burlison [Mo.], Joseph D. Early [Mass.], and Adam Benjamin, Jr. [Ind.]), who vote, to some extent, with the liberal Democrats in Faction 1 ($r = .32$) to form a partisan coalition.

The continuity in the cleavage patterns within the committee is reflected in the two-dimensional representations of the major dimensions of committee conflict (figures 32a and 32b). During the Ninety-third and Ninety-fourth Congresses, we observed a wide dispersion in

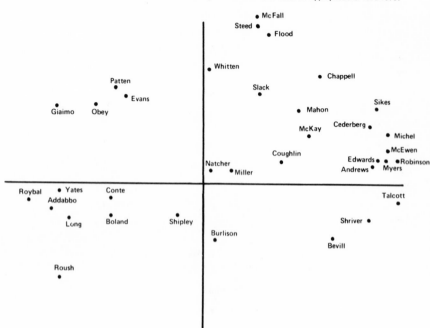

Figure 32a. Two-Dimensional Representation of Cleavages in the House Committee on Appropriations: 1973-1976.

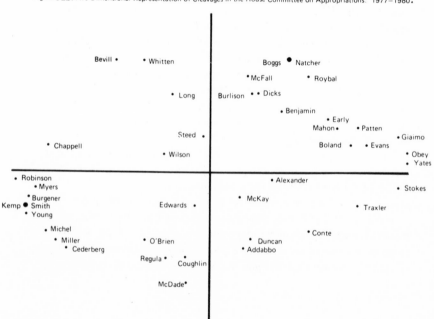

Figure 32b. Two-Dimensional Representation of Cleavages in the House Committee on Appropriations: 1977–1980.

partisan loyalties. While some conservative Democrats (George Mahon [Tex.], McKay, McFall, and Natcher) have moved closer to their Democratic colleagues and farther from the core of Republican support, the diffusion in partisan loyalties persists during the Ninety-fifth and Ninety-sixth Congresses. As in the earlier period, liberal Democrats (right end of horizontal axis) and conservative Republicans (left end of horizontal axis) anchor the ideological extremes of the vote space; the remaining committee members fall between these polar positions.

Armed Services

Partisan pressures had little impact on the formation of cleavages in the Armed Services Committee during the Republican administrations (1973–76). While some conservative Democrats (Richard H. Ichord [Mo.], Charles E. Bennett [Fla.], Melvin Price [Ill.], Mendel J. Davis [S.C.], and Bill Nichols [Ala.]) move closer to their liberal colleagues during the Carter years, intense partisan cleavages fail to materialize. Democrats and Republicans continue to vote together, while each faction maintains an identifiable partisan core; hence, although partisanship has minimal impact, it is not totally inconsequential in the formation of committee factions. Faction 1 (table 36) represents a bloc of (ADA, $r = -81$) Republicans and conservative Democrats (G.V. "Sonny" Montgomery [D-Miss.], Larry McDonald [D-Ga.], Bob Stump [D-Ariz.], Richard C. White [D-Tex.], W. C. Daniel [D-Va.], Robert H. Mollohan [D-W.Va.], and Jack Brinkley [D-Ga.]); Faction 2 is equally conservative, but with a core of committee Democrats. The positions and stands taken by Faction 1 are frequently opposed by liberal committee Democrats Lucien N. Nedzi (Mich.), Patricia Schroeder (Colo.), and Bob Carr (Mich.); therefore, ideology continues to create antagonisms among some committee members.

While Factions 1 and 2 support administration defense policies (Policy Dimension I), Faction 2 is not as supportive as Faction 1 of attempts to *increase* defense expenditures (Increases in Defense Spending). The difference between the two prodefense factions is sharpest in the area of aircraft procurements, where Faction 2 strongly opposes the attempts of Faction 1 to increase aircraft procurements (Increases in Aircraft Procurements, $r = .62$). Four of the members of

221

TABLE 36. Factions in the Armed Services Committee;
1977–1980

Committee Member	Factions		Explained Variation (%)
	1	2	
Floyd Spence (R-S.C.)[a]	.87		80
G.V. "Sonny" Montgomery (D-Miss.)[a]	.83		69
Larry McDonald (D-Ga.)	.82		68
Marjorie S. Holt (R-Md.)[a]	.81		67
Paul S. Trible, Jr. (R-Va.)	.80		65
Bob Stump (D-Ariz.)	.79		63
Richard C. White (D-Tex.)	.78		63
G. William Whitehurst (R-Va.)[a]	.77		59
Robert W. Daniel, Jr. (R-Va.)[a]	.76		58
Donald J. Mitchell (R-N.Y.)	.74		63
Robin L. Beard (R-Tenn.)[a]	.72		68
Elwood Hillis (R-Ind.)	.63		40
Bob Wilson (R-Calif.)[a]	.63		46
W.C. Dan Daniel (D-Va.)[a]	.61	.50	63
Robert H. Mollohan (D-W. Va.)[a]	.61		43
David F. Emery (R-Maine)	.59		36
Jack Brinkley (D-Ga.)	.53		29
Jim Lloyd (D-Calif.)		(−.48)	24
Lucien N. Nedzi (D-Mich.)	−.68		49
Patricia Schroeder (D-Colo.)[a]	−.81		66
Bob Carr (D-Mich.)	−.90		90
Richard H. Ichord (D-Mo.)[a]		.77	60
Bill Nichols (D-Ala.)[a]		.65	53
Samuel S. Stratton (D-N.Y.)[a]		.56	44
Charles E. Bennett (D-Fla.)[a]		.55	30
William L. Dickinson (R-Ala.)[a]		.52	32
Melvin Price (D-Ill.)[a]		(.46)	26
Charles H. Wilson (D-Calif.)[ab]			5
Mendel J. Davis (D-S.C.)[ab]			00

Correlates of Factional Alignments		
Presidential support	−.69*	−.22
Conservative coalition	.79*	.36
Party unity	−.72*	−.23
ADA	−.81*	−.39
COPE	−.72*	−.20
CCUS	.48*	.26
ACA	.74*	.23
Administration Recommendations (I)	−.58*	−.45*
Increases in Defense Spending (II)	−.63*	−.21
Increases in Aircraft Procurements (III)	−.43*	.62*

Note: Doublets: Wilson (D-Calif.) and Lloyd (D-Calif.); Ichord (D-Md.) and Dickinson (R-Ala.). Pearson correlations marked with asterisks are significant at the .01 level.
[a]Core committee member during 1973–76 committee analysis.
[b]Does not exhibit an attachment to any of the committee factions.

Faction 2—Nichols, Price, Samuel S. Stratton (D-N.Y.), and W. C. Daniel—are also members of a bloc that supported administration defense policies in the Ninety-third and Ninety-fourth Congresses. Since many of the members of Faction 2 are also subcommittee leaders (Stratton, Nichols, Price, Ichord, and Bennett), this bloc represents an effective means for the administration to articulate and promote its defense policies.

The composition of Faction 2 and the lack of support for budgetary increases in procurements suggest that this bloc is supportive of administration interests. Therefore, ideology and executive-branch pressures continue as major sources of committee conflict. The continuity in committee cleavages is also apparent in the two-dimensional representations of the major divisions within the committee. The conservative skew of the committee's core membership continues (figure 33): most Armed Services Committee members cluster into a single quadrant (upper-right) diagonally opposite a small bloc of liberal Democrats (Schroeder, Nedzi, and Carr).

Post Office and Civil Service

In the earlier period (1973–76), we suggested that party, ideology, and the executive branch create *salient* pressures on members of the Post Office and Civil Service Committee. These same cleavages continue during the Ninety-fifth and Ninety-sixth Congresses, but another source of pressure, constituency interests, creates further divisions among committee members during the Carter years. During the Carter administration, unlike the Nixon-Ford administrations, the committee handled issues that generated intense interest on the part of federal employees (amendments to the Hatch Act, Civil Service Reform). As a consequence of such constituency-interest pressures, a bloc supportive of the interests of federal employees formed: Faction 1 (table 37) is a bloc of liberal (conservative coalition, $r = -.84$) Democrats who are frequently opposed by a more conservative bloc of Republicans—Edward J. Derwinski (Ill.), Tom Corcoran (Ill.), and Jim Leach (Iowa). This bipolar faction captures some of the partisan-ideological conflict that appeared to be present in the committee during the Ninety-third and Ninety-fourth Congresses. The nominal leaders of Faction 1 (Charles H. Wilson [Calif.], Gladys Noon Spellman [Md.], William Clay [Mo.], William D. Ford

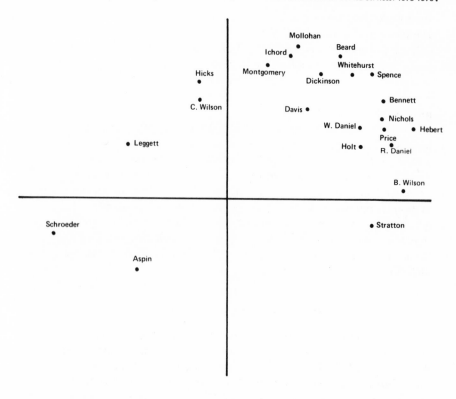

Figure 33a. Two-Dimensional Representation of Cleavages in the House Committee on Armed Services: 1973-1976.

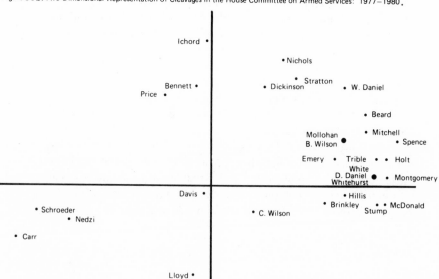

Figure 33b. Two-Dimensional Representation of Cleavages in the House Committee on Armed Services: 1977–1980.

TABLE 37. Factions in the Post Office and Civil Service Committee, 1977–1980

Committee Member	Factions		Explained Variation (%)
	1	2	
Charles H. Wilson (D-Calif.)[a]	.79		64
Gladys Noon Spellman (D-Md.)	.73		53
William Clay (D-Mo.)[a]	.72		62
William D. Ford (D-Mich.)	.69		77
Patricia Schroeder (D-Colo.)[a]	.63		45
James M. Hanley (D-N.Y.)[a]	.54	(.43)	47
Robert Garcia (D-N.Y.)	.54	(.43)	47
Herbert E. Harris II (D-Va.)	.53		30
Stephen J. Solarz (D-N.Y.)	.53	.64	69
Edward J. Derwinski (R-Ill.)[a]	−.80		64
Tom Corcoran (R-Ill.)	−.81		67
Jim Leach (R-Iowa)	−.82		69
Benjamin A. Gilman (R-N.Y.)		−.69	52
Robert N. C. Nix (D-Pa.)		.92	85
William Lehman (D-Fla.)[a]		.82	70
Morris K. Udall (D-Ariz.)		.82	67
Michael O. Myers (D-Pa.)		.78	70
Cecil Heftel (D-Hawaii)		.69	48
Gene Taylor (R-Mo.)	(−.46)		32

Correlates of Factional Alignments			
Presidential support	.51	.49	
Conservative coalition	−.84*	−.40	
Party unity	.74*	.43	
ADA	.64*	.18	
COPE	.80*	.30	
CCUS	−.35	−.57*	
ACA	−.77*	−.53*	
Political Activities of Federal Employees (I)	.70*	.63*	
Civil Service Reform—Executive-Level Employees (II)	−.25	.64*	
Civil Service Reform—Rights and Protections of Employees (III)	.61*	−.34	

Note: Doublet: Spellman (D-Md.) and Harris (D-Va.). Pearson Correlations marked with asterisks are significant at the .01 level.

[a]Core committee member during 1973–76 committee analysis.

[Mich.], and Patricia Schroeder [Colo.]) serve on major subcommittees that deal with federal employee issues: the Civil Service Subcommittee, chaired by Schroeder, and the Compensation and Employee Benefits Subcommittee, chaired by Spellman. The policy interests of the members of Faction 1, as reflected by their subcommittee assignments, suggests that this bloc is susceptible to pressures from federal employees and groups representing public employees.

The policy positions of Faction 1 also suggest that its composition reflects the impact of constituency-interest pressures: Faction 1 opposes threats to the personnel protections and rights of federal employees (Civil Service Reform—Rights and Protections of Federal Employees, $r = .61$), and restrictions placed on the political and union activity of federal employees (Political Activities of Federal Employees, $r = .70$). While Faction 2 (table 37) also opposes such restrictions (Political Activities of Federal Employees, $r = .63$), this bloc is not as supportive of the personnel protections of federal workers. This bloc appears to form from the pressures that result from the interest of the president in issues before the committee: Faction 2 promotes and protects the interests of the president on issues directly affecting executive-branch personnel, such as the recruitment, pay, and responsibilities of presidential "appointees" and Senior Executive Service personnel (Civil Service Reform—Executive Level Employees, $r = .64$). In fact, the policy stands of Faction 2 are the major distinguishing features of this bloc.

This division on the issue of employee rights is not too surprising, since group supporters feel that "the adversary is not other clientele groups, but the executive branch" (Fenno, 1973, p. 37). Faction 1 appears to represent the pressures on the committee that result from the interest of federal employees and their clientele groups in the issues before the committee; the bipolar nature of this faction reflects the continuation of partisan and ideological differences among committee members. Executive-branch pressures also continue to influence committee decisions, as illustrated in the presidential support that Faction 2 provides on personnel decisions within the purview of the president—a policy dimension that has no relationship with party.

The introduction of constituency-interest pressures into the political environment of the Post Office Committee adds pressures on committee members and, therefore, produces a more fragmented cleavage structure during the Ninety-fifth and Ninety-sixth Con-

gresses (figure 34b). A comparison of the two-dimensional representations of committee cleavages reveals a greater dispersion in the
loyalties of committee Democrats. Committee liberals like Schroeder,
Wilson, and Clay continue to anchor the right (liberal) end of the
horizontal axis; in the Ninety-fifth and Ninety-sixth Congresses, a
bloc of Republicans (Corcoran, Leach, and Derwinski) cluster directly opposite this liberal group (figure 34b). The remaining committee Democrats fall somewhere between these ideological extremes.
Thus, the cleavage structure appears more fragmented during the
Ninety-fifth and Ninety-sixth Congresses than during the Nixon-
Ford years (figure 34a), perhaps as a result of the introduction of
additional pressures (constituency-interest) on committee members.

Ways and Means

During the Ninety-third and Ninety-fourth Congresses, party and
ideology were salient sources of committee cleavages in Ways and
Means; the strong intercorrelations between party and ideology make
it difficult to disentangle these cleavages from those created by executive-branch pressures. Partisan and ideological pressures continue
to divide committee members during the Ninety-fifth and Ninety-
sixth Congresses, and they remain strongly intercorrelated (r) .90).
As a result, executive-branch pressures are also obscured during the
Carter administration.

Faction 1 (table 38) represents the intensely partisan and ide-
ological conflicts within the committee: the opposition of liberal
Democrats, with nominal leaders Fortney H. "Pete" Stark (Calif.)
and William M. Brodhead (Mich.), to the positions of conservative
(ACA, $r = .91$) Republicans, with nominal leadership from Guy
VanderJagt (Mich.), Philip M. Crane (Ill.), and Bill Archer (Tex.).
Faction 2 represents a bloc of liberal (conservative coalition, $r = -.88$), partisan (presidential support, $r = .89$) Democrats, with
nominal leaders Joseph L. Fisher (Va.), Dan Rostenkowski (Ill.), and
Al Ullman (Oreg.). We characterize this faction as reflecting the
impact of the executive branch on committee decision making. Our
empirical evidence is basically the same as that which prompted us to
characterize a bloc of leadership Republicans as representing presidential pressures on the committee during the Nixon-Ford period:
Faction 2 is led by ranking majority member Rostenkowski and the

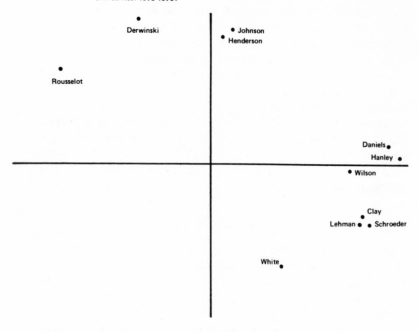

Figure 34a. Two-Dimensional Representation of Cleavages in the House Committee on Post Office and Civil Service: 1973-1976.

Figure 34b. Two-Dimensional Representation of Cleavages in the House Committee on Post Office and Civil Service: 1977-1980.

TABLE 38. Factions in the Ways and Means Committee, 1977–1980

Committee Member	Factions			Explained Variation (%)
	1	2	3	
Guy VanderJagt (R-Mich.)	.88			81
Philip M. Crane (R-Ill.)	.87			88
Bill Archer (R-Tex.)[a]	.87			85
Bill Frenzel (R-Minn.)	.83			68
James G. Martin (R-N. C.)	.79			66
John J. Duncan (R-Tenn.)	.78			67
Skip Bafalis (R-Fla.)	.77			64
Barber B. Conable (R-N.Y.)	.75			57
Richard T. Schulze (R-Pa.)	.72			62
Bill Gradison (R-Ohio)	.72			55
Abner J. Mikva (D-Ill.)	−.50	.58		68
Harold E. Ford (D-Tenn.)	−.51	.58		61
James C. Corman (D-Calif.)[a]	−.51	.52		55
Charles A. Vanik (D-Ohio)[a]	−.56	.50		57
Charles B. Rangel (D-N.Y.)	−.57	.52		64
William M. Brodhead (D-Mich.)	−.65			59
Fortney H. "Pete" Stark (D-Calif.)	−.66			58
Joseph L. Fisher (D-Va.)[a]		.65		52
Dan Rostenkowski (D-Ill.)[a]		.65		51
Al Ullman (D-Oreg.)[a]		.62		57
Richard A. Gephardt (D-Mo.)		.58		35
William R. Cotter (D-Conn.)		.55		37
Raymond F. Lederer (D-Pa.)		(.43)		28
Sam Gibbons (D-Fla.)[a]		(.31)	(.31)	21
Ed Jenkins (D-Ga.)			.73	57
J. J. Pickle (D-Tex.)			.69	57
Ken Holland (D-S.C.)			.62	42
James R. Jones (D-Okla.)			.53	48
Andrew Jacobs, Jr. (D-Ind.)	(.44)		(.38)	26

Correlates of Factional Alignments

	1	2	3
Presidential support	−.86*	.89*	−.05
Conservative coalition	.90*	−.88*	.33
Party unity	−.92*	.88*	−.05
ADA	−.89*	.86*	−.35
COPE	−.95*	.89*	−.14
CCUS	.76*	−.70*	.31
ACA	.91*	−.86*	.06
Taxing Oil Profits (I)	−.75*	.82*	.09
Individual Income Tax Deductions (II)	.56*	−.38	.53*

NOTE: Doublets: Gephardt (D-Mo.) and Lederer (D-Pa.); Gibbons (D-Fla.) and Jacobs (D-Ind.). Pearson correlations marked with asterisks are significant at the .01 level.

[a]Core committee member during 1973–76 committee analysis.

chairman of the committee during the Carter years, Ullman. It may be difficult to disentangle the partisan and ideological pressures on members of Faction 2 from the pressures generated by the executive branch: this bloc supports (table 38) the president's position on legislation (Policy Dimension I, $r = .82$) that is both partisan (party unity, $r = .76$) and ideological (ACA, $r = -.74$)—oil taxation (e.g., windfall profits tax).

Faction 3 (table 38) represents the voting agreement among conservative Democrats—Ed Jenkins (Ga.), J.J. Pickle (Tex.), Ken Holland (S.C.) and James R. Jones (Okla.); this bloc is distinguished by its support of business interests in the areas of deductions and taxes (Policy Dimension II, $r = .53$). This is an attitude that Faction 3 shares with committee Republicans (Faction 1). Aside from this issue, however, there is little voting agreement between these two conservative factions. Membership turnover, and perhaps a southern Democrat in the White House, have strengthened party allegiance among Democrats. While southern Democrats Joe D. Waggonner (La.), Omar Burleson (Tex.), and Phil M. Landrum (Ga.) joined the Republicans to form a conservative coalition during the Nixon-Ford period, their southern replacements (Jenkins, Pickle, Holland, and Jones) are far less supportive of Republican positions during the Ninety-fifth and Ninety-sixth Congresses.

The two-dimensional representation of committee cleavages suggests that the committee is less polarized during the Carter presidency (figure 35b) than during the Ninety-third and Ninety-fourth Congresses (figure 35a). The major change between these periods is that conservative Democrats move farther from the cluster of Republicans and closer to the Democratic core of the committee. Thus, the increased partisanship of the conservative Democrats recently added to the committee enhances the cohesion among committee Democrats. As a result, conservative Democrats Pickle, Jones, Jenkins, and Holland are cross-pressured by their ideological and partisan loyalties; like other cross-pressured members, they are positioned (figure 35b) between the clusters of conservative Republicans (lower-right quadrant) and liberal Democrats (upper-left quadrant). In conclusion, partisan and ideological pressures continue to create cleavages within the Ways and Means Committee, and there is also reason to suspect that the executive branch continues to place pressures on committee members to support administration policies.

Figure 35a. Two-Dimensional Representation of Cleavages in the House Committee on Ways and Means: 1973-1976.

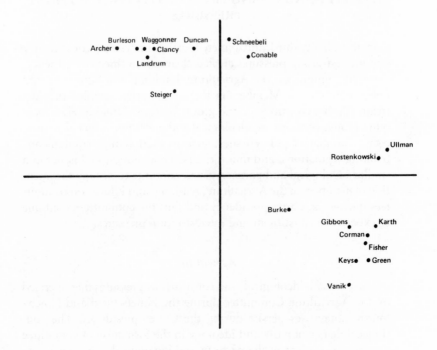

Figure 35b. Two-Dimensional Representation of Cleavages in the House Committee on Ways and Means: 1977-1980.

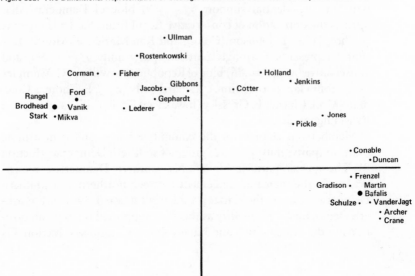

STABILITY AND CHANGE IN CONSTITUENCY-INTEREST PRESSURES

In the Ninety-third and Ninety-fourth Congresses, constituency and interest-group pressures created cleavages in three constituency-oriented committees: the Agriculture, Banking, and Education and Labor committees. Members of these committees divided over the treatment that constituency and group interests should receive. As in other House committees, ideological and partisan conflict also arose over a number of policy issues, such as food stamp requirements, banking regulations, and union rights. These issues, and issues of a similar ideological and partisan genre, continue to occupy the attention of members in the Agriculture, Banking, and Education committees during the Carter presidency and thus the committees continue to experience constituent and interest-group pressures.

Agriculture

The partisan, ideological, and constituency pressures that operated on the Agriculture Committee during the Ninety-third and Ninety-fourth Congresses persist during the Carter presidency. The continued salience of party and ideology in the formation of committee cleavages is evident in the partisan and ideological correlates of the individual factions. Faction 1 (table 39) is a liberal (ACA, $r = -.91$), partisan (presidential support, $r = .89$) bloc of Democrats that attracts the opposition of conservative Republicans Steven D. Symms (Idaho), James P. Johnson (Colo.), and Ron Marlenee (Mont.). Faction 2 represents a strongly partisan (party unity, $r = -.90$) and conservative (ACA, $r = .85$) bloc of Republicans: William C. Wampler (Va.), Tom Hagedorn (Minn.), Richard Kelly (Fla.), E. Thomas Coleman (Mo.), Charles E. Grassley (Iowa), Paul Findley (Ill.), and Edward R. Madigan (Ill.).

Membership changes in the committee have resulted in a more partisan (party unity, $r = .42$) group of southern Democrats (Faction 3). The greater partisanship of this southern Democratic bloc is evident in the increased agreement between northern and southern Democrats: during the Carter presidency Faction 3 votes with northern Democrats *as frequently* as this bloc supported Republican positions in the Ninety-third and Ninety-fourth Congresses. Faction 3 is

TABLE 39. Factions in the Agriculture Committee, 1977–1980

Committee Member	Factions 1	2	3	4	Explained Variation (%)
Tom Harkin (D-Iowa)	.76				80
Alvin Baldus (D-Wis.)	.72				70
Berkley Bedell (D-Iowa)	.71				60
Frederick W. Richmond (D-N.Y.)	.71				71
Floyd J. Fithian (D-Ind.)	.70				54
George E. Brown, Jr. (D-Calif.)[a]	.69	(−.47)			74
Daniel K. Akaka (D-Hawaii)	.68				74
Thomas S. Foley (D-Wash.)[a]	.55				62
Leon E. Panetta (D-Calif.)	.55				55
Keith G. Sebelius (R-Kans.)[a]	(−.47)	.64			66
Steven D. Symms (R-Idaho)[a]	−.56	.65			81
James P. Johnson (R-Colo.)[a]	−.57	.55			66
Ron Marlenee (R-Mont.)	−.74				70
William C. Wampler (R-Va.)[a]		.78			73
Tom Hagedorn (R-Minn.)		.78			82
E. Thomas Coleman (R-Mo.)		.78			71
Charles E. Grassley (R-Iowa)		.77			70
Edward R. Madigan (R-Ill.)[a]		.76			71
Richard Kelly (R-Fla.)		.71			77
Paul Findley (R-Ill.)[a]		.52			44
Walter B. Jones (D-N.C.)[a]			.84		73
Charles Whitley (D-N.C.)			.83		75
Ed Jones (D-Tenn.)[a]			.82		77
David R. Bowen (D-Miss.)[a]			.75		61
Dawson Mathis (D-Ga.)[a]			.70		58
E. (Kika) de la Garza (D-Tex.)			.69		66
Ike Skelton (D-Mo.)			.69		68
Jerry Huckaby (D-La.)			.68		66
Charles Rose (D-N.C.)			.65		73
Richard Nolan (D-Minn.)				.77	82
James Weaver (D-Oreg.)				.67	75
Dan Glickman (D-Kans.)				.52	49
Glenn English (D-Okla.)				(.45)	26

Correlates of Factional Alignments

	1	2	3	4
Presidential support	.89*	−.81*	.32	.38
Conservative coalition	−.77*	.64*	.05	−.40*
Party unity	.83*	−.90*	.42*	.56*
ADA	.81*	−.68*	−.06	.49*
COPE	.81*	−.76*	.29	.47*
CCUS	−.49*	.38*	.15	−.50*
ACA	−.91*	.85*	−.35	−.47*
Food Stamps and Wheat and Feed Grains Legislation (I)	.88*	−.95*	.62*	.48*

Note: Doublets: Glickman (D-Kans.) and English (D-Okla.); Weaver (D-Oreg.) and Nolan (D-Minn.). Pearson correlations marked with asterisks are significant at the .01 level.

[a] Core committee member during 1973–76 committee analysis.

also more supportive of the partisan-liberal issues that are championed by the liberal Democrats, such as food stamps (Food Stamps and Wheat and Feed Grains Legislation, $r = .62$), an issue that divided northern and southern Democrats during the Ninety-third and Ninety-fourth Congresses.

The increased partisanship of this bloc of southern Democrats should not obscure the constituency interests of the members of this faction—agricultural commodities. As in the Ninety-third and Ninety-fourth Congresses, the leaders of the major commodity subcommittees—Walter B. Jones (D-N.C.; Tobacco), David R. Bowen (D-Miss.; Cotton), Charles Rose (D-N.C.; Livestock and Grains), Dawson Mathis (D-Ga.; Oilseeds and Rice)—vote together as a bloc. Thus, Faction 3 represents a bloc of commodity supporters, commodities important to the constituencies of these members. The remaining committee faction (Faction 4) represents the rather unique voting and agreement of two doublets; James Weaver (D-Oreg.) and Richard Nolan (D-Minn.), and Dan Glickman (D-Kans.) and Glenn English (D-Okla.).

The two-dimensional representations of committee cleavages demonstrate the continuity in committee conflict (figures 36a and 36b). Democrats and Republicans continue to cluster in diagonally opposite quadrants. In the 1977–80 period, Democrats cluster in the upper-right quadrant and Republicans in the lower-left quadrant. The only change is that the southern Democrats are more partisan during the Ninety-fifth and Ninety-sixth Congresses, moving farther from the Republicans and closer to the core of committee Democrats. Thus, the cleavages within the Agriculture Committee are stable throughout the 1970s.

Banking, Finance, and Urban Affairs

During the Nixon-Ford presidencies, party, ideology, and constituency interests were the dominant sources of committee cleavages; these influences continue to create divisions in the Banking, Finance, and Urban Affairs Committee during the Ninety-fifth and Ninety-sixth Congresses. Faction 1 (table 40) is a partisan (party unity, $r = .83$) and liberal (ACA, $r = -.85$) bloc of Democrats who oppose the interests of commercial banks on such issues as the guaranteed loans to the Chrysler Corporation and the regulation of interest rates (Policy

Figure 36a. Two-Dimensional Representation of Cleavages in the House Committee on Agriculture: 1973-1976.

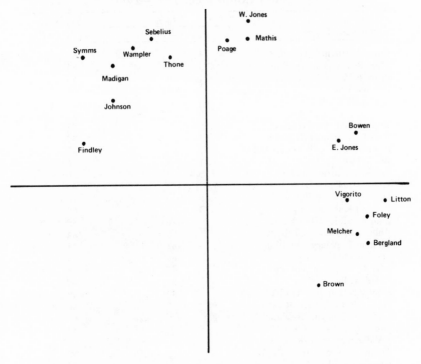

Figure 36b. Two-Dimensional Representation of Cleavages in the House Committee on Agriculture : 1977–1980.

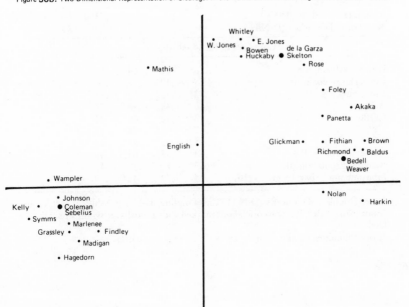

TABLE 40. Factions in the Banking, Finance, and Urban Affairs Committee, 1977–1980

Committee Member	Factions 1	2	3	4	Explained Variation (%)
Parren J. Mitchell (D-Md.)[a]	.74				64
Mary Rose Oakar (D-Ohio)	.73				63
Bruce F. Vento (D-Minn.)	.71				54
Fernand J. St. Germain (D-R.I.)[a]	.70				66
Joseph G. Minish (D-N.J.)[a]	.63				63
Henry S. Reuss (D-Wis.)[a]	.60				52
James J. Blanchard (D-Mich.)	.55				57
John J. Cavanaugh (D-Nebr.)	.54				43
Gladys Noon Spellman (D-Md.)	.52				57
Jim Mattox (D-Tex.)	.51				56
Frank Annunzio (D-Ill.)[a]	.50				50
James M. Hanley (D-N.Y.)[a]	(.48)				49
Henry J. Hyde (R-Ill.)	−.58				50
Richard Kelly (R-Fla.)	−.73				68
John J. LaFalce (D-N.Y.)		.76			59
William S. Moorhead (D-Pa.)		.68			64
Thomas L. Ashley (D-Ohio)		.61			41
Les AuCoin (D-Oreg.)		.60			59
Jerry M. Patterson (D-Calif.)		(.47)			38
David W. Evans (D-Ind.)		(.45)			49
Stanley N. Lundine (D-N.Y.)		(.44)			38
Stewart B. McKinney (R-Conn.)			.78		66
Chalmers P. Wylie (R-Ohio)[a]			.78		67
James A.S. Leach (R-Iowa)			.69		54
J. William Stanton (R-Ohio)[a]			.65		72
Thomas B. Evans, Jr. (R-Del.)			.56		56
Doug Barnard (D-Ga.)				.81	73
Wes Watkins (D-Okla.)				.77	62
Carroll Hubbard, Jr. (D-Ky.)				.73	60
Norman E. D'Amours (D-N.H.)				(.39)	35

Correlates of Factional Alignments				
Presidential support	.78*	.62*	−.64*	−.35
Conservative coalition	−.75*	−.49*	.52*	.56*
Party unity	.83*	.52*	−.73*	−.17
ADA	.66*	.35	−.40*	−.51*
COPE	.83*	.52*	−.60*	−.44*
CCUS	−.67*	−.43*	.49*	.32
ACA	−.85*	−.53*	.65*	.28
Monetary Policy (I)	.63*	.33	−.65*	.40
Banking Regulation (II)	.69*	−.17	−.30	−.41
Housing and Urban Programs (III)	.25	.72*	−.42*	−.59*

Note: Doublets: D'Amours (D-N.H.) and Lundine (D-N.Y.); Ashley (D-Ohio) and Moorhead (D-Pa.). Pearson correlations marked with asterisks are significant at the .01 level.

[a]Core committee member during 1973–76 committee analysis.

Dimension I, $r = .63$) and banking regulations (Policy Dimension II, $r = .69$); another interesting characteristic of this bloc is that the nominal leaders of a similar faction opposed to commercial banking interests during the Nixon-Ford period (Fernand J. St. Germain [D-R.I.], Joseph G. Minish [D-N.J.], Frank Annunzio [D-Ill.], and James M. Hanley [D-N.Y.]) identify with this faction (table 40). Support for banking interests is a significant source of disagreement between the liberal Democrats in Faction 1, who oppose these interests, and the conservative (ACA, $r = .65$) Republicans in Faction 3, who promote the interests of commercial banks (Monetary Policy, $r = -.65$). Thus, the composition of these two factions and the association of these blocs with issues concerned with the interests of commercial banks capture the persistent intermingling of ideological, partisan, and group pressures on the Banking Committee.

A second set of constituency interests also continues to create divisions within the committee: Faction 2 (table 40) represents a bloc of urban Democrats that tends to promote programs and policies that benefit their constituencies, such as housing programs (Housing and Urban Programs, $r = .72$). Most of the members of this faction represent urban areas, or constituencies with a stake in housing programs (John J. LaFalce [D-N.Y.] and Les AuCoin [D-Oreg.]). Thus, the treatment of urban areas continues to divide committee members, even Democrats: southern Democrats (Faction 4) generally oppose programs designed to benefit urban areas (Housing and Urban Programs, $r = -.59$). In short, the Banking Committee continues to reflect the cleavages that result from the preoccupation and interest of urban congressmen in programs that are likely to benefit their constituencies.

Continuity in committee cleavages is evident in the two-dimensional representations of the major dimensions of conflict. The gulf between committee Democrats and Republicans that we observed during the 1973–76 period (figure 37a) is similar to the spatial configuration of Democrats and Republicans in the Ninety-fifth and Ninety-sixth Congresses (figure 37b). Democrats tend to cluster in the lower-right quadrant, directly opposite the core of committee Republicans (upper-left quadrant, figure 37b), and southern Democrats are positioned between these two blocs.

Figure 37a. Two-Dimensional Representation of Cleavages in the House Committee on Banking, Finance, and Urban Affairs: 1973-1976.

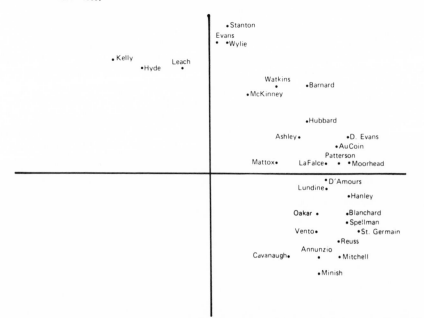

Figure 37b. Two-Dimensional Representation of Cleavages in the House Committee on Banking, Finance, and Urban Affairs: 1977—1980.

Education and Labor

Cleavages within the Education and Labor Committee continue to reflect the pressures of party, ideology, and constituency interests. Faction 1 (table 41) is a bloc of liberal (ACA, $r = -.83$) Democrats who are very supportive of the interests of organized labor (COPE, $r = .93$). The labor orientation of this faction is demonstrated by its sizable correlation with COPE ratings and by the several members of this faction who chair subcommittees that handle labor-related legislation: Employment Opportunities (Augustus F. Hawkins [D-Calif.]), Health and Safety (Joseph M. Gaydos [D-Pa.]), Labor-Management Relations (Frank Thompson, Jr. [D-N.J.], and Labor Standards (Edward P. Beard [D-R.I.]). Members of this faction regularly vote with their liberal colleagues (Faction 2) to form a coalition supportive of Democratic programs in the areas of education and labor legislation $(r = .83)$. The composition and behavior of this faction is consistent with our characterization of a similar labor bloc during the Nixon-Ford period.

The ideological nature of Faction 2 is illustrated by its strong correlation with measures of ideology (r) .70) and by the opposition it receives from conservative Republicans like John M. Ashbrook (Ohio), William F. Goodling (Pa.), and John N. Erlenborn (Ill.). This bipolarization reflects the intertwining of partisan and ideological pressures on the committee—a pattern that mirrors the partisan-ideological conflict that we have observed during the Ninety-third and Ninety-fourth Congresses. The continuity in committee cleavages is demonstrated in figures 38a and 38b: partisan and ideological pressures polarize committee Democrats (upper-right quadrant) and Republicans (lower-end of vertical axis) into opposing clusters of partisans.

THE COMMITTEE SYSTEM, 1973–1980

As we can see from the previous chapters, most House committees were sharply polarized along partisan and ideological lines during the Nixon and Ford administrations (1973–76): liberal Democrats and conservative Republicans often formed tightly knit blocs of adversaries, and conservative Democrats (primarily from the South) fre-

239

TABLE 41. Factions in the Education and Labor Committee, 1977–1980

Committee Member	Factions		Explained Variation (%)
	1	2	
Joseph M Gaydos (D-Pa.)[a]	.88		86
John Brademas (D-Ind.)[a]	.87		83
Frank Thompson, Jr. (D-N.J.)[a]	.84		81
Dale E. Kildee (D-Mich.)	.83		83
William D. Ford (D-Mich.)[a]	.83		75
Carl D. Perkins (D-Ky.)[a]	.75		58
Edward P. Beard (D-R.I.)	.69	.57	80
Austin J. Murphy (D-Pa.)	.68		47
Phillip Burton (D-Calif.)[a]	.57	.68	79
Augustus F. Hawkins (D-Calif.)[a]	.54	.63	69
George Miller (D-Calif.)	.54	.53	57
Michael O. Myers (D-Pa.)	.51	.62	65
William Clay (D-Mo.)[a]	.51	.59	61
Mario Biaggi (D-N.Y.)[a]	.50	.68	71
Ted Weiss (D-N.Y.)	(.46)	.80	85
Paul Simon (D-Ill.)	(.49)	.54	53
John M. Ashbrook (R-Ohio)		−.88	92
William F. Goodling (R-Pa.)		−.87	91
John N. Erlenborn (R-Ill.)[a]		−.80	78
Mickey Edwards (R-Okla.)		−.73	72
James M. Jeffords (R-Vt.)		−.65	43
John Buchanan (R-Ala.)		−.55	31

Correlates of Factional Alignments		
Presidential support	.75*	.72*
Conservative coalition	−.65*	−.80*
Party unity	.89*	.89*
ADA	.67*	.73*
COPE	.93*	.94*
CCUS	−.75*	−.84*
ACA	−.83*	−.84*
Labor and Education (I)	.91*	.92*

Note: Pearson correlations marked with asterisks are significant at the .01 level.
[a]Core committee member during 1973–76 committee analysis.

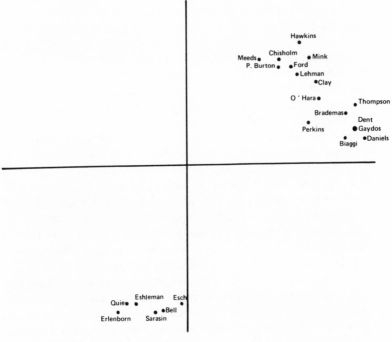

Figure 38a. Two-Dimensional Representation of Cleavages in the House Committee on Education and Labor: 1973-1976.

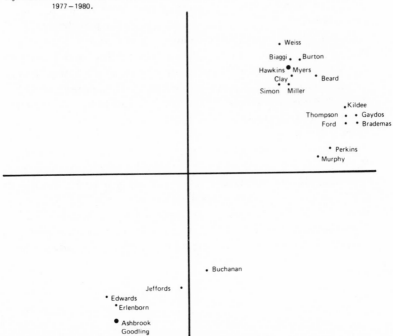

Figure 38b. Two-Dimensional Representation of Cleavages in the House Committee on Education and Labor: 1977—1980.

quently voted with Republicans to form conservative coalitions. The shift in party control of the White House to the Democrats in 1977 induced greater partisanship among both parties, and especially among the recalcitrant southern Democrats. Further, the existing polarization of several committees (Budget, Education and Labor, Interior, Interstate and Foreign Commerce, Ways and Means) continues during the Carter years; on these committees, Democrats and Republicans are sharply divided by political and ideological loyalties.

Democratic control of the executive branch, greater partisanship among recently elected southern Democrats, and perhaps President Carter's southern heritage promote greater adherence to party positions among conservative Democrats during the 1977–80 period. As a result, conservative Democrats, especially southerners, appear to move farther away from the core of committee Republicans and closer to their Democratic colleagues in several of the congressional committees studied (Agriculture, Appropriations, Armed Services, and Ways and Means). In the Appropriations Committee, for example, conservative Democrats Natcher (D-Ky.), Mahon (D-Tex.), McFall (D-Calif.), and McKay (D-Utah) appear to vote more frequently with their Democratic colleagues during the Carter administration than during the previous years under Republican presidents Nixon and Ford. Similarly, in the Armed Services Committee conservative Democrats, Bennett (D-Fla.), Ichord (D-Mo.), Price (D-Ill.), Davis (D-S.C.), and Nichols (D-Ala.), move farther away from the core of Republicans on the committee during the Carter presidency.

In sum, it appears that the change in party control of the White House served to increase the levels of partisanship among congressional Democrats: committees that were previously polarized remain so, and a few House committees become even more polarized than during the Nixon and Ford administrations. In addition, conservative and southern Democrats voted more frequently with their Democratic colleagues, at least in committee. If we were to generalize from these partisan changes in committee voting, we would conclude that Republican presidents have an incentive to build congressional coalitions that follow ideological lines (coalitions of southern Democrats and Republicans) because this salient division within the Democratic party is one that can be easily exploited by a president with a conservative approach to societal issues. Democratic presidents, on the other hand, would benefit most from emphasizing party loyalty in order to mute these divisive ideological rifts within the party. The differences between the composition of many committee factions during Republican and Democratic administrations reflect these opposing strategies.

In three House committees (Government Operations, Interior and Insular Affairs, and Public Works and Transportation) membership changes intensified, rather than reduced, the divisions between conservative and liberal Democrats. The addition of moderately conservative Democrats like Fithian (D-Ind.), English (D-Okla.), Levitas (D-Ga.), and Preyer (D-N.C.) have further increased the diffusion in Democratic loyalties in the Government Operations Committee. Similarly, the division between conservative and liberal Democrats in the Public Works Committee has gained in intensity with the active involvement of several liberal Democrats in committee deliberations. Thus, while membership changes have intensified the cleavages among Democrats in some committees, Democratic control of the White House has strengthened partisanship in several other committees, especially among conservative Democrats.

The emergence of constituency pressures in the Post Office and Civil Service Committee created a higher degree of dispersion of the membership. Although the influences of party, ideology, and the administration remain constant in the committee, issues related to Civil Service reform introduce constituency pressures. This in turn leads to greater fragmentation in party loyalty. These findings suggest that membership turnover, control of the presidency, and the introduction of new issues are potential sources of change in committee divisions.

CHAPTER SEVEN

The Impact of Cleavages
on Coalition Formation

In this chapter we examine the impact of cleavages on committee decision making by focusing on the formation of coalitions in the committees that have been studied. Since cleavages produce factions, and factions are the building blocks of coalitions, we should be able to detect a relationship between the cleavages that exist in committees and the coalitions that form in decision making. Two characteristics of coalitions are of particular interest: the delineation of the factions that coalesce into coalitions, and the size of the coalitions that are successful in decision-making situations. Since the appearance of Kenneth Arrow's (1951) work on the voter paradox, these two questions have been a central focus of much research on decision making.

In each of the examinations of the individual committees, we have provided information suggesting which factions tend to join together to form coalitions. In this chapter, we explore the question of the size of successful coalitions by examining distributions of coalitions in committees displaying different types of cleavage patterns. Once again, two time periods are studied in order to detect stability and change in coalition size. We also show that knowledge of the cleavage structures in the committees is useful in understanding the reasons for the varying sizes of successful coalitions.

One of the earliest theoretic examinations of coalition formation under majority rule conditions was William Riker's (1962) explanation of the nature of winning coalitions that resulted from group decision making. Under certain prescribed situations (an n-person, zero-sum game with side payments), Riker showed that coalitions of minimum winning size could be expected to result. Minimum winning size is defined as coalition where the loss of one member will render it a nonwinning coalition (Riker, 1962). The rationale behind this formation is that the successful coalition divides the benefits that result from winning among the members of the coalition. The larger the coalition, the greater the number of members who must share the benefits; this results in a smaller share of the benefits to members in a large coalition than would result in a small coalition. Thus, it would be more rational for members of a winning coalition to limit the size of the coalition so that each member would receive a larger share of the benefits. The largest share to each member would result from a coalition that was sufficiently large to win, but no larger.

An alternative theory of the size of winning coalitions has recently been proposed by Barry Weingast (1979). Dropping the zero-sum and side-payments conditions imposed by Riker, Weingast (1979) proposes a different model of legislative coalition formation. This model rests on three assumptions: representatives seek reelection; districts respond favorably to beneficial legislation; and the electorate makes decisions based on the amount of benefits provided without considering the consequences for other districts (pp. 249–50). Given these assumptions, Weingast (1979) suggests that

> representatives pursuing their own interests will prefer institutional arrangements (norms) which increase their chances of success in gaining benefits for their district. Universalism is such an institution. Rational self-interested legislators have compelling reasons to prefer decision making by maximal rather than minimal winning coalitions. (p. 250)

Weingast defines universalism as "the tendency to seek unanimous passage of distributive programs through inclusion of a project for all legislators who want one" (p. 249). That is, the uncertainty over whether a member will receive any benefits from a minimum-winning solution is alleviated by solutions that guarantee some benefits for everyone. Thus, faced with uncertainty over receiving any benefits and a solution where there is certainty of receiving some benefits, the rational legislator chooses the solution that guarantees some benefits. The impetus for this solution was the contradiction between theoretic work that predicted the formation of minimum-winning coalitions and empirical studies which found little evidence of such coalitions.

Empirical studies of floor voting in the U.S. House of Representatives, for example, have continued rather than resolved the debate. David Koehler (1972) finds in his study of House floor voting that once an adjustment is made for uncertainty over the number of members likely to participate in a roll-call vote, the coalitions that arise on conflictual issues are minimum winning in size. In contrast, Barbara Hinckley's (1972) examination of floor voting in the House between the Eighty-first and Ninety-first Congresses showed no tendency for minimum-winning coalitions to form.

> To summarize, winning Democratic coalitions increase in size to a point above 60 percent—exhibiting a combination of minimization and maximization effects and neither one alone. As depicted graphically . . . coalition formation in Congress approximates neither the horizontal minimum winning function . . . nor a situation where party size alone determines coalition size.   (pp. 205–206)

Examinations of committee decision making have resulted in some findings supportive of universal solutions and some in contradiction. James Murphy (1974), as noted in Chapter 3, found that House Public Works Committee members acted cooperatively on legislation that could provide benefits to all members but divided on legislation that was not so easily distributed fairly to all. Another example of these differential findings is provided by Fenno's (1973) study of committee decision making. Fenno found that Appropriations Committee members strove to pass legislative proposals agreeable to most members so that the committee could bring its legislation to the floor with a united membership. To do so they followed a norm of minimum partisanship. In contrast, Education and Labor Committee members pursued a norm of "prosecuting partisanship." As a result, committee decision making was highly conflictual, and proposals rarely went to the floor with full committee support.

The experimental findings on the existence and nature of coalitions have been equally ambiguous. While experiments included with the competitive solution (McKelvey et al., 1978) support the notion of minimum-winning coalitions, recent experiments by Gary Miller and Joe Oppenheimer (1982) suggest that the failure to include a universal alternative may have affected the outcomes of those experiments. These authors find that in an experimental setting where a universal solution that provided a high level of expected benefits existed, it was chosen over other alternatives.

This brief literature review reveals that neither the concept of minimum-winning coalitions nor the concept of coalitions of the whole is unambiguously supported by current research. As Miller and Oppenheimer (1982) suggest, "there seem to be at least two modes of committee decision making: a process of competitive coalition formation and a process of cooperative search for alternatives on which everyone can agree" (p. 573). This idea seems to be supported by the empirical literature as well. The present analysis and many of the studies of committee decision making (Fenno, 1973; Murphy, 1974; Parker and Parker, 1979; Price, 1978) suggest that environmental influences, the salience of the issues being debated, the nature of the conflict generated by the issues, and the goals of members impinge upon decision making, producing different decision-making milieus and different patterns of conflict in the committees. It is reasonable to suspect that these differences also could lead to differing coalition formation patterns in the committees.

The hypothesis examined in this section is that the more partisan loyalties of committee members are crosscut by other environmental influences (specifically ideology, administration, and constituent-group interests), the greater will be the proportion of larger-than-minimum coalitions in the committee distribution. Although the same influences can have an impact on different committees, these influences, as the analysis shows, can divide the members of the committee in different ways. For instance, there is a great deal of diversity in the factional structures of the committees examined in Chapter 3 despite the fact that all the committees are influenced primarily by party and ideology. In order to test the hypothesis about the size of winning coalitions presented here, we first categorize the committees according to the cleavage patterns present in committee decision making. We then examine distributions of the size of successful coalitions based on the substantive roll calls to determine the extent to which these distributions are skewed toward minimum winning size or toward universal size (coalitions of the whole). Committees are classified as being polarized-partisan, mixed-partisan, or nonpartisan, based on the cleavage patterns in each committee. The major cleavages uncovered in the committees in the previous chapters are summarized in table 42.

When attachments and loyalties to the majority party are reinforced by other committee cleavages, a successful coalition needs to accommodate few interests other than those associated with the majority party's positions because alternatives that satisfy party interests also tend to satisfy other interests in the committee. Frequently, this pattern of reinforcing cleavages results in a highly polarized committee where the cleavages divide the members in the same ways. Since fewer interests need to be accommodated within a successful majority party coalition in polarized committees, the size of winning coalitions should be skewed toward minimum size. Committees displaying this type of cleavage pattern are classified as polarized-partisan committees.

When the cleavages within a committee crosscut partisanship and divide party members, a greater number of factions need to be accommodated within the majority party's coalition. This often leads to the expansion of the coalition in order to accommodate these divergent views. Under these conditions the value of party for the organization of winning committee coalitions is reduced. When partisan loyalty is insufficient to produce winning coalitions consistently, the majority party's leaders find it necessary to broaden their appeal in order to gain coalition support. This should result in winning coalitions that are beyond the minimal size necessary for victory. These committees are classified as mixed-partisan in nature.

Finally, in the committees where partisanship is minimal, an emphasis is placed on promoting committee consensus because of the collective nature of the policies that the committees handle. The distinguishing characteristics of these committees are bipartisan committee factions. These nonpartisan committees should display unusually large winning coalitions.

Our study departs from other research on the size of successful coalitions in several respects. First, committee decision making is *not* assumed to be a zero-sum game. Indeed, the fact that many commit-

TABLE 42. Summary of the Salient Cleavages within House Committees, 1973–1980

Committee	Party 1973–76	Party 1977–80	Ideology 1973–76	Ideology 1977–80	Executive 1973–76	Executive 1977–80	Constituency Interests 1973–76	Constituency Interests 1977–80
Agriculture	X	X	X	X			X	X
Appropriations	X	X	X	X	X	X		
Armed Services			X	X	X	X		
Banking, Finance, and Urban Affairs	X	X	X	X			X	X
Budget	X	X	X	X				
Education and Labor	X	X	X	X		X	X	
Foreign Affairs			X		X			
Government Operations	X	X	X	X				
House Administration	X	X	X	X				
Interior and Insular Affairs	X	X	X	X				X[a]
Interstate and Foreign Commerce	X	X	X	X				
Judiciary	X	X	X	X				
Merchant Marine and Fisheries		X		X				X
Post Office and Civil Service	X	X	X	X	X	X		X[a]
Public Works and Transportation	X	X	X	X				
Rules	X	X	X	X				
Science and Technology	X	X	X	X				
Standards of Official Conduct				X				
Ways and Means	X	X	X	X	X	X		

[a]New cleavages.

tees handle distributive policies from which many, if not all, members could benefit seems to preclude such an assumption. Second, factions that form in House committees are considered to be the building blocks of coalitions. Factions form because members want to maximize their influence in committee decision making; they can accomplish this objective by organizing into voting blocs. Thus, the legislative alternatives offered are likely to appeal to blocs of members and not just individual members.

These differences can lead to different coalition outcomes than have been previously hypothesized. Riker's (1962) theory of coalition formation rests on the idea that concern over the distribution of benefits would produce minimum-winning coalitions. In a zero-sum game where members of a winning coalition gain what is lost by the unsuccessful coalition, there is a strong incentive to minimize the size of coalitions. In a non-zero-sum situation, however, the incentive to minimize is reduced. As Weingast (1979) notes there is an incentive in non-zero-sum legislative games to expand the size of the winning coalition in order to reduce the risk of winning nothing at all. Further, increasing the size reduces uncertainty over which members will receive payoffs.

The assumption that protocoalitions try to attract other factions in order to build successful coalitions also has implications for the size of such coalitions. First, control over the size of the coalition is an important feature of theories that predict minimum-winning coalitions. If the members of a successful coalition lack the means of controlling entry, the coalition could expand beyond minimum size and thus cut the size of the payoffs to each member. It is for this reason that Riker and Ordeshook (1973) suggests that when oversized coalitions do form, attempts will be made to pare the size of the coalition. When the protocoalitions appeal to factions, the ability to limit the size of a successful coalition is reduced. A basic finding of the previous chapters is that members who are influenced by the same pressures tend to vote together with some regularity, forming factions. Therefore, in building coalitions, accommodating the policy interests of one member of a faction is likely to attract other members of the same faction to the protocoalition. The result is reduced control over the number of members who enter the coalition.

Another factor that impedes minimization, particularly in mixed-partisan committees, is uncertainty over which members will join the coalition. While the presence of several small factions in a committee where cleavages crosscut partisanship might appear to be an ideal situation for the construction of minimum-winning coalitions, uncertainty can reduce this tendency. Crosscutting cleavages result in cross-pressures on committee members. As a result, members can display varying loyalties to several different factions in the committee. That is, a member's primary loyalty to one faction does not preclude his or her having interests in common with members of other factions or voting with another faction.

This fluidity in factional membership poses problems for members of a protocoalition attempting to build a successful coalition. If the policy alternatives proposed by the protocoalition are too narrow, there is a risk not only of failing to attract a sufficient number of factions but also of losing some of the members of the original protocoalition. Hence, fluidity in member loyalties can impede minimization by encouraging a protocoalition to present broader policy proposals that would satisfy several interests in the committee. (See Riker and Ordeshook, 1973, pp. 192–93, for a further discussion of the factors reducing minimization.) These two factors, the inability to control entry to the coalition and the fluidity in membership, increase the tendency for larger-than-minimum-winning coalitions to form in mixed-partisan committees.

Uncertainty over which members will join a coalition and whether the original protocoalition members will defect is reduced in polarized-partisan committees. When the cleavages in a committee coincide with party cleavages, the lines of conflict in the committee are clearly drawn and can be subsumed under party. The reduced number of factions means that fluidity in factional loyalties is diminished. The task of forming a successful coalition should be easier, and less uncertainty should be involved. Members of the successful coalition can narrow their policy appeals without fear of losing members of the original protocoalition. Polarization also reduces the uncertainty of determining which factions will join the protocoalition. In polarized committees there are essentially only two factions, and appeals made along party lines will attract most members of the committee to one or the other protocoalition. In these instances, the larger faction can make narrower policy appeals without fear of creating a coalition too small to be successful. Hence we expect to find minimum-winning coalitions forming more frequently in polarized-partisan committees than in mixed-partisan or nonpartisan committees. Nonpartisan committees are expected to display a *greater* proportion of unusually large coalitions than the other two types of committees.

These hypothetical relationships between cleavage patterns and the size of committee coalitions are summarized in table 43. Since we are dealing with the entire distribution of a committee's votes over an

TABLE 43. The Relationship between Cleavage Patterns and the Size of Winning Coalitions in House Committees

Type of Cleavage Pattern	Committees with Specified Cleavage Pattern	Hypothesized Skew in Size of Winning Committee Coalitions
Polarized Partisan	Budget Education and Labor Interstate and Foreign Commerce Interior and Insular Affairs Ways and Means	Toward minimum size
Mixed Partisan Ideological	House Administration Public Works and Transportation Rules Science and Technology	Minimum to large majorities
Administration	Appropriations Government Operations Judiciary Post Office and Civil Service	Toward minimum size under conditions of unified party control (presidency and House controlled by same party)
Constituency	Agriculture Banking, Finance, and Urban Affairs	
Nonpartisan	Armed Services Foreign Affairs Standards of Official Conduct	Consensus

eight-year period, the size of winning coalitions will vary over the entire spectrum. Our interest is in the frequency (probability) with which coalitions of a certain size arise. Our concern, therefore, is with the shape of the distributions of successful coalitions—whether a committee's distribution of coalition outcomes is skewed toward minimum or maximum size.

In sum, vote distributions are conceptualized as falling along a continuum anchored at one end by coalitions of minimum winning size and at the other by coalitions of universal size. The position of a committee distribution along that continuum is hypothesized to be determined by the existing cleavage patterns in the committee, which in turn are generated by the impact of four environmental influences that impinge upon committee decision making. Two types of comparisons are of primary interest in this analysis: intercommittee comparisons, which help to define the impact of cleavage structures on the size of successful coalitions, and intracommittee comparisons over time, which aid in assessing the impact of partisan control of the presidency and the stability in coalition distributions.

POLARIZED-PARTISAN CLEAVAGE PATTERNS.

Five House committees can be classified as having polarized-partisan cleavage patterns: Education and Labor, Interior and Insular Affairs, Interstate and Foreign Commerce, Budget, and Ways and Means. In these five committees, partisan and ideological cleavages are closely intertwined; unlike other committees with partisan and ideological cleavages, ideological differences reinforce existing partisan divisions. This coincidence between partisan and ideological attachments polarizes the committee membership into tightly clustered factions of members.

In addition to partisan and ideological cleavages that characterize polarized-partisan committees, cleavages in Education, Interior (1977–80), and Ways and Means include other sources of committee conflict, which also reinforce existing partisan cleavages. In the Ways and Means Committee, there is some evidence that administration cleavages divide committee members into supporters and opponents of the president's policy initiatives. While pressures from the president constitute additional sources of committee conflict, the cleavages within Ways and Means remain polarized and tend to reinforce partisan loyalties in the committee. That is, there is a strong collinearity between partisan, ideological, and administration loyalties among Ways and Means Committee members.[1]

The Interior Committee is also characterized by three committee cleavages in the 1977–80 period. In addition to the partisan and

1. Descriptions of the factions that tend to coalesce into coalitions are provided in the explanations of the factional structures for each committee in Chapters 3 through 6. The percentages of votes in each category do not correspond to the figures presented in Chapter 2 because the calculations in Chapter 2 are based on the total number of votes taken in the committees. In contrast, the calculations in this chapter are based on all *non-tied* substantive votes.

Figure 39

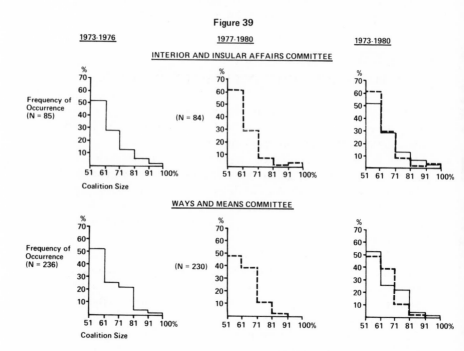

Source: Committee roll-call votes, U.S. House of Representative, 1973-1980.

254

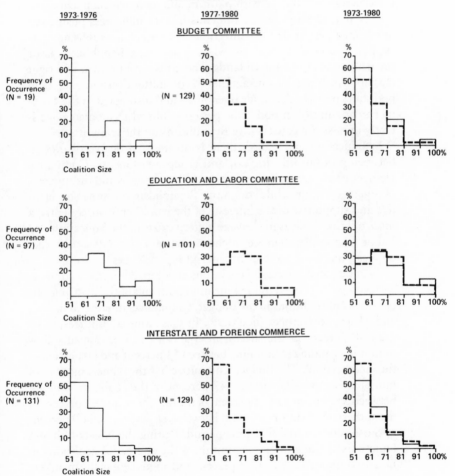

FIGURE 39
DISTRIBUTIONS OF THE SIZE OF SUCCESSFUL COALITIONS IN POLARIZED–PARTISAN
COMMITTEES: 1973-1980

ideological cleavages, members also divide over constituent interests concerned with environmental issues. The members from western states favor exploitation of the mineral, wilderness, and water resources of their states, while members from eastern states seek to restrict such usage. This constituency cleavage does not disrupt the polarized-partisan cleavage pattern within the committee, because the cleavage is collinear with partisan and ideological attachments. Simply put, ideology, party, and constituency influences push committee members in identical directions. As a result, liberal Democrats support conservation policies, while conservative Republicans favor the development of western lands. These two groups form two tight clusters which oppose one another in committee decision making in both time periods. A similar phenomenon is also noted in the Commerce Committee in both time periods—liberal Democrats consistently oppose the conservative Republicans on the committee.

In Education and Labor, there is an unusual degree of overlap between partisan, ideological, and group attachments. Committee Democrats are generally supportive of liberal causes and the interests of organized labor, while committee Republicans are more conservative and supportive of the interests of the employer. Consequently, a more polarized-partisan cleavage pattern exists in the Education and Labor Committee than we might expect of a committee with ideological, partisan, and constituency-group cleavages.

As anticipated, successful coalitions in polarized-partisan committees tend to be skewed toward the minimum end of the distributions of successful coalitions in the Budget, Commerce, Interior, and Ways and Means committees (figure 39). In these four committees, more than 50 percent of the successful coalitions can be considered as minimum-winning (containing between 51 percent and 60 percent of the membership). The Budget Committee has the highest number of minimum-winning coalitions: 47 percent of the coalitions contain between 51 percent and 55 percent of the members, and 63 percent of the successful coalitions contain between 51 percent and 60 percent of those voting in the first time period. During the Ninety-fifth and Ninety-sixth Congresses, one-fourth of the successful coalitions in Budget contained between 51 percent and 55 percent of the members voting.

Generally, between one-fourth and one-third of the successful coalitions in these four committees contain less than 56 percent of the members voting (1973–80). The distributions of successful coalitions in polarized-partisan committees are skewed toward the minimum size (51 percent to 60 percent of the voting membership). Thus, it appears that the reinforcement of partisan cleavages in committees promotes minimum-sized winning coalitions.[2]

The one exception to this generalization is the Education and Labor Committee. Although the committee is fragmented by ideological and constituency-group cleavages, the cleavages tend to reinforce partisanship. Such a polarized cleavage pattern should produce a greater proportion of minimum-winning coalitions. Successful coalitions in the Education and Labor Committee, however, do not exhibit such a pattern. The pattern in Education resembles the pattern in mixed-partisan committees more than the pattern in polarized-partisan committees: a greater concentration of coalitions that extend beyond the minimum size ( ) 60 percent of those voting) necessary to ensure success.

This anomaly *cannot* be explained in terms of the desire of the committee members to improve their chances of floor passage by building larger coalitions. "Education and Labor members' policy goals do not lead them to place a special value on floor success; they do not feel constrained by the institutional prescription of the House; and they do not adopt consensus-building, influence-preserving processes" (Fenno, 1973, p. 235). The greater participation of committee liberals,[3] however, can explain the creation of larger coalitions. This greater involvement by liberals (Chapter 1) could promote larger coalitions by discouraging the participation of conservatives. Conservative Republicans on the committee may feel that they can have a greater impact on committee legislation once it reaches the floor of the

2. The pattern in coalition outcomes in the Merchant Marine and Fisheries Committee also resembles polarized-partisan cleavage structure because of the association of constituency cleavages (environmental concerns) with ideological and partisan divisions within the committee. This committee is not included in the figures because of the small number of votes taken in the committee over the first four-year (baseline) period.

3. Increased voting participation in most polarized-partisan committees tends to reduce significantly the size of successful coalitions. The polarization of cleavages means that the same majority party coalition frequently forms; this group consistently controls committee decisions so that any changes in committee attendance fails to upset the majority party coalition and its control over committee decisions. The only uncertainty about the outcome in polarized-partisan committees is how large the margin of victory will be for the majority party coalition.

House. There, at least, they can subject the committee's legislation to amendment with greater prospects for success, especially in light of the committee's liberal image (Fenno, 1973).

MIXED-PARTISAN CLEAVAGE PATTERNS

A large subset of House committees have cleavages that are not mutually reinforcing. In these committees, partisanship is fragmented by the existence of ideological, administration, and constituency-group cleavages. Since these cleavages crosscut one another, there is a greater degree of fragmentation of member loyalties. Unlike polarized-partisan committees, partisanship in mixed-partisan committees is not reinforced by the other cleavages operating in the committee. Instead, these cleavages crosscut partisan loyalties and reduce the cohesion of partisan groupings. Committee factions tend to reflect the conjoint influences of all committee cleavages.

Mixed-partisan committees can be further classified according to the types of cleavages that tend to disrupt the partisanship of committee members, especially those from the majority party (Democrats). While all committees exhibit ideological cleavages, ideology appears to be the dominant source of divisions among Democrats on four committees: House Administration, Public Works and Transportation, Rules, and Science and Technology. In several other committees, administration cleavages divide majority party members—Appropriations, Government Operations, Judiciary, and Post Office and Civil Service. In these committees, pressure from the president and/or the executive agencies create further divisions among committee members that crosscut partisan loyalties. Finally, two committees exhibit cleavage patterns that include constituency-group pressures in addition to existing partisan and ideological cleavages within the committee: Agriculture and Banking, Finance, and Urban Affairs. Partisanship in these two committees is diluted by the interests of certain types of constituencies, or groups associated with those constituencies, that do not normally follow partisan and ideological lines.

The major ideological divisions in House Administration, Public Works, Rules, and Science and Technology are between conservative and liberal Democrats. In contrast, the ideological loyalties of Republican committee members are less divisive of their partisan loyalties. These committees are similar to those that have been classified as polarized-partisan with respect to the limited number of cleavages within the committees and the partisan and ideological nature of the cleavages. The difference between the two types of committees is that ideology reinforces partisan loyalties among committee Democrats in polarized committees, whereas in mixed-partisan committees ideology is divisive of Democratic partisanship.

The division among committee Democrats in these four committees produces some coalitions that are skewed toward a minimum size, but most of the successful coalitions in mixed-partisan committees with crosscutting ideological cleavages contain majorities larger than minimum size (figure 40). The majority of successful coalitions contain more than 60 percent of the voting members. This contrasts with polarized-partisan committees, where a majority of the successful coalitions contain less than 60 percent of the voting members. Thus, the additional source of committee conflict among Democrats forces successful coalitions to extend beyond the minimum size in order to accommodate the interests of dissident Democrats. It is assumed that compromises and negotiations between various Democratic factions are involved in broadening majority party coalitions. Since liberal and conservative Democrats frequently form a partisan coalition in these committees, minimum-winning coalitions arise with some frequency (about 30 percent of the successful coalitions contain between 51 percent and 60 percent of those voting). Nevertheless, the modal category of successful coalitions is usually composed of coalitions with 61 percent to 70 percent of the committee members voting on the winning side, and the majority of successful coalitions include more than 60 percent of the voting members.

The constituency-group interests that create cleavages in the Agriculture Committee are related to specific commodities (Jones, 1961; Parker and Parker, 1979). In Banking, the interests of commercial banking and savings and loan institutions and the constituency concerns of urban members create constituency and group cleavages within the committee (Salamon, 1975).

Some of these constituency-group cleavages exhibit a degree of convergence with party, but factionalism within the Democratic party normally prevents party-line voting from dominating committee decisions. For instance, while supporters of commodity interests are

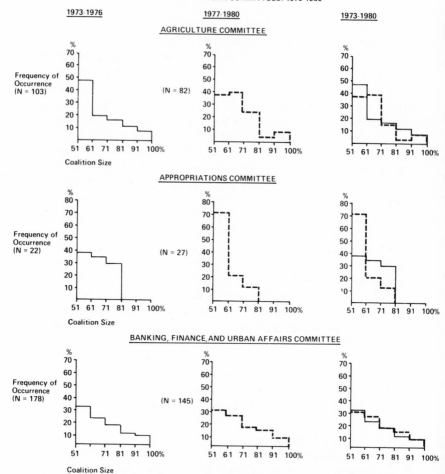

Figure 40
DISTRIBUTIONS OF THE SIZE OF SUCCESSFUL COALITIONS IN
MIXED-PARTISAN COMMITTEES: 1973-1980

260

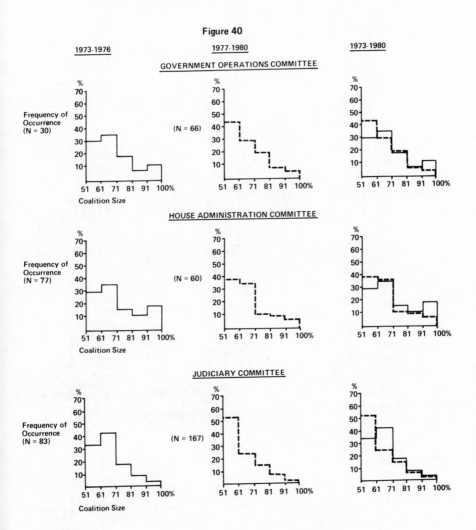

Figure 40

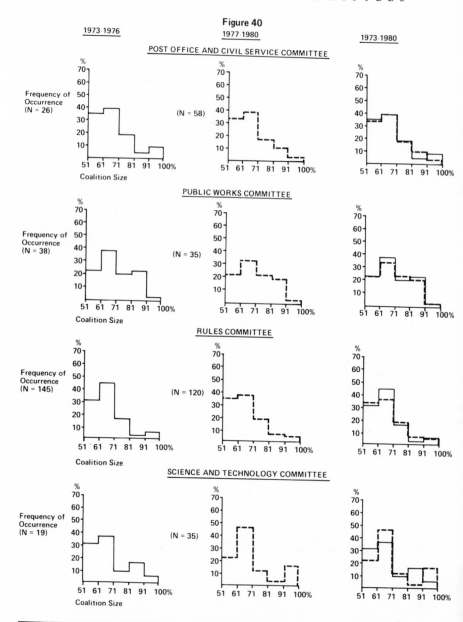

Figure 40

Source: Committee roll-call votes, U.S. House of Representatives, 1973-1980.

predominantly Democrats on the Agriculture Committee, ideology usually prevents the overlap of partisan and constituency cleavages from promoting a polarized-partisan cleavage pattern.

The ideological gap between northern and southern Democrats on Agriculture reached an extreme level between 1973 and 1976. During this period, southern Democrats had more in common with Republican committee members (presidential support, conservative ideological support, degree of support for Democratic policies) than they did with other committee Democrats. This frequently led to successful coalitions of southern Democrats and Republican members. The polarization of ideological, partisan, and constituency interests dissipated during the Carter administration as the areas of agreement between southern Democrats and Republicans narrowed. Still, even in this period (1977–80) differences between northern and southern Democrats on the Agriculture Committee forced partisan coalitions to broaden their appeal. Similarly, urban interests do not receive the same support among southern Democrats on the Banking Committee as they receive from northern Democratic members.

The addition of constituency conflicts to those created by ideology and party should necessitate the formation of coalitions larger than the minimum size necessary to ensure victory, especially where there is divergence between those cleavages. When committee cleavages are not mutually reinforcing, members are cross-pressured by the cleavages within the committee, and successful coalitions extend beyond the minimum size. This situation arises from the need of the majority party to formulate policies capable of satisfying a wider range of interests and a broader band of ideological and partisan attitudes. The number of factions that can be incorporated into the successful coalition thus increases.

Successful coalitions among this subset of mixed-partisan committees also tend to be larger than the minimum size needed for success (figure 40). The skew toward minimum-sized coalitions in Agriculture during the Ford-Nixon years (1973–76) could be anticipated in light of the unusual polarization between partisan, ideological, and constituency cleavages; such a polarized cleavage pattern produces more minimum-sized coalitions.

Coalitions in the environment of the Appropriations and Post Office and Civil Service committees have been described by Fenno (1973) as "executive-led," and administration cleavages have been identified in both of these committees. Administration cleavages co-exist with partisan and ideological differences among members of these two committees. Two other committees that can be added to this subset of mixed-partisan committees with administration cleavages are Government Operations and Judiciary. The policy areas in the jurisdictions of these two committees that attract executive interest are oversight of the operations of the executive agencies by Government Operations and the Judiciary Committee's formulation of federal codes for criminal offenses and illegal practices. Although administration cleavages are generally readily detected in committees with jurisdictions that touch upon executive functions and responsibilities, this is not the case with Government Operations and Judiciary. The pervasive effects of party and ideology tend to obscure administration cleavages in these two committees, but because other research suggests that the executive branch is an important influence in Judiciary (Perkins, 1980) and Government Operations (Henderson, 1970), the two committees have been included in the list of mixed-partisan committees with administration cleavages.

During a Republican presidency, administration cleavages are likely to crosscut partisan loyalties to some degree as the minority party president finds it necessary to seek majority party support for administration policies. That is, when the Democrats control the House, a Republican president quickly recognizes the value of bipartisanship in securing sufficient support for the passage of his policies. A Democratic president, on the other hand, reinforces committee partisanship because of the coincidence between partisan and administration pressures on these committees; both pressures uniformly push committee Democrats and Republicans in opposite directions. Democratic presidents can focus all of their persuasive skills on committee Democrats and ignore the interests of committee Republicans without endangering the prospects for a successful coalition of supporters. Hence, under Democratic presidents and Democratic control of the House, administration cleavages reinforce partisan attachments. Under Republican presidents, with Democratic control of the House, these cleavages are less collinear with party. When administration cleavages reinforce partisan divisions, we can expect a greater concentration of successful coalitions at the minimum level (1977–80). When these cleavages are not mutually reinforcing (1973–76), successful coalitions tend to be larger.

In three of these four committees (Appropriations, Government Operations, and Judiciary), coalition outcomes become skewed toward the minimum size during the Democratic Carter administration (figure 40). For example, during the Nixon-Ford presidencies only about one-third of the successful coalitions in the Appropriations and Judiciary committees contain less than 61 percent of those voting, but during the Carter administration more than one-half of the successful coalitions fall in this range (figure 40). The reinforcement of partisanship when the majority party exercises united control of the government produces a pattern of coalition outcomes that resembles the distribution of successful coalitions in polarized-partisan committees. When administration and partisan cleavages are not mutually reinforcing, as under divided control of the government by the majority and minority parties, coalition outcomes extend over a broader range and the skew toward minimum-sized coalitions is reduced.

The Post Office Committee does not exhibit this pattern of skew toward minimum-sized coalitions during the Carter administration. The emergence of a constituency cleavage in the committee divides the loyalties of committee Democrats and prevents minimum-sized coalitions from arising frequently. The cleavage reflects the divergent interests of federal workers and President Carter over the rights of federal employees. Such issues as Civil Service reform and the political rights of federal workers occupied the committee's agenda during this latter time period (1977–80). The division among committee Democrats served to offset the pressures that would normally reinforce committee partisanship during Democratic administrations. Thus, the pattern of successful coalitions in Post Office is the same under both Democratic and Republican administrations: successful coalitions are most likely to contain more than 60 percent of those voting (figure 40).

NONPARTISAN CLEAVAGE PATTERNS

Nonpartisan cleavage patterns are found in committees that place a premium on achieving committee consensus by minimizing partisanship. The policy-making responsibilities of these committees tend to deal with collective goods, such as foreign policy (Foreign Affairs Committee), national defense (Armed Services Committee), and congressional ethics (Standards of Official Conduct Committee).[4] While ideological cleavages are evident in these committees, there are only traces of partisanship. In the Armed Services Committee, for example, Democrats and Republicans frequently form bipartisan factions that are supportive of defense spending. When factions appear in Armed Services, the differences between them center on the degree of agreement with administration procurement and spending allocation policies. Similarly, in the area of foreign policy, presidents also seek to promote consensual support for their policies: "Executive officials place great emphasis on nonpartisanship in day-to-day dealings with the (Foreign Affairs) Committee on the theory that procedural nonpartisanship will stimulate substantive bipartisanship" (Fenno, 1973, p. 29).

The policy responsibilities of the Standards Committee force its members to seek unusual levels of committee consensus because the committee is charged with investigating the ethics violations of House members. These investigations have the potential of embarrassing not only the individuals involved but also the political parties and the House. In order to minimize the pervasive fear of politically motivated retribution, attempts are made to achieve bipartisan support for committee decisions and to ensure that any decisions are based on fact rather than political rancor. In order to promote objective investigations and to prevent one party from using a numerical advantage to embarrass the opposition party unjustly, the committee, unlike others in the House, maintains an equal ratio of Democratic and Republican members.

The drive for bipartisanship in these three Committees reduces the influence of party as a vehicle for organizing committee majorities. The result is a skew in the size of successful coalitions toward consensus (universalism). That is, a large proportion of the successful coalitions will contain more than 70 percent of those voting (figure 41). In Armed Services, for instance, almost one-half (47 percent) of the successful coalitions between 1973 and 1976 contain more than 80 percent of those voting. During the same period, three-fifths of the

4. There are insufficient votes within the Foreign Affairs Committee and the Standards Committee during the 1977–80 period to permit analysis of coalition size.

The Impact of Cleavages on Coalition Formation

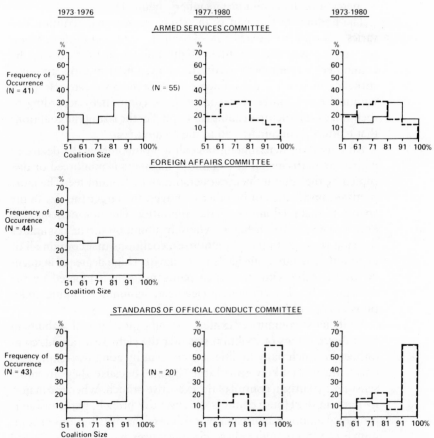

Figure 41
DISTRIBUTION OF THE SIZE OF SUCCESSFUL COALITIONS IN NONPARTISAN COMMITTEES

Source: Committee roll-call votes, U.S. House of Representatives, 1973-1980.

267

winning coalitions in the Standards Committee contained more than 90 percent of the voting members. Finally, in the least consensus-oriented committee of this subset, Foreign Affairs, about one-fifth of the successful coalitions (21 percent) contain between 71 percent and 75 percent of the committee members (figure 41).

The findings of this part of the study suggest that coalition size varies according to the structure of conflict within committees. Members of a committee are differentially influenced by forces in the committee's environment—party, ideology, administration, and constituency influences; the influence of these forces creates cleavages within the committee. Categorization of committees according to their cleavage structures enables us to predict the size of the coalitions that tend to predominate within the committees.

An important determinant of coalition outcomes is the degree to which the partisanship of committee members is reinforced or disrupted by the other influences operating in the committee. The more partisanship is crosscut by other cleavages, the larger the size of the coalitions that predominate in the committee. The most extreme case occurs when partisanship is relatively unimportant in committee decision making. In these committees, coalitions that contain all or most voting members are likely to form with a high degree of frequency. At the other extreme, when partisanship is reinforced by the overlap with other committee cleavages, minimum-winning coalitions are most likely to predominate.

While most committees exhibit a significant degree of stability in their distributions of coalition size over the eight-year period, committees in which party loyalties are crosscut by administration influences are most likely to exhibit change, because they are most sensitive to partisan control of the executive branch. When the majority party in the House controls the executive branch, partisanship is promoted among majority party members. The distributions of committee coalitions under these circumstances tend to skew toward minimum winning size. Divided control of the government promotes broader coalitions as the president seeks opposition support.

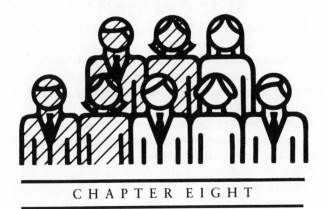

CHAPTER EIGHT

Some Concluding Observations on Factions

The major part of this analysis has now been completed. In the preceding chapters we have demonstrated that in making decisions on conflictual issues, the members of House committees break into distinct voting blocs composed of members who frequently vote together. These blocs or factions arise as members are pushed and pulled by salient influences within the committee's environment. Underlying the factions are cleavages, or lines of division, in committee decision making along which members split. When legislation touches upon salient cleavages, members divide into factions, and these factions can be detected in the voting patterns of committee members. In this chapter we review the sources of cleavage in committees and the relationship between cleavages and coalitions. In addition, we return once again to the question of stability and change by examining the sources of change in committee decision making. Finally, we explore the implications of this analysis for the study of policy change.

THE SOURCES OF CLEAVAGES IN COMMITTEES

Four influences have been found to exert a significant and differential effect on committees: party, ideology, the administration, and constituency and group interests. Most prominent among these influences are party and ideology, which are found in conjunction with one another in most House committees. Our analysis suggests that despite the weakened position of political parties in Congress and the decline in party unity, partisanship still plays an important role in the operation of the committee system. Party is an important influence in the creation of factions and cleavages, as well as an important force in the organization of coalitions in decision making. We note that party influences can either be reinforced by other influences in the committee or fragmented by those influences. For instance, in committees like Commerce and Budget we find that party and ideology are the predominant influences in decision making. Further, in these committees ideology tends to reinforce party sentiments among most members. As a result, we also note in these two committees strongly bipolar factions. Decision making in these committees tends to be conflictual in nature with a substantial proportion of minimum-winning coalitions forming.

By contrast, in committees such as House Administration, Public Works, Rules, and Science and Technology, which are also influenced predominantly by party and ideology, ideology fragments rather than reinforces committee partisan loyalties. We say that ideology crosscuts rather than reinforces party. The consequences of the cross-pressuring created by ideology is evident in the committee factional structures; the membership is more dispersed than in polarized committees and more factions appear in committee decision making. These committees are also distinguished from the more polarized committees by the types of coalitions that form in decision making. In committees where partisanship is crosscut by other influences, larger-than-minimum coalitions appear. Finally, in committees where partisanship is minimal, such as Armed Services, Foreign Affairs, and Standards, we find evidence that ideology is a more important influence on decision making. Decision making appears to be more consensual in these committees as evidenced by the number of unusually large coalitions that form.

The importance of ideology in committee decision making is our second major finding. Previous studies of floor voting in the House have suggested that ideology was not very influential in that context. In committee decision making, we find its influence in every committee examined. Such influence is probably due to the fact that the committee system encourages representatives to specialize, which increases their ability to discern the ideological content in the legislation presented to the committee. Ideology has been shown to be an important factor in the divisions that exist between party members on the committees. When ideological cleavages crosscut partisanship, party becomes less effective as a means of aggregating members into coalitions. As a result, coalitions must expand to include more divergent points of view.

The influences of the executive branch and constituency interests are also discernible in several committees. When the administration exerts an influence on committee decision making, its impact takes one of two forms. First, such influence may be seen in factions. For example, in Appropriations we detect a bloc of members who appear to display loyalties to the executive agencies. Similarly, we detect the influence of the executive branch in a faction in the Post Office and Civil Service Committee. In other committees, like Ways and Means, the influence of the administration is harder to detect because it tends to be collinear with party and ideological influences. In two committees, Government Operations and Judiciary, we suspect that the executive branch influences decision making, although its influence on the formation of committee factions is difficult to detect. Finally, in Armed Services and Foreign Affairs, administration and ideological influences crosscut partisan loyalties and fragment the committee membership. In these two committees, we also find a large proportion of unusually large coalitions.

The administration exerts a second type of influence on committee decision making. A switch from divided to united control of government is reflected in the behavior of southern Democrats. When Democrats control the Congress and Republicans the presidency, southern Democrats are cross-pressured by their partisan and ideological loyalties. This makes them more vulnerable to appeals for presidential support than other Democrats. In such situations, they often vote with the Republicans. Under united control of government, the southern members tend to join their Democratic colleagues when voting in committee. The switch to united control is also reflected in the

271

coalition patterns of committees in which we detect administration influences. When the Democrats control both Congress and the presidency, the coalitions in these committees tend to decline in size, and the distributions of coalitions tend to skew toward the minimum winning end of the continuum. The partisan and administration influences in these committees become more collinear under united control; as a result, coalitions need not expand their appeals to committee members to accommodate as many factions. In response, the coalitions in these committees attenuate.

Constituency influences that are tied to the policies decided by the committees can lead to further divisions among committee members. Three committees display the influence of constituencies and group interests—Education and Labor, Agriculture, and Banking. Constituency influences crosscut partisan loyalties in Agriculture and Banking, and hence these two are classified as mixed-partisan committees in our examination of coalitions. In both of these committees, coalitions tend to be larger than minimum (60 percent) but smaller than in committees like Armed Services or Foreign Affairs. Education and Labor is classified as a polarized committee because of the overlap between labor and ideological influences on the committee. The overrepresentation of liberal members, however, results in coalitions beyond minimum winning in this committee. Therefore, although the nature of committee cleavages suggests a polarized committee with a large proportion of minimum-winning coalitions, the skew in the distribution of coalition size is more similar to mixed-partisan than polarized committees. We also note that the emergence of a constituency faction in Post Office continued to disperse the membership even when the switch to united control should have caused the committee factions to become more collinear. Finally, in the Interior Committee during the 1977–1980 period we detect the influence of constituency that is tied to environmental issues, but in this committee these influences are collinear with party and ideology. Therefore, we continue to observe a high percentage of minimum-winning coalitions even with the presence of this influence.

As this brief summary suggests, an important finding of this study is the differential effect of the various influences on the committees. Not only do we find differences in the types of influences that impinge upon committee decision making, but we also note differences in the ways the same influences divide members. Thus, while we find in some committees that party and ideology are the predominant influences, for instance, we also note differences among these committees in the degree to which ideology crosscuts partisanship. This crosscutting leads to differences in the degree of dispersion of the membership of committees affected by the same influences. Thus, committees can be distinguished from one another not only on the basis of the predominant influences on decision making but also by the degree to which these influences independently divide the membership.

By using the second type of distinction to categorize committees according to the degree to which partisanship is crosscut by other influences, we are able to suggest an explanation of the size of coalitions that form in committees. That is, the more that partisanship is reinforced by the other influences in the committee (creating a polarized membership configuration), the greater the likelihood minimum-winning coalitions will form in the committee. Conversely, the greater the factionalization of the membership, as a result of influences that crosscut partisanship, the greater the likelihood of larger-than-minimum coalitions.

STABILITY IN COMMITTEE CLEAVAGES AND COALITIONS

The factions that form in committees reflect the nature of the forces acting to influence legislation within the committee. These factions, and the cleavages that create them, represent the *salient* divisions within committees. Most of the committee cleavages that we analyzed during the eight-year span of this analysis exhibit little change in saliency. Perhaps the most important influence on the continuity in committee cleavages is the committees' jurisdictions and responsibilities.

Committee jurisdictions help to determine the types of forces that will be salient in the committee's environment. For example, committees that touch upon important executive functions such as foreign affairs, defense, revenues, and expenditures exhibit factions supporting or opposing the president and individual agencies. Further, some jurisdictions (Rules, for instance) are explicitly partisan in their duties and responsibilities; that is, partisanship has become an institutionalized feature of the environments of these committees. Jurisdictions also determine which committees will have to deal with some of the most controversial issues within society. For instance, the Education and Labor Committee cannot avoid large doses of liberal-conservative committee conflict, since its responsibilities cover the ideologically divisive issues of labor-management rights and federal involvement in education. Thus, we can speak of *partisan, ideological, executive, agency, group,* and *constituency-pressured* committee jurisdictions as a way of characterizing the major sources of salient cleavages within individual House committees.

Committee jurisdictions are stable for at least two reasons. Fears about the loss of power, responsibilities, and/or "turf," provide an adequate rationale for most congressional committees to resist changes in their jurisdictions. Not surprisingly, where such changes have been suggested, committees have vigorously campaigned against them. Even if these political problems could be resolved to the satisfaction of the committees involved, there is no assurance that the conciliation would pave the way for modifications in committee jurisdictions. As one of the most recent attempts to reform the committee system in the House demonstrates, interest groups with established and supportive relations with a congressional committee will mobilize to resist attempts to upset these well-nurtured relationships (Davidson and Oleszek, 1977):

> The unions, like other special interest groups, opposed the jurisdictional changes basically because they would destroy, as chief AFL-CIO lobbyist Andrew Biemiller phrased it, "some old relationships between established committees, and legislative functions vital to our membership." "Carefully nurtured contacts with key congressmen and their aides, as well as years of selective campaign contributions," one journalist wrote, "will all come loose when a new unfamiliar committee takes jurisdiction." (P. 196)

Thus, there are internal and external forces to promote stablity in committee jurisdictions. The consequence has been a "hardening" of committee jurisdictions and responsibilities; stable jurisdictions tend to solidify attachments, commitments, and loyalties, and thereby promote continuity in the divisions among committee members.

The jurisdiction of a committee also appears to be a major component in a committee's attractiveness to different members. While some committees, like Appropriations, Rules, and Ways and Means, appeal to just about every member, the attractiveness of most committees varies from member to member. Congressional committees with jurisdictions that can acommodate individual goals and policy interests are sought by members. The diversity in goals and policy interests makes different congressional committees attractive to different House members. Those with similar goals and policy interests tend to gravitate to the same committees.

The stability of committee jurisdictions means that the attractive features of committees have also remained relatively stable. That is, the differential attraction of individual committees has remained fairly constant over time. Thus, congressional committees are likely to appeal to the same types of congressmen. Those attracted to the committee are likely to take an active part in the committee's business and, therefore, help to guide its deliberations. When members are assigned to committees they perceive as useful to their career objectives, they are more likely to allocate their scarce resources (principally time and staff) to committee-related activities. Conversely, members assigned to committees where activities do not mesh well with their individual goals are likely to shift resources at their disposal to activities unrelated to committee work (Shepsle, 1978, p. 244).

As those attracted to the committee become actively involved, they are pushed and pulled in the same directions as others with similar policy perspectives, goals, and loyalties. In the process, the majority of members find that their views can be accommodated within the existing factional structure of the committee, and new factions, therefore, do not emerge.

The distributions of successful coalitions tend to mirror the stability of committee cleavages. If cleavage patterns displayed by the committees are not seriously disrupted, committee coalitions appear to remain fairly stable over time (with the exception of committees where administration influences are particularly salient). This stability occurs because the cleavages that divide the committee tend to remain stable over time, and hence, the same types of factions tend to form. By extension, it means that the same types of coalitions form as well. Further, if the cleavage patterns within the committee remain stable, the same committees will continue to produce minimum-winning, larger-than-minimum, or universal size coalitions.

In short, committee jurisdictions serve to attract members with views that can be represented by the existing factions within the committee. As a consequence, cleavages within committees remain fairly stable. Those not attracted to the committee but nevertheless assigned to it (perhaps as a minor assignment) will rarely seek to be actively involved in the committee's deliberations. As a consequence, they do not *consistently* confront the panoply of pressures that operate on those actively participating in committee decision making. The behavior of members is more erratic, and their factional attachments are less stable and more random in appearance.

Finally, we can expect voting alignments to remain fairly stable, because there is a large degree of continuity in the voting behavior of congressmen (Asher and Weisberg, 1978) and in the membership of committees. The stability in the voting patterns of congressmen promotes continuity in the cleavages that exist within the committee. In addition, since members are now more likely to receive a preferred assignment earlier in their congressional careers (Gertzog, 1976), those attracted to a committee are likely to remain on that committee for a longer period of time. This stability in membership also produces continuity in the cleavages within the committee. In fact, the greatest turnover in House committees appears to occur among those committees with the least attractive jurisdictions (in terms of the breadth of responsibilities and in the variety of goals that can be satisfied through committee membership). Hence, the policy interests and legislative goals that entice committee membership promote member participation in committee decisions and stability in the core of members that guide committee deliberations. In sum, the observed stability in committee cleavages can be attributed to the stability in the types of individuals that take an active interest in committee deliberations, in the jurisdictions of House committees, and in the voting behavior of congressmen.

CHANGE IN COMMITTEE CLEAVAGES AND COALITIONS

While committee cleavages exhibit substantial continuity over time, several conditions promote changes in these cleavages. New issues, for example, can arise within a committee to alter the existing factional structure either by enhancing (e.g., Interior Committee) or by diminishing the saliency of an existing environmental influence. The increased saliency of an environmental influence (e.g., Post Office Committee) produces additional pressures on committee members and, therefore, serves as another potential source of committee conflict. Issues with this capacity are extremely controversial in nature; while a committee might have an incentive to avoid such issues, their significance forces the members to make policy decisions on them.

The mere emergence of new issues on the committee's agenda, however, does not ensure that the existing factional structure will be altered. Issues may change within a committee, but as long as they touch upon the same types of cleavages that already exist within the committee the factional structure will remain intact (e.g., Science and Technology Committee). Likewise, the disappearance of certain types of issues from the committee's agenda can neutralize an existing cleavage by reducing the pressures on committee members.

If the emergence of new issues results in changes in the cleavage patterns such that the cleavages become more collinear or become more crosscutting, the coalitions that tend to form will change as well. For instance, if ideology were to become more collinear with party in a committee where ideology currently crosscuts party, the skew in the distribution of successful coalitions would be expected to move closer to the minimum-winning end of the continuum. Conversely, if party and ideology become more independent as the result of the emergence of new issues, the skew in the distribution in a polarized-partisan committee would be expected to move from the minimum-winning end of the continuum toward larger-than-minimum coalition size.

In sum, where new issues systematically create additional salient pressures on committee members, we can expect new cleavages to appear within the committee. Of course, such issues must demonstrate a degree of continuity over time to produce stable committee factions. That there is little change in a committee's factions, even when the issues that a committee deals with have changed, is because most of the salient issues that a committee handles create the same types of environmental presures on committee members.

Another factor that has the potential of changing both cleavage and coalition patterns is membership change. There are four ways in which a change in membership could alter the cleavage and coalition patterns in committees. A change in the attractiveness of the committee could result in members with divergent goals joining the committee. As Fenno (1973) notes, similarity of member goals leads to agreement on the strategic premises employed in committee decision making. An influx of members with different goals could disrupt such agreement and lead to new divisions within the committee. This analysis suggests that shifting cleavage patterns can significantly affect the nature of coalitions that form in the committee.

Changes in the ideological or partisan nature of the committee membership can also introduce new cleavages or exacerbate older lines of cleavage. The Democratic leadership's efforts to liberalize the Democratic membership on the Budget Committee in the early 1970s served to strengthen the partisan-ideological cleavages in the committee. In this instance, coalition patterns did not change, because the membership changes strengthened rather than disrupted the cleavage patterns already present in the committee. Introducing more ideological divergence into a polarized committee, however, might alter the lines of cleavage and change the pattern of coalitions. Similarly, introducing more partisanship into committees like Foreign Affairs and Armed Services by means of membership changes could significantly alter decision making in those committees.

A significant change in the electoral fortunes of one of the parties could also alter the coalition patterns in the committees. For instance, replacement of members of one party by members of the other can lead to policy changes (Brady and Lynn, 1973). Therefore, the addition of a significant number of new party members could lead to new cleavage patterns and hence new coalition patterns. Even if cleavage patterns did not change, a lopsided majority, by virtue of its numerical advantage, could lead to larger coalitions. In this case, while we would expect the mean size of coalitions to become larger, we would not necessarily expect the skew of the coalition distributions to change. This expectation is based on Hinckley's (1972) finding that the size of the majority in the House did affect the size of floor coalitions, but it alone was not sufficient to explain coalition size. Further, incumbent electoral safety in the House has to some extent limited the number of new members entering the chamber.

Finally, a realigning election that produced a new party coalition could be expected to disrupt older lines of cleavage and produce different coalition patterns. For example, Paul Beck (1979) suggests that the majority party leadership is more effective and partisan loyalties are stronger after a realignment than when a majority coalition has maintained power for an extended period. Increased partisanship does have the potential of producing new cleavage patterns in committees where partisan loyalties are crosscut by other cleavages. In these committees, increased partisanship might significantly influence coalition patterns.

The ideological and partisan complexion of the executive branch also appears to influence committee factions. For example, under the administration of a conservative Republican president, there is a large degree of partisan-ideological conflict within congressional committees. As a result, conservative Democrats, particularly those from the South, participate more frequently in Republican coalitions. The shift to a Democratic president increases the partisanship of most committees and reduces the association of the conservative Democrats with Republican factions. Admittedly, Jimmy Carter's southern heritage could also be responsible for the diminished responsiveness of southern Democrats to the conservative coalition; however, since partisanship in House committees increases generally during Carter's administration, we can attribute a significant proportion of the increased loyalty of southern Democrats to partisan control of the White House. We also note changes in the distributions of coalitions in those committees where administration influences crosscut partisan loyalties. In these committees unified control of the government produces more minimun-winning coalitions as administration and party cleavages become more collinear. Thus, the ideological and partisan composition of the executive branch can alter the nature of committee coalitions, even while the major divisions within the committee remain intact.

Finally, committee cleavages may change as the divisions among members are muted through the resolution of underlying conflicts. This can occur with the emergence of consensus among committee members, or the resolution of conflict through a partisan-mutual adjustment process. In addition, conflict can disappear as committees change responsibilities and/or jurisdictions. As noted earlier, however, changes in committee jurisdictions are rare.

It appears from this analysis that changes in committee cleavage patterns and coalition outcomes are the exception rather than the rule in most House committees. Two important factors in the stability of coalition outcomes are jurisdictional and membership stability. Both promote stability in cleavage patterns within the committee, and hence, stability in the size of coalitions that form.

IMPLICATIONS FOR POLICY CHANGE

Stability in factional patterns and coalitions appears to be far more common than change. The types of policies and alternatives that emerge from committees would thus seem to be fairly stable as well. When changes do occur that could have an effect on policy, they tend to be isolated to a few committees and to occur over a period of time. Innovative policy changes of a comprehensive nature seem to be more likely to occur during realignment periods rather than in more normal political periods (Burnham, 1970; Brady, 1978; Sinclair, 1982). The reason such periods are more conducive to "clusters of policy change" is suggested by David Brady. His analysis points to several conditions that result from critical elections that promote such changes. In order to enact major policy changes, the majority party must be capable of building legislative majorities both on the floor and in the committees that will pass such changes. Two obstacles to this ability under normal conditions are the party-constituency cross-pressures to which many members are subject and the insulated nature of the committee system, which cushions it from rapid and massive changes. Realigning elections, however, reduce party-constituency cross-pressuring and disrupt the committee system.

> Specifically, critical elections change the constituency bases of the congressional parties along a continuum which reflects the changes that are occurring in the "party in the electorate," thereby helping to diminish party-constituency cross-pressures. Such elections also effectively rearrange the committees of the House so that the party leadership is able to perform its function of organizing coherent majorities for legislative programs.   (Brady, 1978, p. 81)

Brady notes three major changes in the committee system during the realignments of the 1890s and the 1930s that disrupted the committees sufficiently to produce clusters of policy changes. The first was a high level of membership turnover. Additionally, turnover led to the emergence of new committee leaders who were not prominent immediately prior to the realignment period. Under normal electoral conditions, the membership on committees changes slowly over time. New members, therefore, are socialized to the norms, and committee continuity tends to be reinforced. In contrast, critical elections are associated with rapid and massive committee membership changes which disrupt this continuity and bring in new committee leaders who themselves are not well socialized. Finally, the newer members who join the committees are more supportive of the party, because they also tend to come from districts most affected by the critical election. That is, the polarization of the electorate in these districts reduces the cross-pressures that a member normally feels from the often-conflicting pressures of the party and the constituency.

The explanations of committee decision making presented here suggest the mechanism that translates such changes into a greater potential for nonincremental policy changes. The reduction of cross-pressures during realignments should result in a greater overlap of the influences on decision making in committees. In this study, when the cleavages in a committee are overlapping rather than crosscutting, the factional structure in the committee tends to be polarized. Further, this type of factional structure is associated with minimum-winning coalitions. The reason for this is that the majority party coalition needs to satisfy fewer interests. The overlap in cleavages means that policy appeals made along party lines are apt to satisfy other interests in the committee.

A second factor leading to smaller coalitions in polarized committees is the increased certainty with which party leaders can build a coalition. In committees with crosscutting cleavages and a more dispersed factional structure, members generally maintain a primary loyalty to one faction, but at the same time they can display lesser loyalty to one or more other factions in the committee. This dispersion increases the degree of uncertainty in coalition formation. A majority coalition not only must expand its policy appeals to attract a sufficient number of members but also must broaden its appeals to be sure of holding those members who, while maintaining a primary loyalty to that faction, also have loyalties to other factions. In this situation, the majority coalition cannot be certain whether the issue being debated is one on which some of its membership may defect. In a polarized committee, loyalties are not so divided. Hence there is more certainty that coalition members will remain loyal. Policy appeals can be narrower without endangering the changes of winning.

When several interests must be satisfied in building a winning coalition, the chance for policy change decreases because policy alternatives must take into account several influences. Compromises are necessary, and policy can be expected to be more moderate and less innovative. The chance for innovative changes, therefore, would appear to be greater when fewer interests need to be satisfied. This situation appears to occur in committees where the influences on decision making reinforce rather than crosscut one another. Thus, conditions that reduce cross-pressuring would tend to increase the likelihood of polarized committee factions and of nonincremental policy changes. Under these conditions party would be an effective vehicle for mobilizing a majority coalition.

We also note, like Brady (1978), that membership change is a potential source of disruption in committees. When new members are different (because of their goals, their ideology, their party loyalty, or their sensitivity to influences on decision making) from the continuing committee membership, they are more likely to introduce new conflicts into the committee that cannot be subsumed under the normal cleavage structure. The number of new members entering under normal electoral conditions is generally limited, and thus the potential for change is reduced. Further, the conflicts introduced by new members have the potential of dispersing as well as polarizing the committee membership. Hence, in interalignment periods, changes in the committees tend to be gradual and would be as likely to disperse as to polarize the membership. By contrast, realignment periods are associated with rapid and extensive membership changes, and the nature of the changes would tend to be systematic; that is, the new members tend to be more partisan thereby increasing the polarization of committees. Realignment periods, could be expected, therefore, to create systematic changes in the committee system that increase the likelihood of nonincremental policy change.

Finally, critical elections generally involve the introduction of new issues that cannot be handled by politics as usual (Burnham, 1970; Sundquist, 1983). The issues that emerge during these periods polarize the electorate and lead to changes in the party coalitions. As illustrated in Chapter 2, new issues that emerge during more normal electoral periods are generally subsumed under the existing committee cleavages and rarely result in the disruption of the factional structures. The same is not true of realigning periods; issues introduced in these periods have a greater potential for disrupting more stable lines of cleavage and factional patterns. In addition, since such issues tend to polarize the electorate, they would appear to have a greater potential for also polarizing the committee membership.

Under normal electoral conditions, the three factors that have a potential for changing committee decision making (changes in the nature of influences on decision making, changes in membership, and changes in the issues debated by committees) can lead to either greater dispersal or greater polarization in the committees. The difference during realignment periods is that all three forces have the potential of systematically changing the committees in the same manner: all three forces tend to appear in conjunction with one another during realignment periods, and all three have the potential of producing greater polarization in the committees. As the earlier discussion suggests, the possibility for nonincremental policy changes appears to be greater in committees with a polarized factional structure. If all or most of the committees were to move in the direction of greater polarization, there would be a concomitant rise in the possibility that clusters of policy change would emerge from the committees. It would appear, therefore, that forces which have the potential for producing systematic changes in the nature of conflict in the committees also have a higher potential for producing policy change.

THE STUDY OF COMMITTEE FACTIONS AND CLEAVAGES

In addition to providing information about committee decision making, this study should prove useful to future researchers whether or not they use roll-call data in their analyses. Interviews with committee members, for example, have proven to be a valuable method for collecting information about member goals, strategies, and perceptions of external influences on committee decisions (Fenno, 1973). Unfortunately, interviews are quite costly in terms of the time spent both by the interviewer and the congressmen. Access to and availability of committee members often become major criteria in their selection, but such a pragmatic approach often means that the members selected to be interviewed are not representative of the committee members or of the dominant committee factions. Hence, inferences about committee decision making may be misleading. The use of this analysis to "target" for interviews certain members who represent the major circles of power within the committee could minimize the problems associated with interviewing an unrepresentative or "inactive" subset of members, or a group of members that cluster into only a few of the committee factions.

Studies of the voting behavior of House members form a substantial segment of our literature, and the availability of recorded committee votes should increase the attention given to roll-call studies of committee decision making. The present analysis can serve as a starting point or baseline for diachronic studies of committee factionalism. Future studies of individual committees can compare their descriptions of committee factions with those provided by this analysis. These comparisons can aid in determining the nature of changes in committee cleavages and of shifts in the factional structure within the committee. As a result, we may be better able to understand the dynamics of committee changes and their impact on committee decision making.

In many cases, studies of congressional committees have taken a case study approach by focusing on individual committee decisions. The value of these studies rests in the detail and specification that they supply about the actors involved in committee decisions and the processes that guide committee deliberations. In organizing a case study, consideration must be given to the decisions or policies to be studied. The analysis of committee cleavages can aid in the systematic selection of committee decisions and policies for study, because it isolates important, conflictual committee decisions. Further, using salient conflict as a criteria for case study selection can strengthen the comparability of such studies by ensuring that committee studies would analyze the same types of decisions—those that create significant cleavages within the committee. Since the findings of one case study could be readily compared and contrasted with those based on other case studies, the generalizability of the findings derived from such studies, often limited, could be increased.

In conclusion, the definition of cleavages within a committee provides a general guide to the forces operating within congressional committees. It is a sketch of the basic contours of committee decision making; further topographic detail can be supplied by future studies of individual committees or specific policy decisions. The importance of our analysis is that it provides congressional scholars with a view of the "lay of the land," suggesting questions to be addressed and researched and decision-making processes that warrant further investigation.

Procedures for Analyzing Committee Votes

The methods employed in our study demonstrate a strategy for analyzing committee votes that entails the use of Q (component)-factor analysis to identify factions within a committee. Q-factor analysis consists of factor analyzing a matrix in which variables refer to entities (i.e., committee members) and the cases (roll-call votes) are the characteristics. This procedure delineates the voting blocks within the committee and can provide a visual interpretation of the factional structure of the committee (Grumm, 1963). The accuracy and validity of such a visual interpretation can be corroborated by examining the demographic, political, and electoral correlates of the individual committee factions. The R(component)-factor analysis of the same data describes the salient policy cleavages within the committee. R-factor analysis consists of factor analyzing a matrix with the variables (roll-call votes) referring to the characteristics of entities (committee members); the cases are the committee members. The policy dimensions capture the impact that the nature of issues can have on the organization of a committee's factions. Thus, the research strategy provides for: (1) definition of committee factions, (2) corroboration of visual interpretations of the factional structure, and (3) determination of factional stability within committees.

The factional alignments within a committee are analytically defined as the dimensions (factors) derived from a principal component analysis of the non-(near) unanimous substantive roll call votes (amendments) within each committee. A principal component analysis is performed in lieu of other factor-analysis models because this technique appears to be best suited for the definition of the independent dimensions of a committee's vote-space. In an earlier analysis, we examined and compared the results of image, alpha, and common-factor analysis to determine the impact that different factor solutions might have in defining the factional alignments; this procedure was subsequently dropped after no notable differences in the dimensional structure appeared in different factor-analysis solutions for several committees. In this study, a committee's factional alignments correspond to the dimensional structure within the committee's votes—each faction is associated with an extracted *factor*. All factors with an eigenvalue greater than 1.00 are retained unless they appear to capture the unique voting behavior of individual committee members.[1]

Since the analysis attempts to delineate patterns of vote agreement among committee members, a Q-component analysis of committee votes is performed in which the committee members serve as "variables" and each roll-call vote becomes an "observation" or "case." The Q-component analysis produces factor loadings that represent the correlation between dimensions (factions) and variables (committee members). The square of a factor loading represents the propor-

---

1. A popular criterion for determining the number of factors to be extracted is to retain unities in the principal diagonal of the correlation matrix and limit the factors to those with eigenvalues greater than unity—the total variance of one variable. The sum of the eigenvalues is equal to the sum of the principal diagonal elements of the matrix factored. If the matrix is a correlation matrix with unities in the main diagonal, the sum of the eigenvalues will equal the number of variables; the *average* eigenvalue will therefore be unity. This implies that if there is sufficient correlation within the data for a few eigenvalues to be much larger than unity, then a greater number of eigenvalues less than unity must exist to maintain an average eigenvalue of unity. The decision to expand or contract dimensions, or factors, is designed to distinguish unique voting styles from general patterns (voting blocs). Occasionally, two members vote together to an unusual extent, and this agreement is unique within the committee; in these cases, we have listed these members as "doublets" beneath the tables describing the factional alignments and correlates.

tion of variation that a variable shares with a dimension or factor. We can interpret a squared factor loading as reflecting the extent to which a committee member votes with a particular faction. Therefore, *factor loadings serve as measurements of the attachment of each committee member to the various factions within that committee*; the vectors of the factor loadings (one vector for each extracted factor) are the dependent variables in the analysis of each committee's voting pattern.

A varimax rotation, generally regarded as the best analytic orthogonal rotation, is performed on each committee's factional structure in order to simplify the interpretation of the alignments. The varimax criterion for orthogonal rotation comes closest to a simple structure solution. A strong feature of varimax is its ability to discern the same cluster of variables regardless of the number or combination of other variables in the analysis. The rotation of the factor solution delineates the voting blocs (factions) within the committee and simplifies the interpretation of the factional alignments. Clearly, a varimax rotation ignores the empirical correlations among factors and, therefore, may obscure important relationships within a committee's factional structure. However, the effects of ignoring the relationships among factors (factions) are not serious, since the correlations among a committee's factions that appear if we allow the factors to assume a fairly oblique (correlated) solution are normally quite weak.

All substantive, nonunanimous amendments voted upon by at least 70 percent of the committee members included in the analysis are also subjected to an *R*-component analysis to delineate the policy dimensions in committee voting. Each committee member can be scored on the various policy dimensions. In extracting the policy dimensions, those factors which fail to account for at least 10 percent of the variation in committee voting are eliminated; this cut-off point serves to delineate the reliable from the unique factors. In order to *simplify* and *sharpen* the interpretation of these dimensions, only those votes which are strongly correlated with an underlying policy dimension are selected for study—that is, any vote with a factor loading greater than .82. If an issue has a factor loading greater than .82, the underlying dimension can explain approximately two-thirds of the variation in the votes on the issue. The application of this criterion improves the interpretation of the issue dimensions by illuminating the major issue components of the dimension. This restricted pool of issues is subsequently refactored into the same number of extracted issue dimensions, and factor scores that summarize a committee member's position on the various policy dimensions are obtained. In the study, these factor scores are referred to as *policy-dimension scores*.[2] These dimension scores serve as explanatory variables that help to define the nature of factional alignments in House committees.

2. The factor scores are computed as a weighted product of the existing data: factor score = (number of committee votes/nonmissing committee votes) $\times$ $_i F_i z_i$, where F_i is the factor-score coefficient, z_i is the standardized variable, and the summation occurs over all nonmissing votes. We have replaced absences with the mean vote for the issue where a committee member has missed less than one-third of the votes; otherwise, the committee member's issue-dimension score is defined as missing data. These calculations are necessary due to the uneven vote participation of committee members.

APPENDIX B

Partisan Divisions in Conservative Coalition Support

TABLE B-1. Mean Conservative Coalition Support Scores Showing Partisan Divisions in House Committees for the 91st–96th Congresses

Committee	Overall Score	Democrats	Republicans
	91st Congress		
Agriculture	66.81	57.76	77.06
Appropriations	54.56	46.93	65.25
Armed Services	58.97	52.13	68.81
Banking, Finance, and Urban Affairs	42.86	31.55	57.93
District of Columbia	54.00	45.00	64.63
Education and Labor	32.4	11.2	60.66
Foreign Affairs	38.55	19.5	59.76
Government Operations	33.58	24.00	46.57
House Administration	46.91	30.53	68.20

Appendix B: Partisan Divisions in Conservative Coalition Support

Committee	Overall Score	Democrats	Republicans
		91st Congress	
Interior and Insular Affairs	45.84	30.89	66.14
Interstate and Foreign Commerce	52.20	36.80	72.73
Judiciary	37.70	24.05	56.21
Merchant Marine and Fisheries	44.26	36.75	55.00
Post Office and Civil Service	41.00	22.66	66.0
Public Works and Transportation	56.72	41.53	73.93
Rules	45.26	30.9	74.0
Science and Technology	45.61	38.27	55.77
Standards of Official Conduct	58.41	41.33	75.5
Un-American Activities	49.38	39.6	65.6
Veterans Affairs	53.25	46.46	61.27
Ways and Means	45.78	33.2	69.35
		92d Congress	
Agriculture	60.19	47.45	80.21
Appropriations	54.72	43.00	72.31
Armed Services	59.28	50.68	69.00
Banking, Finance, and Urban Affairs	43.29	30.45	62.13
District of Columbia	44.20	29.07	65.40
Education and Labor	34.57	15.95	60.19
Foreign Affairs	42.10	29.42	60.23
Government Operations	39.92	29.65	54.69
House Administration	46.48	30.8	70.00
Interior and Insular Affairs	47.74	33.48	69.60
Internal Security	60.00	38.50	81.5
Interstate and Foreign Commerce	50.60	31.56	77.05
Judiciary	37.86	17.81	65.44
Merchant Marine and Fisheries	45.57	39.36	54.66

Committee	Overall Score	Democrats	Republicans
		92nd Congress	
Post Office and Civil Service	53.62	37.60	75.45
Public Works and Transportation	50.27	34.00	77.00
Rules	49.13	36.10	75.20
Science and Technology	37.83	45.50	62.18
Standards of Official Conduct	67.00	50.66	86.60
Veterans Affairs	53.53	42.37	71.40
Ways and Means	50.32	30.40	80.20
		93d Congress	
Agriculture	60.02	50.05	72.50
Appropriations	53.65	43.90	68.27
Armed Services	62.04	50.04	77.21
Banking, Finance, and Urban Affairs	38.34	21.50	61.50
District of Columbia	42.04	20.38	67.36
Education and Labor	36.08	17.45	59.38
Foreign Affairs	40.90	27.59	57.16
Government Operations	42.15	27.91	60.33
House Administration	45.73	31.90	64.55
Interior and Insular Affairs	49.53	31.14	69.84
Internal Security	60.00	46.00	77.50
Interstate and Foreign Commerce	52.27	35.04	74.05
Judiciary	41.79	20.80	67.71
Merchant Marine and Fisheries	47.97	37.86	61.05
Post Office and Civil Service	43.84	22.67	75.60
Public Works and Transportation	54.66	35.64	80.81
Rules	47.86	34.70	74.20
Science and Technology	50.87	42.53	61.77
Standards of Official Conduct	58.25	40.50	76.00

Appendix B: Partisan Divisions in Conservative Coalition Support

Committee	Overall Score	Democrats	Republicans
		93rd Congress	
Veterans Affairs	54.65	46.40	65.91
Ways and Means	51.60	34.07	77.90
		94th Congress	
Agriculture	53.05	43.57	72.0
Appropriations	52.98	41.16	77.28
Armed Services	60.64	51.27	79.38
Banking, Finance, and Urban Affairs	42.47	27.71	72.0
Budget	49.24	34.41	80.75
District of Columbia	37.45	31.73	49.71
Education and Labor	34.97	20.73	63.46
Foreign Affairs	37.23	24.22	61.08
Government Operations	38.98	27.72	62.28
House Administration	48.80	32.76	82.88
Interior and Insular Affairs	49.83	35.19	77.00
Interstate and Foreign Commerce	45.51	31.00	75.57
Judiciary	40.94	23.87	76.64
Merchant Marine and Fisheries	35.13	37.57	60.23
Post Office and Civil Service	39.60	22.79	75.11
Public Works and Transportation	50.97	34.40	82.85
Rules	44.13	27.82	80.00
Science and Technology	46.46	36.56	67.08
Small Business	38.14	27.76	59.75
Standards of Official Conduct	64.92	46.33	83.50
Veterans Affairs	48.61	37.00	73.11
Ways and Means	47.81	32.52	79.67
		95th Congress	
Agriculture	55.52	46.0	75.2
Appropriations	50.72	37.54	77.83
Armed Services	64.65	54.56	84.07

Committee	Overall Score	Democrats	Republicans
		95th Congress	
Banking, Finance, and Urban Affairs	40.56	29.51	63.4
Budget	42.56	22.29	85.63
District of Columbia	38.57	33.92	48.66
Education and Labor	37.19	22.91	65.75
Government Operations	40.32	25.78	70.5
House Administration	43.76	28.17	76.88
Interior and Insular Affairs	45.02	30.93	74.21
International Relations	37.94	23.64	67.75
Interstate and Foreign Commerce	42.79	27.55	74.35
Judiciary	45.97	33.43	72.18
Merchant Marine and Fisheries	47.55	36.11	71.30
Post Office and Civil Service	40.52	21.52	80.87
Public Works and Transportation	57.09	44.65	82.85
Rules	39.37	24.09	73.00
Science and Technology	47.90	37.69	68.30
Small Business	41.81	31.17	63.06
Standards of Official Conduct	55.25	49.5	61.0
Veterans Affairs	55.75	46.94	74.33
Ways and Means	49.81	35.2	80.25
		96th Congress	
Agriculture	57.83	48.74	74.20
Appropriations	46.15	36.44	76.61
Armed Services	62.72	55.54	76.13
Banking, Finance, and Urban Affairs	45.31	31.41	70.33
Budget	43.32	23.88	84.63
District of Columbia	36.07	21.33	62.60
Education and Labor	42.47	25.00	73.38

Appendix B: Partisan Divisions in Conservative Coalition Support

Committee	Overall Score	Democrats	Republicans
		96th Congress	
Government Operations	44.13	28.12	72.71
House Administration	43.24	26.13	73.33
Interior and Insular Affairs	47.30	30.81	77.93
International Relations	40.38	25.95	64.42
Interstate and Foreign Commerce	49.88	33.56	79.27
Judiciary	46.97	29.68	76.82
Merchant Marine and Fisheries	41.85	32.52	58.50
Post Office and Civil Service	46.77	26.08	76.67
Public Works and Transportation	60.47	47.07	84.12
Rules	38.63	22.27	74.60
Science and Technology	53.26	43.28	71.07
Small Business	47.56	34.96	70.07
Standards of Official Conduct	65.00	51.83	78.16
Veterans Affairs	65.31	58.19	78.91
Ways and Means	45.56	30.04	76.58

APPENDIX C

Percentages of Successful Coalitions in House Committees, by Size of Coalition

TABLE C-1. Percentages of Successful Coalitions in House Committees, by Size of Coalition, 1973–1976

| | Size of Winning Coalition | | | | | | | | | | |
	51–55%	56–60%	61–65%	66–70%	71–75%	76–80%	81–85%	86–90%	91–95%	96–100%	r^a
Polarized-partisan committees											
Education and Labor	12	16	16	16	12	11	3	3	4	7	−.22*
Interior and Insular Affairs	34	17	14	14	8	6	5	1	0	1	−.37*
Energy and Commerce	22	31	23	12	5	5	2	0	0	1	−.40*
Budget	47	16	5	5	16	5	0	0	0	0	−.75*
Ways and Means	28	24	14	11	9	9	2	3	0	1	−.25*

Appendix C: Percentages of Successful Coalitions in House Committees, by

Size of Coalition

	Size of Winning Coalition										
	51–55%	56–60%	61–65%	66–70%	71–75%	76–80%	81–85%	86–90%	91–95%	96–100%	r^a
Mixed-partisan committees											
Agriculture	28	21	11	7	10	7	7	4	3	3	−.10
Appropriations	14	23	18	18	23	5	0	0	0	0	.34
Banking, Finance, and Urban Affairs	17	15	17	16	10	8	8	2	3	5	−.05
Government Operations	17	13	13	23	10	7	3	3	0	10	−.17
House Administration	12	17	22	9	7	7	1	9	9	8	−.19*
Judiciary	17	16	15	27	10	6	4	5	2	0	−.18*
Post Office and Civil Service	12	23	19	19	8	8	4	0	4	4	−.06*
Public Works and Transportation	13	8	26	11	5	13	8	13	0	3	−.21
Rules	10	10	21	24	22	9	7	1	0	1	−.02
Science and Technology	21	11	16	21	5	5	16	0	5	0	.41*
Nonpartisan committees											
Armed Services	5	15	2	12	7	12	15	15	10	7	−.10
Foreign Affairs	11	16	9	14	21	9	5	5	2	9	.09
Standards of Official Conduct	7	0	5	7	5	5	2	9	2	58	−.34*

Note: [a]Pearson product-moment correlation coefficient between size of successful committee coalition and number of committee members voting; those marked with asterisks are significant at the .05 level.

TABLE C-2. Percentages of Successful Coalitions in House Committees, by Size of Coalition, 1977–1980

	Size of Winning Coalition										
	51–55%	56–60%	61–65%	66–70%	71–75%	76–80%	81–85%	86–90%	91–95%	96–100%	r^a
Polarized-partisan committees											
Education and Labor	8	17	17	17	21	9	4	2	3	3	−.18*
Interior and Insular Affairs	35	26	25	4	7	0	0	1	0	2	−.22*
Energy and Commerce	36	25	16	8	9	2	4	0	1	0	−.37*
Budget	25	28	12	18	6	6	1	1	2	1	−.40*
Ways and Means	24	25	24	13	7	3	2	2	0	0	−.06
Merchant Marine and Fisheries	32	18	18	12	9	3	6	3	0	0	−.48*
Mixed-partisan committees											
Agriculture	17	20	21	17	10	6	1	2	2	4	.00
Appropriations	52	19	15	4	11	0	0	0	0	0	−.35*
Banking, Finance, and Urban Affairs	17	15	17	11	9	9	9	6	5	3	−.19
Government Operations	21	21	15	14	14	5	3	3	5	0	−.31*
House Administration	10	28	23	13	8	2	5	3	2	5	−.23*
Judiciary	24	28	13	11	10	5	5	5	2	1	−.05
Post Office and Civil Service	12	21	21	17	7	9	7	3	3	0	−.24*
Public Works and Transportation	11	11	14	20	11	11	14	3	3	0	−.19
Rules	13	23	12	25	13	6	2	3	1	3	−.14
Science and Technology	9	14	20	26	3	9	3	0	0	17	.10
Non-partisan committees											
Armed Services	11	7	18	11	15	16	9	6	6	2	.10
Foreign Affairs	15	31	8	0	23	0	8	8	0	8	
Standards of Official Conduct	0	0	5	10	20		0	5	0	60	.25

*Correlations marked with asterisks are statistically significant at the .05 level.
aPearson correlation coefficient between size of successful committee coalition and number of committee members voting.

REFERENCES

Arnold, R. Douglas. 1979. *Congress and the Bureaucracy.* New Haven: Yale Univ. Press.

Arrow, Kenneth. 1951. *Social Choice and Individual Values.* New York: Wiley.

Asher, Herbert B. 1974. "Committees and the Norm of Specialization." *Annals of the American Academy of Political and Social Science* 411 (Jan.):63–74.

Asher, Herbert B., and Herbert F. Weisberg. 1978. "Voting Change in Congress: Some Dynamic Perspectives on an Evolutionary Process," *American Journal of Political Science* 22 (May):391–425.

Bacheller, John M. 1977. "Lobbyists and the Legislative Process: The Impact of Environmental Constraints." *American Political Science Review* 17 (Mar.):252–62.

Beck, Paul Allen. 1979. "The Electoral Cycle and Patterns of American Politics." *British Journal of Political Science* 9:129–56.

Bibby, John F. 1966. "Committee Characteristics and Legislative Oversight of Administration." *Midwest Journal of Political Science* 10 (Feb.):78–98.

Bibby, John, and Roger Davidson. 1967. *On Capitol Hill.* New York: Holt, Rinehart and Winston.

Bowler, M. Kenneth. 1976. "The New Committee on Ways and Means: Policy Implications of Recent Changes in the House Committee." Paper presented at the Annual Meeting of the American Political Science Association, Chicago, Sept. 2–5.

Brady, David W. 1978. "Critical Elections, Congressional Parties and Clusters of Policy Change: A Comparison of the 1896 and 1932 Realignment Eras." *British Journal of Political Science* 8 (Jan.):79–100.

Brady, David W., and Charles S. Bullock III. 1980. "The Conservative Coalition: Origin, Causes, and Consequences." *Journal of Politics* 42 (May):549–59.

Brady, David W., Joseph Cooper, and Patricia Hurley. 1979. "The Decline of Party in the U.S. House of Representatives: 1887–1968." *Legislative Studies Quarterly* 4 (Aug.):381–406.

Brady, David W., and Naomi B. Lynn. 1973. "Switched Seat Congressional Districts: Their Effect on Party Voting and Public Policy." *American Journal of Political Science* 17 (Aug.):528–43.

Broder, David. 1971. *The Party's Over.* New York: Harper and Row.

Bullock, Charles S., III. 1970. "Apprenticeship and Committee Assignments in the House of Representatives." *Journal of Politics* 32 (Aug.):717–20.

———. 1971. "The Influence of State Party Delegations on House Committee Assignments." *Midwest Journal of Political Science* 15 (Nov.):525–46.

———. 1972. "Freshmen Committee Assignments and Re-election in the United States House of Representatives." *American Political Science Review* 66 (Sept.):996–1007.

———. 1973. "Committee Transfers in the United States House of Representatives." *Journal of Politics* 35 (Feb.):85–120.

Burnham, Walter Dean. 1970. *Critical Elections and the Mainsprings of American Politics.* New York: Norton.

Clausen, Aage R. 1973. *How Congressmen Decide: A Policy Focus.* New York: St. Martin's Press.

Cooper, Joseph. 1965. "Jeffersonian Attitudes toward Executive Leadership and Committee Development in the House of Representatives, 1789–1829." *Western Political Quarterly* 18 (Mar.):45–63.

———. 1970. *The Origins of the Standing Committees and the Development of the Modern House.* Rice University Studies (Sumner), vol. 56, no. 3.

Cooper, Joseph, and David W. Brady. 1981. "Institutional Context and Leadership Style: The House from Cannon to Rayburn." *American Political Science Review* 75 (June):411–25.

Dahl, Robert A., and Charles E. Lindblom. 1953. *Politics, Economics, and Welfare.* New York: Harper.

Davidson, Roger H. 1974. "Representation and Congressional Committees." *Annals of the American Academy of Political and Social Science* 411 (Jan.):48–62.

_____. 1976. "Congressional Committees." *Policy Analysis* 2 (Spring):299–323.

Davidson, Roger H., and Walter J. Oleszek. 1977. *Congress Against Itself.* Bloomington: Indiana Univ. Press.

Dawson, Raymond. 1962. "Congressional Innovation and Intervention in Defense Policy: Legislative Authorization of Weapons Systems." *American Political Science Review* 56 (Mar.):42–57.

Dodd, Lawrence C. 1972. "Committee Integration in the Senate: A Comparative Analysis." *Journal of Politics* 34 (Nov.):1135–71.

Dyson, James W., and John W. Soule. 1970. "Congressional Committee Behavior on Roll Call Votes: The U.S. House of Representatives, 1955–64," *Midwest Journal of Political Science* 14 (Nov.):626–47.

Ehrenhalt, Alan. 1975. "House Agriculture: New Faces, New Issues." *Congressional Quarterly Weekly Report* (Feb. 22, 1975):379–84.

Ehrenhalt, Alan (ed.). 1981. *Politics in America.* Washington, D.C.: Congressional Quarterly Press.

Eidenberg, Eugene, and Roy D. Morey. 1969. *An Act of Congress: The Legislative Process and the Making of Education Policy.* New York: Norton.

Ellwood, John W., and James A. Thurber. 1981. "The Politics of the Congressional Budget Process Re-Examined." In Lawrence C. Dodd and Bruce I. Oppenheimer (eds.), *Congress Reconsidered.* Washington, D.C.: Congressional Quarterly Press.

Entin, Kenneth, 1973. "Information Exchange in Congress: Case of the House Armed Services Committee." *Western Political Quarterly* 26 (Sept.):427–39.

_____. 1974. "The House Armed Services Committee: Patterns of Decision Making during the McNamara Years." *Journal of Political and Military Sociology* 2 (Spring):73–88.

Fenno, Richard E., Jr. 1962. "The House Appropriations Committee as a Political System: The Problem of Integration." *American Political Science Review* 56 (June):310–24.

_____. 1963. "The House of Representatives and Federal Aid to Education." In Robert L. Peabody and Nelson Polsby (eds.), *New Perspectives on the House of Representatives,* 1st ed., 195–236. Chicago: Rand McNally.

————. 1966. *The Power of the Purse: Appropriations Politics in Congress.* Boston: Little, Brown.

————. 1973. *Congressmen in Committees.* Boston: Little, Brown.

————. 1978. *Home Style,* Boston: Little, Brown.

Ferejohn, John A. 1974. *Pork Barrel Politics: Rivers and Harbors Legislation, 1947–1968.* Palo Alto, Calif.: Stanford Univ. Press.

Finley, James J. 1975. "The 1974 Congressional Initiative in Budget Making." *Public Administration Review* 35 (May-June):270–78.

Fox, Douglas, and Charles H. Clapp. 1970. "The House Rules Committee's Agenda-Setting Function, 1961–1968." *Journal of Politics* 32 (May):440–43.

Fox, Harrison W., Jr., and Susan W. Hammond. 1979. *Congressional Staffs.* New York: Free Press.

Froman, Lewis A., Jr., and Randall B. Ripley. 1965. "Conditions for Party Leadership: The Case of the House Democrats." *American Political Science Review* 59 (Mar.):52–63.

Furlong, P. J. 1968. "Origins of the Houe Committee on Ways and Means." *William and Mary Quarterly* 25 (Oct.):587–604.

Gawthrop, Lewis C. 1966. "Changing Membership Patterns in House Committees." *American Political Science Review* 60 (June):366–73.

Gertzog, Irwin N. 1976. "The Routinization of Committee Assignments in the U.S. House of Representatives." *American Journal of Political Science* 20 (Nov.):693–712.

Goodwin, George. 1970. *The Little Legislatures.* Amherst: Univ. of Massachusetts Press.

Gordon, Bernard K. 1961. "The Military Budget: Congressional Phase." *Journal of Politics* 23 (Nov.):689–710.

Goss, Carol F. 1972. "Military Committee Membership and Defense-Related Benefits in the House of Representatives." *Western Political Quarterly* 25 (June):215–33.

Grumm, John G. 1963. "A Factor Analysis of Legislative Behavior." *Midwest Journal of Political Science* 7 (Nov.):336–56.

Havemann, Joel. 1975. "Budget Report/Committees Seek Stimulus but Call for Spending Curbs." *National Journal* 7 (Apr.):495–508.

Henderson, Thomas A. 1970. *Congressional Oversight of Executive Agencies: A Study of the House Committee on Government Operations.* Gainesville: Univ. of Florida Press.

Hersh, Seymour. 1969. "The Military Committees." *Washington Monthly* 1 (Apr.):84–92.

Hinckley, Barbara. 1972. "Coalitions in Congress: Size and Ideological Distance." *American Journal of Political Science* 16 (May):197–207.

———. 1975. "Policy Content, Committee Membership, and Behavior." *American Journal of Political Science* 19 (Aug.):543–58.

Huitt, Ralph K. 1957. "The Morse Committee Assignment Controversy: A Study in Senate Norms." *American Political Science Review* 51 (June):313–29.

Jahnige, Thomas P. 1968. "The Congressional Committee System and the Oversight Process: Congress and NASA." *Western Political Quarterly* 21 (Mar.):227–39.

Jewell, Malcolm, and Chiu Chi-Hung. 1974. "Membership Movement and Committee Attractiveness in the U.S. House of Representatives." *American Journal of Political Science* 18 (May):433–41.

Jones, Charles O. 1961. "Representation in Congress: The Case of the House Agriculture Committee." *American Political Science Review* 55 (June):358–67.

———. 1968. "Joseph G. Cannon and Howard W. Smith: An Essay on the Limits of Leadership in the House of Representatives." *Journal of Politics* 30 (Sept.: 617–46.

Kaiser, Fred. 1977. "Oversight of Foreign Policy: The U.S. House Committee on International Relations." *Legislative Studies Quarterly* 2 (Aug.):255–79.

Kelman, Herbert. 1958. "Compliance, Identification, and Internalization: Three Processes of Attitude Change." *Journal of Conflict Resolution* 2:51–60.

Kingdon, John W. 1973. *Congressmen's Voting Decisions.* New York: Harper and Row.

Koehler, David H. 1972. "The Legislative Process and the Minimal Winning Coalition." In Richard G. Niemi and Herbert F. Weisberg (eds.), *Probability Models of Collective Decision Making.* Columbus, Ohio: Charles E. Merrill.

Kofmehl, Kenneth. 1962. *Professional Staffs of Congress.* West Lafayette, Ind.: Purdue Univ. Press.

Kolodziej, Edward A. 1966. *The Uncommon Defense and Congress, 1945-1963.* Columbus: Ohio State Univ. Press.

Kravitz, Walter. 1969. "A Short History of the Development of the House Committee on Rules." Washington, D.C.: Legislative Reference Service, Library of Congress. Mimeographed.

Lacy, Donald P., and Philip Martin. 1972. "Amending the Constitution: The Bottleneck in the Judiciary Committees."

Harvard Journal on Legislation 9 (May):666–93.

LeLoup, Lance T. 1979. "Process Versus Policy: The U.S. House Budget Committee." *Legislative Studies Quarterly* 4 (May):227–54.

Lindblom, Charles E. 1965. *The Intelligence of Democracy.* New York: Free Press.

Lowi, Theodore J. 1969. *The End of Liberalism: Ideology, Policy, and the Crisis of Public Authority.* New York: Norton.

McKelvey, Richard D., Peter C. Ordeshook, and Mark D. Winer. 1978. "The Competitive Solution for N-Person Games, without Transferable Utility, with Application to Committee Games." *American Political Science Review* 72 (June):599–615.

Maffre, John. 1971. "Congressional Report/New Leaders, Staff Changes Stimulate House Foreign Affairs Committee." *National Journal* 3 (June 19):1314–22.

Malbin, Michael J. 1974. "Congress Report New Democratic Procedures Affect Distribution of Power." *National Journal* 6 (Dec. 14):1881–90.

Manley, John F. 1965. "The House Committee on Ways and Means: Conflict Management in a Congressional Committee." *American Political Science Review* 59 (Dec.):927–39.

———. 1968. "Congressional Staff and Public Policy Making: The Joint Committee on Internal Revenue Taxation." *Journal of Politics* 30 (Nov.):1046–67.

———. 1969. "Wilbur D. Mills: A Study of Congressional Influence." *American Political Science Review* 63 (June):442–64.

———. 1970. *The Politics of Finance: The House Committee on Ways and Means.* Boston: Little, Brown.

Masters, Nicholas. 1961. "Committee Assignments in the House of Representatives." *American Political Science Review* 55 (June):345–57.

Matsunaga, Spark M., and Ping Chen. 1976. *Rulemakers of the House.* Urbana: Univ. of Illinois Press.

Matthews, Donald R., and James A. Stimson. 1975. *Yeas and Nays: Normal Decision-Making in the U.S. House of Representatives.* New York: Wiley.

Mayhew, David R. 1966. *Party Loyalty among Congressmen.* Cambridge, Mass.: Harvard Univ. Press.

———. 1974. *Congress: The Electoral Connection.* New Haven: Yale Univ. Press.

Miller, Gary J., and Joe A. Oppenheimer. 1982. "Universalism in

References

Experimental Committees." *American Political Science Review* 76 (Sept.):562–74.

Murphy, James T. 1974. "Political Parties and the Porkbarrel: Party Conflict and Cooperation in House Public Works Committee Decision Making." *American Political Science Review* 68 (Mar.):169–85.

Murray, Michael. 1969. "The House Education Labor Committee and the 1967 Poverty Controversy: A Study of Congressional Avoidance." Ph.D. diss., Univ of Illinois.

Nader, Ralph. 1972. *Citizens Look at Congress.*

Neustadt, Richard E. 1960. *Presidential Power.* New York: Wiley.

Niskanen, William A. 1971. *Bureaucracy and Representative Government.* Chicago: Aldine-Atherton.

_____. 1975. "Bureaucrats and Politicians." *Journal of Law and Economics* 18 (Dec.):617–43.

Norton, Bruce. 1970. "The Committee on Banking and Currency as a Legislative Subsystem of the House of Representatives." Ph.D. diss., Syracuse Univ.

O'Keefe, Dennis J. 1969. "Decision-Making in the House Committee on the District of Columbia." Ph.D. diss., Univ. of Maryland.

Oleszek, Walter J. 1978. *Congressional Procedures and the Policy Process.* Washington, D.C.: Congressional Quarterly Press.

Ornstein, Norman J., and David W. Rohde. 1977. "Shifting Forces, Changing Rules and Political Outcomes: The Impact of Congressional Change on Four House Committees." In Robert L. Peabody and Nelson W. Polsby (eds.), *New Perspectives on the House of Representatives,* 3d ed. Chicago: Rand McNally.

Parker, Glenn R. 1979. "The Selection of Committee Leaders in the House of Representatives." *American Politics Quarterly* 7 (Jan.):71–93.

Parker, Glenn R., and Suzanne L. Parker. 1979. "Factions in Committees: The U.S. House of Representatives." *American Political Science Review* 73 (Mar.):85–102.

_____. 1981. "The Comparative Study of Factions in the House Committee System." Paper presented at the Annual Meeting of the Midwest Political Science Association, Cincinnati, Ohio, April 15–18.

Peabody, Robert L. 1963. "The Enlarged Rules Committee." In Robert L. Peabody and Nelson W. Polsby (eds.), *New Perspectives on the House of Representatives,* 1st ed. Chicago: Rand McNally.

Perkins, Lynette P. 1980. "Influence of Members' Goals on Their Committee Behavior: The U.S. House Judiciary Committee." *Legislative Studies Quarterly* 5 (Aug.):373–92.

———. 1981. "Member Recruitment to a Mixed Goal Committee: The House Judiciary Committee." *Journal of Politics* 43 (May):348–64.

Poke, Carl. 1968. "Congress and Outer Space." Ph.D. diss., Univ. of Pittsburgh.

Pressman, Jeffrey L. 1966. *House vs. Senate: Conflict in the Appropriations Process*. New Haven: Yale Univ. Press.

Price, David E. 1972. *Who Makes the Laws?* Cambridge, Mass.: Schenkman.

———. 1975. *The Commerce Committees: A Study of the House and Senate Commerce Committees*. New York: Grossman.

———. 1978. "Policy Making in Congressional Committees: The Impact of 'Environmental' Factors." *American Political Science Review* 72 (June):548–74.

———. 1981. "Congressional Committees in the Policy Process." In Lawrence C. Dodd and Bruce I. Oppenheimer (eds.), *Congress Reconsidered*. Washington, D.C.: Congressional Quarterly Press.

Ralph Nader Congress Project. 1975. *The Environment Committees: A Study of the House and Senate Interior, Agriculture, and Science Committees*. New York: Grossman.

Ray, Bruce A. 1980a. "Federal Spending and the Selection of Committee Assignments in the U.S. House of Representatives." *American Journal of Political Science* 24 (Aug.):494–510.

———. 1980b. "The Responsiveness of the U.S. Congressional Armed Services Committees to Their Parent Bodies." *Legislative Studies Quarterly* 5 (Nov.):501–15.

Riker, William H. 1962. *The Theory of Political Coalitions*. New Haven: Yale Univ. Press.

Riker, William H., and Peter Ordeshook. 1973. *An Introduction to Positive Political Theory*. Englewood Cliffs, N.J.: Prentice-Hall.

Ripley, Randall B. 1978. *Congress: Process and Policy*. 2d ed. New York: Norton.

Robinson, James A. 1962. *Congress and Foreign Policy Making*. Homewood, Ill.: Dorsey.

———. 1963. *The House Rules Committee*. Indianapolis: Bobbs-Merrill.

Rohde, David, and Kenneth Shepsle. 1972. "Democratic

Committee Assignments in the House of Representatives: Strategic Aspects of a Social Choice Process." *American Political Science Review* 66 (Sept.):889–905.

Salaman, Lester. 1975. *The Money Committees: A Study of the House Banking and Currency Committee and the Senate Banking, Housing, and Urban Affairs Committee.* New York: Grossman.

Schattschneider, E.E. 1960. *The Semi-Sovereign People: A Realist's View of Democracy in America.* New York: Holt, Rinehart and Winston.

Schick, Allen. 1975. "The Battle of the Budget." In Harvey C. Mansfield (ed.), *Congress Against the President.* New York: Academy of Political Science.

_____. 1980. *Congress and Money.* Washington, D.C.: Urban Institute.

_____. 1981. "The First Five Years of Congressional Budgeting." In Rudolph G. Penner (ed.), *The Congressional Budget Process after Five Years.* Washington, D.C.: American Enterprise Institute.

Schneider, Jerrold E. 1979. *Ideological Coalitions in Congress.* Westport, Conn.: Greenwood.

Schuck, Peter H. 1975. *A Study of the House and Senate Judiciary Committees.* New York: Grossman.

Shepsle, Kenneth A. 1978. *The Giant Jigsaw Puzzle.* Chicago: Univ. of Chicago Press.

Sinclair, Barbara. 1976. "Political Upheaval and Congressional Voting: The Effects of the 1960s on Voting Patterns in the House of Representatives." *Journal of Politics* 38 (May):326–45.

_____. 1981. "Agenda and Alignment Change: The House of Representatives, 1925–1978." In Lawrence C. Dodd and Bruce I. Oppenheimer (eds.), *Congress Reconsidered.* 2d ed. Washington, D.C.: Congressional Quarterly Press.

_____. 1982. *Congressional Realignment, 1925–1978.* Austin: Univ. of Texas Press.

Smith, Howard. 1965. "In Defense of the Rules Committee." In Joseph S. Clark (ed.), *Congressional Reform: Problems and Prospects.* New York: Thomas Y. Crowell.

Spohn, Richard. 1975. *The Revenue Committees: A Study of the House Ways and Means and Senate Finance Committees and the House and Senate Appropriations Committees.* New York: Grossman.

Stephens, Herbert W. 1971. "The Role of the Legislative

Committees in the Appropriations Process: A Study Focused on the Armed Services Committees." *Western Political Quarterly* 21 (Mar.):146–62.

Strom, Gerald S. 1975. "Congressional Policy Making: A Test of a Theory." *Journal of Politics* 37 (Aug.):711–35.

Sundquist, James L. 1983. *Dynamics of the Party System.* Rev. ed. Washington, D.C.: Brookings Institution.

Swanson, Wayne R. 1969. "Committee Assignments and the Nonconformist Legislator: Democrats in the U.S. Senate." *Midwest Journal of Political Science* 13 (Feb.):84–94.

Truman, David B. 1951. *The Governmental Process.* New York: Knopf.

_____. 1959. *The Congressional Party: A Case Study.* New York: Wiley.

Unekis, Joseph K., and Leroy N. Rieselbach. 1984. *Congressional Committee Politics.* New York: Praeger.

U.S. House of Representatives. 1980. *Toward the Endless Frontier: History of the Committee on Science and Technology, 1959–1974.* Washington, D.C.: Government Printing Office.

Vinyard, Dale. 1968. "The Congressional Committee on Small Business: Pattern of Legislative Committee-Executive Agency Relations." *Western Political Quarterly* 18 (Sept.):391–99.

Wagner, James R. 1971. "Interior Subcommittees Move Slowly on Legislation to Reform Public Lands Policy." *National Journal Reports* 3 (Aug.):1768–73.

Weingast, Barry. 1979. "A Rational Choice Perspective on Congressional Norms." *American Journal of Political Science* 23 (May):245–62.

Westphal, Albert C.F. 1942. *The House Committee on Foreign Affairs.* New York: Columbia Univ. Press.

Wildavsky, Aaron. 1974. *The Politics of the Budgetary Process.* 2d ed. Boston: Little, Brown.

INDEX

Factions in House Committees has been set into type on a Linotron 202 digital phototypesetter in ten point Sabon with two points of spacing between the lines. Serif Sabon was selected for display. The book was designed by Judy Ruehmann, composed by Typecraft Company, printed offset by Thomson-Shore, Inc., and bound by John H. Dekker & Sons. The paper on which the book is printed carries acid-free characteristics for an effective life of at least three hundred years.

THE UNIVERSITY OF TENNESSEE PRESS : KNOXVILLE